Praise for *Tunnel, Smuggle, Collect: A Holocaust Boy*

TUNNEL, SMUGGLE, COLLECT:
A HOLOCAUST BOY

(Second Edition)

Other books by Jeffrey N. Gingold:

Facing the Cognitive Challenges of Multiple Sclerosis,
Second Edition

Mental Sharpening Stones:
Manage the Cognitive Challenges of Multiple Sclerosis

TUNNEL, SMUGGLE, COLLECT: A HOLOCAUST BOY

(Second Edition)

JEFFREY N. GINGOLD

HenschelHAUS Publishing, Inc
Milwaukee, Wisconsin

Maps of Warsaw ghetto used with permission from the
Polish Center for Holocaust Research (www.ghetto.pl)

Published by HenschelHAUS Publishing, Inc.
www.henschelHAUSbooks.com

All HenschelHAUS titles, imprints, and distributed lines are available at
special quantity discounts for educational, institutional, fund-raising,
or sales promotion.

100% of author royalties will be donated to the
Nathan and Ester Pelz Holocaust Education Resource Center

ISBN: 978159598-405-0
E-ISBN: 978159598-406-7
LCCN: 2015942971

Publisher's Cataloging-In-Publication Data
(Prepared by The Donohue Group, Inc.)

Gingold, Jeffrey N.
Tunnel, smuggle, collect : a Holocaust boy / Jeffrey N. Gingold.
pages : illustrations ; cm
Issued also as an ebook.
Includes bibliographical references.
ISBN: 978-1-59598-405-0
1. Gingold, Sam. 2. Holocaust survivors--Poland--Biography. 3. Political prisoners--Russia
(Federation)--Siberia--Biography. 4. Holocaust, Jewish (1939-1945)--Poland--Warsaw. I.
Title.
DS134.72.G56 G564 2015
940.5318092   2015942971

Cover photography: Pam Ferderbar
Author photograph: Peggy Morsh

Printed in the United States of America.

*For Terri, with her kind heart and steadfast love,
holding tight with balance.*

*For Lauren and Meredith,
remembering the past and sharing their joy for life
with endless, sweet hugs.*

And Mickey, too, again.

TABLE OF CONTENTS

AUTHOR'S NOTE

This is the true story of Sam Gingold's childhood during World War II, told from his point of view. It is based on video and audio recordings of interviews of the author's father, Sam Gingold, and grandmother, Lilly (Leah) Gingold. The names of some individuals and other identifying characteristics have been changed to protect their privacy.

Please enjoy the morsels of Yiddish from my father [Sam], adding a layer of texture to the Jewish life in Warsaw. The Gingolds' Yiddish is in the rich Warsaw (*varshever*) accent of Southern Yiddish, varying in most of its vowels from Northern, or "Standard" Yiddish. Sam's accent is reflected in the transliterations provided. The Yiddish in this book was interpreted from recordings transcribed by Hershl Hartman. Mr. Hartman has translated numerous Yiddish documents, letters, diaries, and memoirs, including a notebook of Nobel laureate Issac Bashevis Singer, as well as scores of poems, essays, and several full-length Yiddish books.

100 percent of the author's royalties from the sale of this publication will be directly donated to the Nathan and Ester Pelz Holocaust Education and Resource Center (HERC).

—Jeffrey N. Gingold

FOREWORD

There are two events that were both liminal and seminal in the history of the Jewish People. The first event was the *Shoah*, more commonly referred to as the Holocaust, the attempted utter annihilation and destruction of the Jews. The second event was the establishment of modern State of Israel, the reconstituting of a Jewish commonwealth in the Jewish People's historic, national homeland, the Land of Israel.

Many link the two events, claiming that the former is the reason for the latter. While the Shoah was certainly a catalyst for the United Nations Security Council vote that established a partition of Palestine into two states—one Jewish, the other Arab—it was never the overarching or primary factor.

The Jewish People had been yearning to return home since 70 C.E. when the Romans destroyed the Second Temple, the center of Jewish religious and political life, and sent the Jewish People into exile, creating the Jewish Diaspora. For the next two millennia, Jews throughout the Diaspora experienced degradation, discrimination, deportation, oppression, and attempted genocide.

It is against this backdrop that the narrative of Jeffrey Gingold's *Tunnel, Smuggle, Collect: A Holocaust Boy* unfolds. Jeffrey's father, Sam; his grandparents, Duvid and Leah; and his uncle, Baruch, are a Jewish family living in Warsaw, Poland, at the start of the World War II. They are Polish citizens, they speak Polish—they even dress like Poles—but the fact that they are Jewish (a fact easily discerned from their Jewish sounding names and their use of Yiddish (the vernacular of Ashkenazi Jews) makes them vulnerable to the anti-Semitic sentiments of the Polish neighbors.

Their somewhat precarious, careful, and rather guarded existence only becomes more tenuous and existential on September 1, 1939, when Nazi Germany invades Poland. The Nazis sought to subdue a conquered people. But the Nazis also worked diligently to address the presence of the Jews they had now brought into the sphere of their control. With fiendish precision, they dehumanized and objectified the Jews of Poland by passing discriminatory legislation. They concentrated Poland's Jews into ghettos within cities like Warsaw and Lodz (later deporting other Jews from other countries into those ghettos). The ghettos were essentially holding pens which the Nazis used to liquidate Jewish families like Gingold's through starvation, disease, hard labor, and vicarious and brutal murder.

Gingold captures, in searing detail through the voices of his family, the frightening days that marked Germany's capture of their city, Warsaw, their failed attempt to flee, their horrific life in the ghetto, their fateful decision to escape (like other ghettos, the Warsaw Ghetto was eventually liquidated by the Nazis. Its inhabitants were sent by railway to the Treblinka death camp), the kindness and sanctuary they encountered by a number of Polish Christian peasants while on their trek toward the Soviet border, their lives as refugees in Siberia, and their post-war experience in Germany and America.

I have known Jeffrey Gingold, his father, Sam, the "Holocaust Boy" who tunneled, smuggled, and collected to keep himself, his family and his neighbors alive in the midst of horrendous, inhuman conditions, for many years. I knew that they were a child of survivors and a survivor, respectively. I did not know the extraordinary saga that was their story until I read the narrative Jeffrey finally committed to paper after completing his exhaustive research and his interviews with the members of his family who lived through an event that neither Hayyim Bialik nor Theodore Hertzl could have imagined.

Jeffrey Gingold's *Tunnel, Smuggle, Collect: A Holocaust Boy* will make you cry. It will make you seethe in anger. Most importantly, it will make you remember.

—Rabbi Jacob Herber

Rabbi Jacob Herber is a Senior Rabbinic Fellow and iEngage Consultant at the Shalom Hartman Institute of North America. He served for 15 years as the spiritual leader of Milwaukee's conservative synagogue, Congregation Beth Israel Ner Tamid.

ACKNOWLEDGMENTS

I am at a loss of how to properly thank relatives who are no longer with us, yet by their resilience; they have left an indelible example of faith and love of family.

I especially want to thank my grandmother and father for the years of video interviews and conversations, sharing the unimaginable horror and trauma of living in the Warsaw ghetto. There were good reasons why their memories and pain were buried, but it's vital that they are preserved to keep our family's survival through the Holocaust on a true course. We will never forget.

For Jerry (*in memoriam*) and Louise Stein, inspiring outreach to remember the humanity lost in the Holocaust.

I am also grateful to Arleen Peltz, Shay Pilnik, PhD, Executive Director, and the **Nathan and Esther Pelz Holocaust Education Resource Center,** as well as Ellie Gettinger and the **Jewish Museum Milwaukee,** for their guidance and support.

Especially for Sandy Hoffman (*in memoriam*) and her inspiration to share this true story. And Leo Kleiner for his enthusiasm to preserve family memories by spending time with relatives, asking questions and listening. For Peggy Morsch and her vision to capture my father's spirit and strength. And for Hershl Hartman, who brought life to a murdered era, while ensuring that Yiddish remains a living language. Also to Josh Becker and his sharp eye.

To my literary mentor, Kurt Chandler, who encourages me to let the writing show it. And for HenschelHAUS Publishing for giving this journey a home.

—Jeffrey N. Gingold

PREFACE

As if there were not enough of a reason to write this book and encourage others to delve into their family history, another reason surfaced. I was just informed that Hitler's *Mein Kampf* will be re-printed and released. Certainly, many copies of this vile and delusional publication already exist on bookshelves, but the decision to further spread its twisted, anti-Semitic thoughts goes far beyond royalties. In fact, it answers a question.

As a teenager in the 1970s, I stood with the Jewish community and faced down uniformed Nazis marching up Prospect Avenue in Milwaukee. Their swastika flags waved in the faces of Holocaust survivors and their families, who stood on the curb as silent witnesses to the incarnation of the Nazis' homicidal message. The ongoing propaganda of Hitler's intent was unchanged and so was the answer. Vigilance against such irrational hatred must be as constant as the scapegoat justification for strewing an absence of morality. Genocide remains prevalent, often disguised as political, social, or economic differences. It is never justified, period.

Within the generations that followed the exodus from Egypt, the Emancipation Proclamation, and 9/11, I imagine there are individuals who question why these significant events need to be recalled and honored every year. It's the same answer: vigilance against deniers and conspiracy theorists, thriving on altering a well -established narrative to support a vengeful agenda.

While starving with his family in the Warsaw ghetto, my grandfather, Duvid Gingold, frequently said: "What's happening to us doesn't make sense, but we must go on." Lesson learned and remembered, so never again, means *never*.

As a dear friend or relative of a survivor, you have an obligation to research and ask about what happened to them and their family in the Holocaust. You will probably find that the questions are welcome and overdue.

—Jeffrey N. Gingold

PROLOGUE
DEATH KNOCK

W hen Himmler and Goebbels were dead, Leah thought the Holocaust had ended.

* * * * *

"How could you just call like that?" asked Sam. "You didn't tell them, did you?" He pinched his lower lip and looked at the floor. The call cut deep and reached a scarred-over wound.

"I got your number from your parents," said the man's voice on the phone. Like an unanticipated meteor strike, Sam's life would be leveled.

"You called them?" said Sam, almost yanking the cord out of the wall phone. He had just returned home from his office in his un-air-conditioned Pontiac. After tossing his tie and blue sport coat on a chair, Sam sat down for dinner. When the phone rang, Sam's wife, young daughter, and two teenage boys all put down their silver-ware and stared at him from the kitchen table. Sam gestured to turn down the volume on the black-and-white kitchen television, silencing Walter Cronkite and the evening news.

Listening intently to the phone call, Sam nodded his head and turned his chair away from the table.

"Could I have some more tomatoes?" Jeffrey asked his mother. The length of his thirteen-year-old grasp held out his plate toward his mom and the dish of sliced tomatoes, but Jeffrey continued to watch his father. Something was very wrong with Dad.

Sam angled his chair toward the open kitchen window behind him, but the short phone cord did not let him leave the family dinner table. The summer evening breeze wafting through the screen was welcome, but not the phone call. Tomato slices plopped down on the plate.

"They didn't understand me," continued the man's voice on the phone, "but the woman gave me your number."

With his back tilted toward his wife and boys, Sam stared out the window and began to clench his teeth. "I am calling long distance from Princeton, New Jersey," continued the voice, "and needed to reach his family in Milwaukee."

As his eyes welled, Sam wanted to know details, but didn't want to know. As the words continued, his eyebrows rose and his cheek was numb to the falling tear. In an instant, the warm summer evening disappeared from his mind except for one thought: *he had to get to his parents*. Sam didn't know what to do and couldn't just call his parents, but he needed to get there. Be there. He reached over and hung up the phone with a slam on its base, but didn't let go of it.

"I have to get to Bobe and Papo's house to warn them," said Sam, standing up from the table. "I can't do this alone and have to make two quick calls. I'll use the other phone." He stood and glanced at his wife, Sue, and their three children, then tossed his crumpled dinner napkin onto his chair.

"But you didn't finish your dinner," said Bruce. "Remember, I have that AZA meeting tonight to see if I get in the new Chapter. Jeffrey's turn is next year."

"Is everything O.K.?" asked Sue. Sue used both hands to tuck her Laura-Petrie-styled red hair behind her ears. Sam avoided direct eye contact and shook his head.

"No, it's horrible."

"All done?" asked Lainie. She tried to push away from the table, but her blue and white trimmed Keds couldn't reach the floor.

"No," answered Sue, "first finish your carrot sticks and fries, then you can go back outside and finish drawing on the sidewalk. Remember, you left the chalk out there."

Sue stood up and pulled back around a corner and into the hallway, waiting for Sam. He followed her and then the children heard their mother gasp and a door slam. When Sue re-entered the kitchen, the attention of all three children snapped back to their plates.

"Finish up," she said, and walked to the sink to look out the window.

"Sorry," said Sam. He walked back into the kitchen and glanced at the children's confused faces. "I'll call you from their house."

He turned and held up his hand, not knowing whether to wave or be hugged, but decided to keep the details of the call from their kids. Sam winged the kitchen door closed behind him and darted toward the garage. It would be a fifteen-minute breath to hold until he arrived at his parents' home.

Although their experiences in the Holocaust had been buried by the rubble of time, Sam knew that his sixty-one-year-old mother, Leah, would collapse or worse. His sixty-four-year-old father, Duvid, would implode with the torment of long-lost generations. It was like a Gestapo throat clench had reached through time to rip out the family heart. Survival was never closure.

* * * * *

The warm weather had prompted Duvid to hang the screens on the windows, bringing inside the fresh June breeze. After bundling against a harsh Wisconsin winter, the moist air and atmosphere of neighborhood bustle was welcome into their home.

Leah tightened the waist cord of her flowery kitchen apron and unrolled the sleeves of her white blouse, which she re-tucked into a light blue summer skirt. The skirt was below the knee, but she still felt the sudden chill. The sounds of several car doors slamming caused Leah to turn away from the chrome-edged kitchen table.

She placed the gallon of 2% milk on the yellow-flowered Formica table top, next to the fresh-cut rhubarb salad. They weren't expecting company, so what was all of the street noise? She shook off the noise and laid two plates, cups, silverware, and napkins on the table.

Leah paused when she heard several men's voices murmuring from the street. The unidentified voices chanted low like the invisible approach of an unstoppable subway train. Leah leaned her head against the kitchen screen window to identify the echoing conversations. It was time for dinner and Duvid had already disappeared with the evening *Milwaukee Journal*. She jumped when another car door slammed, followed by the sound of hard-shoed footsteps on the asphalt street. The street conversation had a soft familiar undertone, but remained hushed.

Duvid clicked on the phonograph in the living room and watched the Barry Sisters album drop onto the turntable at 33⅓ RPM. The needle shifted into place and gently lowered onto the first groove. The album jacket rested on the console speaker, revealing a photo of the sisters exiting the stairs of an El Al airplane. *"Ztena, ztena"* filled the flat with the music of an old promise fulfilled.

Duvid entered the kitchen from the hallway and sat down at the table on one of the yellow cushioned chrome chairs. He ran his fingers back through his slicked gray hair, as if pushing the day's work further behind.

The cheerful color of the table set made Leah feel happy at any meal served in the kitchen. The street voices seemed to stop for the moment, so she carefully placed a bowl of bright red borscht in front of Duvid. He grabbed his spoon, scooped sour cream out of the plastic container, and plopped the dollop into his bowl. The creamy white blob seemed to cling to itself, not wishing to be stirred into the borscht. He then grabbed a salted rye roll out of the basket in Leah's hands and broke it open for a slice of butter.

As Duvid took a bite out of the roll, he noticed that Leah was back at the window, curious for a hint about the voices. "What's all the fuss?" asked Duvid, tipping his head toward the street. He finished the borscht and used the roll to wipe the creamy remnants from the edges of the bowl.

"Not sure," answered Leah, "but I heard Yiddish."

"Not from this neighborhood," said Duvid. Their cream brick duplex was located on the West side of Milwaukee.

"I'm finished with the borscht," he said. Duvid pushed away from the table, rose slowly, and placed his bowl in the sink. Then he continued to clear the table. A cool breeze blew through the screen window, causing Leah to step back from the screen and cross her arms to hold onto warmth, but she stayed by the window.

"Go to the door see what all of the tumult is about," said Duvid, "if you're that curious." The extended daylight hours made his work day on the steel factory line seem longer. With the sun still up, sitting down for dinner seemed like a work break. Duvid continued to work the slow grind of long hours, knowing that his retirement was approaching and that every saved dollar would ease their remaining years. At the end of the work day, Duvid was glad to get out of his dark blue work shirt and enjoy the evening in a fresh white t-shirt.

As Duvid continued to clear the kitchen table, placing the milk back in the refrigerator, Leah walked into the living room for a glance at the street out the front window. She reached to slightly part the front curtains, peered out the window and quickly retracted her hand. The men were approaching. Leah had survived certain death in the Warsaw Ghetto, but she sensed that this would be worse. She had felt fear, but knew this was different. There was no escape.

Duvid heard a strangled "No!" screeching down the hallway and quickly dropped two dinner glasses in the sink. It was a gasp for air choked by a dying scream. Duvid rushed to find Leah and bolted toward the living room with their silverware still clutched in his hand.

"What's wrong?" asked Duvid, as he caught sight of Leah. She was clutching the front crimson curtain with both hands and pressing it against her neck. He slowly entered the room, but Leah didn't acknowledge that Duvid had appeared, slowly walking toward the stereo player to catch her eyes.

"No, no," she gasped. Her eyes darted around the room, glancing at the front door, side window and hallway. There was no escape from time itself. Duvid stopped moving and watched her desperate glances across the room. He put down the silverware on the television stand and lifted the blonde wood lid of the Grundig record player console, switching off the record, and gently returning the record player arm to its rest. The lifted needle unveiled a silent room filled with trepidation. Duvid turned on a table lamp, revealing Leah's wide-eyed terror.

Her face was a pale death mask. Leah's mouth was slightly ajar from her last gasp of life and her empty stare was locked on the far wall, as if looking through it into another time. It was a look of frozen terror that Duvid had not seen on her face since they had hidden in a barn from black leather Gestapo boots.

Duvid walked over to the picture window for a peek at the street.

"No," Leah repeated. "Please."

"What did you see?" asked Duvid.

Another car door slammed and Duvid reached over Leah's tight embrace to slightly part the curtain. Duvid knew that it was something horrible and it couldn't be stopped. Leah could hear the clicking of heels walking down the sidewalk toward their front cement stairs. They held onto each other and the open edge of the curtain. Spying their own neighborhood, they were puzzled by the sight of their oldest son, Sam, walking in front of a line of dark suits coming to the house.

Duvid could see the Rabbi's dark-green Ford LTD parked at the curb, and he knew that God was involved. The street conversation stopped. Doctors Asher and Jerome Cornfield were each grasping the handles of their black physician's satchels, walking toward the house close behind Sam and Rabbi Lerer.

Leah pulled away from the picture window, startled by the sight of Sam and Rabbi walking up the cement steps to the front door, followed by the doctors. Leah trembled and screamed with the dread of watching a live execution. She shrieked a long, cutting cry and clenched Duvid's arm with both hands.

The doorbell rang once. Leah's knees buckled, but Duvid grasped her arms and held her close.

"Let me open the door," said Duvid.

She pulled away and ran toward the front door. The screen door creaked as it was pulled open. Leah pressed her open hands against the inner wooden door and closed her eyes, panicked by an unknown disaster on the other side.

"Are you going to let them in?" asked Duvid.

She looked up and out the narrow pane of glass running across the top of the door and noticed the mezuzah gently nailed into the outer door frame. The bell rang again.

As she bit into her lip, Leah's small, brown eyes popped open, as if bracing for the impact of a highway collision. The soft, creaseless skin of her round face pulled tight from her jaw clenching. Her hand instinctually pulled her gray hair tighter into the teeth of the hair clip. She then untied the kitchen apron, tossing it over the back of the living room couch. Their oldest son, Sam, the Rabbi, and both family doctors waited on the other side of the door. The bell rang again, then a knock.

Leah recalled when their Warsaw apartment front door and building were blown to pieces by Luftwaffe bombing, but she feared that opening this door would be worse. Duvid came up behind Leah, held onto one of her arms, reached around her, and opened the door. Now staring into Sam's eyes, Duvid was perplexed by the visitors standing on his porch in the evening dusk. They were there to face something too and said nothing about it.

"*Oy, Got!*" screamed Leah. She squirmed to flee anywhere and Duvid held her waist from behind. Sam leaned against the aluminum frame of the open screen door, grabbed his mother's hand, and held firm.

"*Wus is eas?*" asked Leah. She looked at Sam with inquiry in her eyes.

"*Setz ech*", answered Sam. "Let's all sit down." He held the screen door open as the Rabbi and doctors silently entered the home. Their heads were bowed and they avoided eye contact with Leah and Duvid. She fought, standing next to Duvid as everyone came in, but he held her waist firm.

"Let's sit down on the couch," said Sam again, gesturing his parents to sit down first.

While one doctor had on a blue sport coat and the other a gray suit, they each wore white, rumpled shirts, no ties, and dark khaki pants. Their black loafers were well worn in the heels from miles of hospital rounds. It wasn't clear whether they were friends with their patients or if patients became friends, but their dedication to both extended practice hours. A casually wrapped stethoscope protruded from Dr. Asher Cornfield's jacket pocket. The brothers hugged their medical bags and leaned against the living room wall next to the Rabbi, watching as Leah tried to shake off the grip of Duvid's hand.

Rabbi Lerer's black, pin-striped suit and freshly shined black shoes confirmed the somber tenor of the evening. More and more frequently, Duvid had seen this funeral suit. The Rabbi pressed his dark-blue yarmulke in place, straightened his maroon tie, and re-fastened the tie clip. He held a *siddur*, a Jewish prayer book, against his chest, waiting for the right moment for prayer and to offer comfort. There was nothing right about the moment.

Duvid sat on the couch and pulled on Leah's arm to sit her down next to him. She turned her body toward the hallway and tried to twist her arm out of Duvid's grip. No words were spoken, but Leah grunted with her twisting effort to flee, bumping a small glass bowl of flowers to the edge of the coffee table. She frequently left fruit or freshly cut flowers in bowls, reminding her to have colorful life. She liked to see life.

Sam tossed the white couch pillows on the carpet, and grabbed her other hand, gently pulling her down onto the couch between himself and Duvid.

"What is it?" asked Leah again, this time in English.

Rabbi Lerer pulled one of the sitting chairs to the other side of the solid-wood coffee table and sat down, pushing the bowl away from the edge to prevent its crashing to the floor. He placed his *siddur* on the table and ran his forefinger down his black moustache, as if preparing to speak.

"What is it?" repeated Leah more frantically. "Tell me." Sitting on the couch, Duvid held his grip on her arm and Sam clenched her hand, bracing for impact. She looked at the doctors and the Rabbi, Duvid, and then turned toward Sam.

"He was at that conference in Princeton, New Jersey," said Sam, "and they called me to say, we lost him."

Asher opened his black bag and reached inside, searching for something. Sam looked into the open well of his mother's eyes. Duvid stopped breathing and the color of his face turned bleach white as the blood drained from his being. The words cut out the marrow of his splayed soul.

"What happened?" she screamed at Sam. It was a visceral response to the impossible and irreparable damage.

"I'll get details and tell you when I know," answered Sam, gasping through the choke in his voice, "but he died." He covered his head with both hands and began to sob.

"The younger brother?" whispered Dr. Jerome to his own brother. Dr. Asher nodded his head.

"He was a blessing for them surviving," said Dr. Asher.

"Where is he? I want to see him!" said Leah, and yanked her hands clear of any hold. With one hand, she grabbed a clump of her hair tucked behind her ear and yanked it hard out of her scalp. She didn't scream from the ripping pain and threw the clump on the floor, then reached back for more.

Rabbi Lerer extended his reach and took her free right hand, then dropped to his knees in front of her, looking up into Leah's eyes.

"Don't punish yourself," said Rabbi Lerer. "We are all here for you." He held her hand tight. There was no amount of pain to end the pain. Surviving against the odds, she fought to never bury their boys, but her new reality was like a slow and endless guillotine chop.

"Let's have her lie back," said Dr. Asher. Duvid pulled himself into the corner of the couch and turned Leah to lean back against him. Sam stood up to make room for the doctor and his medical bag. The Rabbi let go of her right hand and Sam stationed himself behind the couch, holding his mother's left hand and shoulder, while Duvid locked his grip around her waist.

"I'll sit here," said Dr. Asher as he sat in Sam's place and put his open black bag on the tan carpet between his feet. Dr. Jerome stood close behind Duvid's head.

They collectively held their breath in disbelief of the moment.

"Leah," said Dr. Asher, "try to lie still. This will help you feel better." He rolled up her right sleeve, while Dr. Jerome crouched down at her side and gently held her arm straight.

Dr. Asher stood and slid her feet onto the couch where he was sitting. Dr. Jerome lifted her head off Duvid's lap, so he could get a blanket from the hallway closet, and laid a pillow in Duvid's place. She began to look up at the faces surrounding her and slowly absorbed their presence. It was a nightmare.

"Why didn't I go first?" asked Leah, "Before any of them?"

Glances were exchanged, but there was no answer.

Dr. Asher was holding the syringe and inserted the needle into the glass vial to draw in the sedative.

"Hold still, Leah," said Dr. Asher, "just relax and you will feel a little poke." He taped white gauze over the blood spot and dropped the empty needle into a small, red Sharps container.

To the others, he said, "This should calm her down for several hours, but it won't put her to sleep." He glanced at Duvid, who was holding a blanket, waiting for an acknowledging nod.

Leaning away from the couch, Sam shuffled his feet and wiped a tear away with the back of his wrist.

Duvid brushed Leah's hair back over the exposed torn roots. His face was still white, but focused on Leah. It was no time for his emotions or tears. Leah bled for both of them.

With the gauze in place, Leah reached over and clenched the cloth of her opposite sleeve. With one powerful downward yank, the fabric's shoulder seam split open. Sam looked at Duvid, who was still holding her tight. She lay still, but her heart continued to open wide. Her hand slid over to grab her breast pocket and tore it completely off the blouse.

Duvid and Sam exchanged darting glances with the doctors and Rabbi, but didn't react to the ripping, waiting for the medicine to kick in. As if swishing away an attacking pest, Leah's hand bounced around her white collar to find a grip. She let out an exasperated shriek and closed her eyes on a pool of tears. Her hand fell to the side and was cradled by Dr. Asher. Painful silence filled the room.

"Do you smell something burning?" asked Dr. Jerome. He spun around and began sniffing the air.

"The brisket!" said Duvid. "She left the oven on!" Sam sprang toward the kitchen and switched off the Kenmore oven. As he walked back to the living room, he began to switch on some lights.

Suddenly Leah sat up, rolled off the couch, and walked to her bedroom. She flipped on the ceiling light and closed the door behind her. Sam started to follow his mother, but Duvid grabbed his arm.

"Maybe let her be alone for a moment," said Duvid. "Let's listen and we'll see."

The wood floor in the bedroom rhythmically creaked as Leah slowly paced the narrow space between the queen-sized bed and the dresser. Back and forth, then again and again. She turned her back toward the mirror hanging on the closet door, knowing the surface must be covered. There was nothing to fight and nowhere to go. Tears followed by tears rushed down her soft cheeks. His death was final.

Emptiness overcrowded the bedroom. Two dressed baby dolls rested on the bed, each seated against a pillow. The dolls were the only items brought with her from Germany at the end of the war. They always remained seated on the light-gray bed quilt. Safe.

"Oh, my God," said Leah, "my God." Her hoarse and fatigued voice continued to plead for a response. Her hands remained open at her sides as if waiting for an embrace. With the ferociousness of a blown-open, once-dormant volcano, Leah screamed with a guttural pain of her burning heart. The sound rose from a desperate horror without escape. Her survivor's apprehension came true. The Holocaust was not over for Leah.

She let out a pained screech with the wounded terror of a trapped animal. Duvid cracked opened the door, leaned his head into the opening and asked, "*Bist du..........?*" She grumbled a response and screamed, while ripping apart the sleeves of her blouse, leaving them in shreds on the floor.

Duvid pushed the door wide open and stepped into the room to see Leah looking out the window at the darkened sky, pleading with the heavens. The shrieks of exasperation filled the room.

"Doctors, please come!" Duvid cried out to the Cornfield brothers. Doctors Jerome and Asher rushed into the room, black bags in hand. Rabbi Lerer and Sam remained poised at the door, waiting to aid. Duvid walked over to the nightstand and switched on the lamp. The Rabbi opened his *siddur* and began to quietly sway, silently chanting a prayer.

"Leah, come sit on the bed," said Duvid, gathering the dolls with a swoop of his hand. She started to pace and walked into the arms of the incoming doctors.

"With the sedative, Leah," said Dr. Asher, "you should sit down and rest." She tried to shake off the hands that supported her arms. The Rabbi and Sam stepped further back into the hall.

"Do you know what happened to him?" asked Rabbi Lerer.

Sam nodded his head and gestured that they moved into the hallway shadows.

"During a break at the conference," answered Sam, "he was shooting hoops outside and collapsed on the court. His knees buckled and he went down in front of friends, but they couldn't resuscitate him. His heart stopped." The Rabbi raised his hands over his eyes and they both bowed their heads.

"Don't fight the medication, Leah," said Dr. Asher. "Just lie down and let it help you relax." He placed one hand on her back and the other on her shoulder, and gently eased her onto the bed. She reached over and opened the nightstand. Her hand shuffled through some Kleenex, Sucrets, and photos, and she pulled out an age-yellowed envelope. Gently, she pressed it to her chest and lay back.

Leah closed her eyes and thought about their apartment building in Warsaw and how quickly it had fallen to rubble when the first Luftwaffe bombs struck the city. She recalled dive-bombing planes with the giant swastikas painted on their wings . . . a newborn infant . . . corpses in the streets . . . and running for their lives with handfuls of belongings. Her hand fell to her thigh, still clutching the envelope.

* * * * *

Duvid and Leah were grateful to be settled in Milwaukee and proud to own their home. The sandstone brick house on 52nd Street gave them the sense that this structure could provide a stable place to enjoy retirement years with visiting children. Leah had survived with shredded hope, but it alone wouldn't be life's end point.

"Hitler took everything away," whispered Leah. How could she lose it again and survive? *Why bother?* she wondered. She was living through her heart being torn out and not being allowed to die.

"Not the baby," said Leah. He had died and there was nothing to change that fact. Life was smashed. The envelope slipped from Leah's grip and fell to the floor. Duvid slowly reached down and picked it up off the carpet. He stared at the time-worn envelope resting in his hand.

"She still has it," said Duvid.

"What's in there?" asked Dr. Jerome, offering his hand to hold it.

"A reminder," said Duvid. He turned and opened the nightstand drawer, then slid the envelope under a stack of Polaroid color photos of their grandchildren. "Let's keep it sealed."

EUROPE IN 1939, JUST BEFORE THE OUTBREAK OF WORLD WAR II.
(SOURCE: HTTP://ADRIANCHAPMAN.COM)

CHAPTER ONE

STREET GAMES

Our strength is our quickness and our brutality
(T)he aim of this war does not consist in reaching certain
designated [geographical] lines,
but in the enemies' physical elimination."

Unsere Stärke ist unsere Schnelligkeith und unsere Brutalität ...
das Kriegsziel besteht nicht im Erreichen von bestimmten Linien,
sondern in der physischen Vernichtung des Gegners.
—Adolf Hitler, Obersalzberg Speech
August 22, 1939, one week prior to the German occupation of Poland

WARSAW: SEPTEMBER 1, 1939

S lam! Sam wasn't quite seven years old, but he closed the oak apartment front door with the desperate force of saving a life. Ramming the door into its wooden frame made an ear-piercing crack, like firing a hand-gun. Sam quickly turned around and bolted shut the entrance. Pressing his back against the door, he looked around for help, oblivious to the street mud caked on his brown boots and laces. The doormat, a tattered, square piece of burlap, caught a few chunks as he pounded his feet in place.

"Ma!" yelled Sam. He locked his legs and pressed his back into the door, expecting it to be kicked open. "Ma!" He was so out of breath that he could only call out the one syllable. His lungs were burning from panting so fast and frantically heaving in the cool autumn air.

The water in the iron pot on the stove was just starting to steam, so she couldn't be far away. Fresh-cut potatoes were sitting on the cutting board, ready to be plopped into the boiling water.

"Sammy, *kim aheyr*," said Leah, beckoning the boy. *Not again*, she thought. At the sound of his voice, she swallowed her fear and tempered her anger. Her firm, soft tone was a mix of concern and alarm that something happened to her son when he disappeared from the courtyard.

"I'm fine," answered Sam, "I'm right here." He avoided his mother's gaze and remained fixated on the cracks in the wood floor at his feet, as he continued to heavily pant.

"Where have you been?" She gently embraced him, while checking for any bruises or blood. "You disappeared and I didn't know where to look for you. You know I can't chase you." He started to cough from being out of breath. "Settle yourself and drink some water."

She picked up a tin cup from the sink and scooped some water out of the bucket. Her calm manner was in stark contrast to Sam's racing panic. "You're in a sweat." Leah brushed his damp, brown hair off his forehead and held his full, bright-red cheeks in the palms of her hands.

As she looked down from the front window in their third-floor apartment, Leah could see several boys running out the courtyard entrance into Wolynska Street. They fled, darting around a push cart with a busted wheel propped against the curb. The last boy held the brim of his cap and reached down to scoop a rock from the curb. He spun around, yelled something, and tossed it at their building.

Leah listened for a crash, but instead heard a "thud" as the rock bounced off the bricks. "We don't need any broken glass here," she said.

"Broken glass?" Sam asked. He looked up at her with squinted eyes.

"Far away, but getting closer, I fear," she answered. "They're not from around here," Leah mumbled, as she walked away from the window. "*Gib a kik vus es iz in droysn ayder di gayst.*"

"I always check first if anyone's out there," said Sam. "Josh says his mother tells him the same."

"You must both watch to stay away from them." Leah walked to the kitchen window and looked down into the empty inner courtyard. She gently massaged her swollen stomach and guided Sam away from the door.

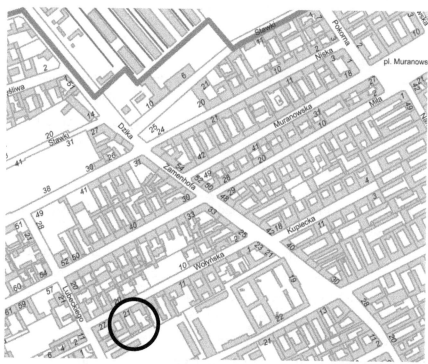

MAP OF WARSAW SHOWING 21 WOLYNSKA STREET, WHERE THE GINGOLD FAMILY LIVED BEFORE THE WAR.
(SOURCE: POLISH CENTER FOR HOLOCAUST RESEARCH)

"Wipe all the mud off your boots and hang up your jacket," she continued. "You should stay inside until we go to the market."

She looked straight into Sam's deep brown eyes and again brushed back his sweaty dark curls. She slowly shook her head from side to side.

"Where's your hat?" she asked. Saying nothing, Sam pulled the wool cap out of his coat pocket and proudly exhibited it to his mother.

"Where were you?" asked Leah. "When I looked down to see you, you were gone. That cannot happen again, if you want to play with Josh." Sam averted her eyes and unbuttoned his coat to let out the heat. "Do you understand?"

"We're in September," she continued, "it's already cold outside and you're sweating. You need to wear a hat and not get sick." She walked over to the coal bin and picked out a few pieces from the black chunky pile with the iron tongs.

"Now go wash with the water left in the bucket, but remember, the carp is still in the tub. We will have fresh fish with Schabes dinner tonight." Leah could only lean forward a bit to grab a towel to hold the stove's handle and pull open the hot oven door.

"Your sleeve is ripped, too," she noted. "Now how did that happen if you were just playing with Josh?" Sam's cheeks were bright red and his eyes scanned the room for a quick answer, but there was none.

"I can sew this up again, but remember it's your only coat for winter. Those pants have to last, too, because your other pair is for *shul*. Did Josh make it home?" asked Leah.

Sam moved toward the kitchen window, peering down on the empty courtyard and rusted stairs.

"We made it to the steps and he ran up toward his door," answered Sam. From such a promising early morning, Leah recalled how it had filled with so much sweat and trauma . . .

* * * * *

"Are you done in the kitchen?" asked Leah. She had been startled awake by the sound of Duvid coming back into the bedroom and the creak of the closing door.

"Not light yet outside," answered Duvid, "and almost done. Sorry for waking you. I wanted to get my work clothes on so I didn't have to finish tinkering in my undershorts. It's still early and you need your rest," Duvid whispered into Leah's ear. She sat up and swung her thin, white legs out from under the warm quilt.

He sat on the corner of their bed and reached for his gray work pants, draped over the back of an armless wooden chair.

The suspenders snagged one of the decorative knobs attached to the top rail on the back of the chair.

"Is that what those are for," he said, "to catch things?"

Duvid yanked the pants into his lap, almost rocking the chair off the ground. He quickly stood to get his legs into the pants and dinked the back of his head into the dangling ceiling light. "Aaaaah!" He swatted at the light and was reminded that being well over six feet tall had it disadvantages, especially in a small apartment.

Standing beside her husband, Lead laughed, "I never had that problem, or anyone else in my family." She proudly held her hand next to the height of her head and looked up, smiling at Duvid. Like many Warsaw residents, she was more than a foot shorter than Duvid and the fact that he stood out made him very uncomfortable in crowds. Rubbing the back of his head, Duvid decided to sit down again and safely put on his work boots.

"Someday," said Duvid, "I would like to have knee-high, black boots like your father. They're not for work, but I like how Sam stares at them when your parents visit. The heels make such a pounding thud on the wood floor that he watches as if the boots were moving by themselves."

"Sorry," said Leah, slowly sitting down on the bed next to Duvid, "maybe you first have to be a grandpa to have nice boots." She reached behind herself and grabbed her back with both hands, and slowly began to press and rub her lower back muscles.

Leah recalled how she had hesitated when her friend introduced her to Duvid for the first time. She had looked directly into his chest and when she looked up, she caught herself glaring at his large nose. Leah didn't instantly imagine a future with him, but now looking at her growing family, she couldn't see it any other way.

"I may not know about the baby things," said Duvid, "but I remember when you were with Sammy at this point, the doctor always said that you need to stay off your feet and get rest."

Sitting back down on the bed, Leah groaned slightly with effort to roll back onto her left side and re-stuff the pillow under her head. "I am still in my twenties and already move like a fat, old lady."

"I'm almost finished with it," said Duvid. "Stay in bed and rest, but keep an eye out for Sam and make sure he doesn't get up and come into the kitchen." The morning sun had cracked through a gap in the bedroom curtain.

"You want me to sleep and stay awake?" chuckled Leah. She wiggled under the covers, awkwardly rolled to one side, and propped up her head with one hand.

"I can't sleep anyway," she continued, "and I miss sleeping on my stomach. Last few weeks of this, maybe."

Duvid smiled at her, gently gathered her unbraided glossy, black hair and pulled up the blanket over her shoulder. There was enough light in the room for her to see that he was now dressed in his lightly grease-stained gray overalls and a white sleeveless shirt. He had been up since 4 o'clock and had stowed himself in an empty kitchen corner with some hand tools, a few short boards, and a clinky sack of metal pieces.

"He is going to be *meshuge* over this," said Duvid, "and I should be done in a few minutes." He dropped to his knees and blindly reached under the bed and pulled out another brown sack from behind boxes of winter clothes. He jumped to his feet and smiled with the excitement of holding a mined bag of gold.

"Where did you get all of the parts?" asked Leah.

"Mostly junk pieces from the shop," answered Duvid, "but the right-sized wheels and bearings were the most difficult to find."

He held open one hand and in the other, held a brown bag, cinched closed with a tied piece of string. "I've been digging through the scrap piles at work for months, hoping that something useful would be thrown out."

Standing in his work boots, Duvid's industrial and muscular frame towered over their bed. When standing together with Leah, his height dwarfed her. Her soft and now round frame was in contrast to his fiercely focused expression, highlighted by a larger, angular nose. They were opposite pieces that fit together into one picture.

Leah and Duvid were expanding their young family, and they were proud to have two bedrooms with a corner W.C. to help accommodate the hopeful addition. Their brick apartment building had been built in the late 1800s, but had useful modern conveniences for their growing family, including an electric ceiling light in each room, and a kitchen with a coal-burning stove for cooking and heat.

"I'm not sure who will be more excited with your surprise *tchotchke*, you or Sammy."

"Probably me," said Duvid, "but he'll like being a big brother even more." Duvid leaned over and gave Leah a confirming kiss on her forehead. "This will give him something fun to do, so he doesn't feel pushed aside by the baby. All he has are little pebbles in his pocket to play against the wall, while other kids in the park have so much. This will be his."

"I know you have worked hard on this, but don't you think it will bring him trouble?" asked Leah. "He is still a little boy and any attention on the street gets rough."

"As long as the boys stay with it in the courtyard and you can see them, he'll be fine." Duvid's fingers brushed his slick, black hair off his forehead. He opened the top dresser drawer and pulled out a white handkerchief, snapped it open, and stuffed it into his back right pants pocket, then grabbed both clanking sacks lying on the foot of the bed. "I'll quick finish this so we can give it to him before breakfast and I can run to the factory."

Leah rolled back to her side, closed her eyes, and tried to pretend that the sun wasn't rising. She heard the low and heavy hum of airplane engines and tried to ignore that, too.

"Rest?" she mumbled. *Tap, tap, tap.* Leah struggled to roll to her other side and sit up. *Tap, tap, tap.* The rhythmic pounding of a ball-peen hammer beating nails into soft wood was too much to ignore.

She struggled to lean forward and gently rock off the bed to stand. With one step, she reached for her thinning ivory robe, which was hanging on a metal hook on the back of their bedroom door. She heard more airplane engines overhead and slipped on the robe.

"Can't reach anymore," she said to no one. She struggled to overreach around her back, carefully pulling in the worn drawstrings around her waist and quickly tying them around her extended stomach.

"Have you dropped from yesterday?" she inquired of the unborn child. "Soon, we hope."

"Where are they going so early in the morning?" asked Leah.

Duvid had stepped back in the room and tossed the empty sacks back under the bed.

"I don't know," answered Duvid, "but maybe our air force has to practice when no one else is up there. They seem to all being going West." He lifted the shade and bit down on his lower lip, looking up at the passing sight in the early morning gray sky. "Go wake Sammy and let's give it to him before breakfast, then I will go to work."

"Don't leave so fast," said Leah, as she reached for Duvid's hand and started to tip toward the wall. He quickly reached back and grabbed her hand to steady her upright. They both froze in the awkward position and looked into each other's eyes. Leah smiled at his quick thinking and their moment of tenderness.

"What?" asked Duvid. "You were about to hit the wall."

"That's not it. I forgot, but the Lipinskys never came for their bread order yesterday, so I was given the two extra rye loaves when we closed up the bakery yesterday." Her smile continued. "We can't eat that much before it gets moldy, but they think I'm eating for two, so I couldn't say no. Take one to work and trade it for a bit of meat or something that I can add to the pot."

"I'll see what I can get, "he said.

Grabbing one of the empty sacks, Duvid looked down at Leah's bare feet and shook his head. "Your ankles still look swollen, and you know what the doctor said about keeping your legs up."

"We need the zloty," said Leah, "and the extra bakery pieces are also good for me and the baby. If I didn't have this job, we wouldn't eat so well."

Together, they walked into the kitchen. She went to the lower cupboard near the iron stove, swung open the door, and pulled out a large brown clay pot and cover. Leah grabbed the clay pot by its molded handles and hobbled to the small kitchen table.

Duvid quickly moved to the table, grabbed his folded copy of the *Haynt* newspaper, closed the evening performance listings, and tossed it on one of the chairs.

"I'll finish reading it when I get home," said Duvid.

Leah placed the empty covered pot on the small kitchen table next to the blue cup of wooden matches.

"My mother walks so far for the few bread crumbs that we give them, so how can I stop?" Leah walked back to the cupboard and pulled open one of the wooden drawers and began picking through the jumbled metal utensils.

"But you can barely walk or bend your ankles," said Duvid.

"I already took today off," said Leah. "Next week will be my last until after the baby, and don't complain when we are back to steaming stale crusts."

"Why complain? We'll have a healthy baby and mother, if you stay off your feet," said Duvid.

Leah shrugged her shoulders in a non-committal fashion. She walked to the cabinet by the sink and pulled a large wooden ladle and serrated knife out of the drawer, and laid them next to the pot.

"After you leave, I'll chop the vegetables we got from the market yesterday. It would be helpful if you could bring up some water before you go," continued Leah. "I just can't make it up the stairs with a full bucket of water."

"And you shouldn't have to," said Duvid, as he peeked into the sink. "Where's the bucket?"

"It's where you left it yesterday," answered Leah, "next to the tub. And check that the carp is still moving, too. Please leave a full bucket next to the stove."

"Can you get the pot to the bakery before closing?" asked Duvid.

"Uncle Aaron turns off his ovens for Schabes early afternoon, so if I get our cholent pot to him before everyone else shows up, he'll push ours in before he closes the doors. I'll take Sam with me after he eats something and maybe they will let me in before the line forms."

"I've never seen the Friday oven rush," said Duvid, "so how does he know who belongs to which pot?"

"Simple," answered Leah, "Each of the ladies knows her pot by the cloth left on the handle. When Aaron turns off the oven and closes the iron doors, nothing gets in or out until Saturday afternoon. He's funny that way and treats it like a bank vault, so nothing will steal the heat."

"I thought you weren't going into work," said Duvid, "and staying off your feet."

"It will be a quick visit," said Leah, "I'll be in and out, before everyone lines up with their pots."

Then Leah pulled all of her hair behind her head and reached into her robe pocket. She pulled out a brown headscarf to cover her hair and tie in back. The scarf had a blue thread that ran the length of the fabric and appeared as a circle when resting across the top of her forehead.

She struggled to slightly lift up onto her toes to pull out a sack from behind an upper cabinet door, and then drop it on the counter. She began shaking out end chunks of carrots, turnips, potatoes, and celery, and placed them near the knife.

Duvid leaned the newly crafted contraption against the wall near Sam's door.

Leah kept chattering. "If I drop the pot off this morning, then I can quick say *Gut Schabes* to everyone at work, and Rebecca can push it in the oven, until we pick it up after services tomorrow."

It wasn't a religious part of their Jewish orthodox rituals, but retrieving the warm cholent after *shul* on Saturday morning was an embedded habit for Leah, as much as it was for the observant bearded men to wear a black-and-white tallis for the morning services.

"That is a lot of running around for someone who is supposed to rest," said Duvid.

Snick, snick, snick. Leah had started chopping the vegetables into even smaller bite-sized pieces, and scraped them off the warped cutting board into the pot.

"You can't leave work to get to the bakery," said Leah, "and I need fresh air. And speaking of visits," continued Leah, "Chava will stop by next week, so we can talk about her taking care of Sam when I'm in the hospital."

"How is your sister going to get here by herself, since Froim works during the day?" asked Duvid.

"Chava is almost 17 and insists she is old enough to walk here by herself. In the morning, she can walk part way with my brother on his way to work and just be alert for the rest. She is on her own to get back to my parents' house, but I'm not arguing with her. She's careful, knows the safe streets, and wouldn't listen to me, Froim, or our parents anyway."

Duvid brought his hand to his lips in a thoughtful manner and tried to think of other safe transportation. He knew the same streets.

"Sam loves playing with Chava and soon, we are going to need her help. So even if I could get word to her, I'm not going to tell her *not* to come. Still need the water bucket, please."

Duvid started to say something, then stopped and nodded his head.

Leah took the pot to the sink and sprinkled in something from a small bag that had been hidden behind the pan and large boiling pot in the lower cupboard.

"I know that's not another hidden sack of parts," said Duvid. "What's in the bag?"

"These are some beans my mother got from her neighbor a few weeks ago," answered Leah, "and I thought if you swapped the bread for some meat, it would bake together well. Our best dinner all year, I think, and a little different from the Friday night fish and soup."

"Sounds delicious, so let's not forget the pot tomorrow," said Duvid. "Let's wake Sam."

Their son found himself cajoled out of bed and prodded into the kitchen by his mother. They were both standing barefoot on the cool, wooden kitchen floor, waiting for the reason to be there. Sam was wearing his father's old dress shirt, which was now his nightshirt, and was tugging at the fabric that was twisted at his shoulders.

He started rubbing one of his eyes and remembered a piece of his dream, something about finding a pile of shiny pebbles left in a backstreet gutter. The memory of the dream began to slip away with each moment.

"Sam," said Duvid, with a loud, morning voice. From Duvid's perspective, Warsaw was a dirt-poor city and they were at best common and scraping by life. At a time and in a city where it was cruel to dream, there were few treasured moments, and this would be one.

"We have *something special to give you*, but you must promise to listen and be very careful with it."

Sam scrunched down his eyebrows and gazed at his father's serious expression. He had never heard those five words before, and wondered if it was a continued dream about pebbles. But there was something hiding behind his father's legs and work boots, and a piece caught and reflected the early light.

It gleamed.

Duvid stepped aside and Sam looked straight at the shiny wheels, mounted in front under the one-inch-thick foot slat. The handmade creation had no markings or colors on the charcoal-dusted wooden frame, but Sam knew it was a scooter and that it was meant for him. The splintered wood of the crossbar handle had blue rags wrapped and tacked onto the left and right grips.

"For me?" screamed Sam, crossing his arms and hugging his shoulders. His mouth hung open and he took two steps backward, and then froze, taking it all in. He looked up at his father's face for confirmation, and Duvid nodded. Their smiles embraced each other in mutual content and disbelief.

"Go get dressed," said Duvid, "and eat some oatmeal for breakfast. You can take it out for a quick ride before you go with Ma to the market."

Sam darted into his room and Leah smiled at the sound of clothes and shoes flying across his room.

Leaning his head into Sam's room, Duvid asked, "You know who to avoid and where you must stay with the scooter, right? I'm very serious about this." Sam's eyes gleamed as he nodded.

Turning back to his wife, Duvid looked toward the window, listening to the hum-and-choke sound of more plane engines. Duvid faced Leah with his arms open and palms turned upward.

"Stay in the courtyard with Josh," said Leah, "where I can see and hear you." She spoke to the same open door and feared that Sam couldn't hear them, deafened by the scooter. She walked into his room to emphasize the point and make sure that Sam's eyes met hers.

"Remember our deal." His sheets and blanket were in a heap on the floor, as if they had been blasted off the bed. Sam jumped into his chair at the kitchen table and began to wolf down the bowl of oatmeal Leah had finished mixing.

"Only go out if Josh is with you, and stay in the courtyard where I can see and hear you from our window," she admonished.

"I know," said Sam with a mouth stuffed full of oatmeal. He stood up, chair legs screeching along the floor, walked to the front coat hook, and grabbed his coat and hat.

"I'll come down soon and get you when I'm ready for the market. There is nothing but trouble for you both on the street. So don't wander off," Leah said.

"I know," said Sam, as he grabbed the scooter handles and went to their front door, rolling the scooter at his side. He knew where to stay within the safe courtyard and to not leave.

"There won't be any other Jewish kids out there yet," said Leah, "and neither of you want to be pushed around again." She waved her finger at the empty courtyard, her voice echoing down the back hall. "*Gib a kik vus es iz in droysn ayder di gayst*," said Leah.

"I'm looking," said Sam, "*Ikh zey nisht kan sakh mentshn.* I don't see anyone."

"If you see them, then you know to come back," said Leah.

Sam paused and looked down at his scooter.

"Those boys are older than you and next time, you may not get away."

Sam turned back and looked into his mother's eyes, then again at the scooter.

"I'm in no condition to go find you," Leah continued, her hand resting gently on her belly. She also looked down at the scooter and its shiny wheels.

"If you see others on the street, come back in right away," she said again. "And don't worry about the scooter."

Both Duvid and Sam looked at her.

"We can fix a scooter," Leah paused, "but you?"

Sam had acquired some bruises from his street smarts, but he could only focus on one spoken word: "Scooter."

* * * * *

While Sam wanted to go to school like the older kids, there was no public school for him, nor did his family have money for religious education. Leah knew that he only had a few friends in the building to play with, so she was happy to let him outside under a watchful eye when there were others in their courtyard.

Sam and Josh were fortunate to enjoy each other's company, since neither boy was invited to other homes to play. They were Jewish and not welcome.

Together, the boys created their own games, which often carried them to the edge of danger. Roll an unused wooden carriage wheel frame down the smooth cement street and see how long it will go until it fell or crashed. The wheel was from a horse-drawn buggy and had a thick rim that was shoulder-height to the boys. A right turn out of the gate took a sharp downhill pitch to the main crossroad, Zarnenhofa Street. The sprint needed to stop well before the intersection, since traffic and the streetcar would cut them off or neighborhood ruffians would pummel them for being Jews.

If the wheel took off uninterrupted, then either Sam or Josh would have to chase and knock it down before it caught runaway speed. Sam was born to explore his environment, and even as an infant, Leah could not get him to sit in a buggy for a free ride. He kept crawling out, insisted on pushing, whether or not anyone else was riding. In his spirit, there was always somewhere else to go. Anywhere.

Josh was a little taller, thinner, and a bit faster than Sam, though not as agile. They frequently picked up street pebbles and gently tossed them a short distance against a near brick wall, so that the small stones bounced back to them. Whoever tossed the second pebble would then use his spread-open hand to try and touch both stones. If it was close enough to touch one another's stone, then the grabber could claim both stones. Of course, each boy aimed for the shiniest pebble, like children with gleaming marbles, and tried to collect the smoothest pieces. While Josh was a year older, taller, and could lean in a bit further, Sam had the balance and a finesse toss in his favor. The pebbles rested in the gutter or in a pocket, but the street wasn't as simple.

* * * * *

"Why can't you and Josh play in the courtyard where I can watch you?" asked Leah.

"The sidewalk and street pavement are smooth," answered Sam. "The chunky cobblestones catch the pebbles, the wheel, and trip us, too."

By giving Sam something to do outside of the apartment, Leah agreed that the boys could play pebbles just outside of their gate without wandering too far astray. However, when the boys played with the wheel in the street, an undesired third game occurred that Sam didn't like to share with his parents.

* * * * *

Jumping into the street to run to the other side was an urgent necessity whenever the two Jewish boys were approached by non-Jewish Polish kids. The risk of being suddenly struck by a moving vehicle, carriage, or push cart was worth the risk to be safe from teenage thugs. It was a fact that they were all Polish kids, but being

Jewish and speaking Yiddish openly on the street labeled you a Jew and unwanted, like street vermin that needed to be harshly stomped.

Yiddish was the language of Warsaw Jews and openly spoken, especially by groups of Jewish men resting outside stores discussing politics or wandering the Jewish neighborhoods. It was also a paranoid survival reality for little Jewish boys, and a seed planted in Sam's earliest instinct.

"You must be careful outside," said Duvid, "because you are Jewish and seen as different."

"But why, Papa?" asked Sam. "We're all just kids."

"It's unfair and has been that way since I was your age," Duvid continued, "but Jews have always got to be on guard to survive. If you speak Yiddish outside of our home, then people will know that you are a Jew and that is a mark for others to see."

Duvid had learned that unless one was in a large group of Jews, speaking Yiddish in public was asking for a beating or worse. When he and Leah had recently attended an evening performance at the Jewish theatre, they decided to cut short the path home and avoid the busier streets. It had been a bad choice.

When Sam's nose had been busted by street bullies earlier that summer, it had taught him to not be noticed by others. There was nothing to hide the blood on his clothes or from his parents' view.

Duvid now had the same problem and scooped a handful of sidewalk winter snow for a cool compression to stem the bruise and bleeding trail leading back home.

Street blood was frequently spilled for being noticed and Sam and his Jewish friends were not invisible, just like the shirt stains. It became instinct for Sam to look over his shoulder, whether up at the window to see his mother, or out through the open courtyard gate or constantly on the street.

Even after several soakings in the sink, Duvid's ripped and bloodied white shirt held stains that ran deep and yielded permanent discoloration. Duvid had agreed with Leah that it was best to throw out his only dress shirt—one less reminder. His facial gashes would heal with time, but not the emotional scars and humiliation of a gang publicly pounding him in front of his wife.

* * * * *

Sam went down the open back hall, heading toward Josh's door and holding the scooter handles to avoid scraping the wall. *Thump, thump.* Sam kept both hands on the handlebar and could only kick the front door of Josh's family apartment. *Thump!* It wasn't difficult for Sam to convince Josh to join him for an after-breakfast courtyard excursion, especially when Josh saw what Sam was holding.

"Is that yours?" asked Josh. His pale complexion seemed to brighten with the thought of scooter-cruising possibilities.

"Yes," answered Sam, "and my parents told me to share it with you." Josh smiled with two teeth missing. "But I get to go first and we need to stay real close or my ma will make me come inside."

"Fair deal!" Josh said, grinning even more broadly.

"I just got it," said Sam, "and don't want to get in trouble. I don't want it taken away on the first day. My *tateh* made it for me." Sam raised his foot over the step board and held both handles with a gleam of anticipation. "He surprised me with it this morning."

Josh was ready in the courtyard with Sam in an instant.

With one foot riding the slat, Sam gave the courtyard cobblestone a backwards push with the other foot and tried to glide. The haphazardly laid out stones immediately caught the front wheel and almost sent Sam to the ground.

"We need it smooth," said Sam, and Josh glanced around for a flat patch of ground.

"Not in here," said Josh. He pointed his thumb at the gate leading to the street, lifted his eyebrows towards the upper apartment window, and flashed a smirk. Sam subtly nodded, lifted the scooter by the handlebars, and walked to the gate, avoiding a direct view from above. Their youthful exuberance was timeless and wouldn't be bounded by parental admonition.

While Sam ignored his own trepidation, he would soon discover the morning's incident would merely be the first tread of descent into the darkest moment of humanity.

Surveying the street outside the gate, Sam noticed that no one was walking casually. Instead, a few doors slammed and people were running everywhere and even in the street, dodging several grayish and muddy trucks—one loaded with wooden crates, one with two cows, and another running open and empty with rusted steel side-rails in place. Its back hatch was open and rattling, as if anticipating receiving a sudden load. Flatbed driftwood push carts were scattered up and down the curb leading toward the main street, forming an obstacle course for the traffic to jockey through a gap down the street.

Two older ladies were quickly walking against traffic and trying to navigate a path up the sidewalk, along with dozens of other residents. They both looked as if their hair had just been especially set for the Sabbath dinner, with fresh bouncing curls and shiny hairclips holding their bangs above their ears.

Since he knew there wasn't a hair salon in this neighborhood, Sam figured the ladies were friends who fixed each other's hair. The lady with the blue scarf tucked in her coat collar held tightly to a younger girl's hand, pulling her along in a quick tow. In the other hand, she grasped a collection of small, empty burlap bags. The women wore heavy, almost-matching black coats that reached below their knees, as if they were expecting colder weather. They weren't talking to anyone or each other, but were driven to not hesitate.

"What's happening?" asked Josh. This was not the normal Friday rush for the market. Sam's family did not own a radio and the torn pieces of newspaper blowing around the street probably contained old news that his father had probably read.

Their families lived in a quiet area, set away from the markets, shops, and the clanging of street cars. The world was disturbed that morning, but for Sam and Josh, scooter business was at hand and all downhill. They stepped onto the street, where there was smooth cement. They turned and smiled at each other, ignoring the obvious and unseen neighborhood barriers.

From the minute they looked out the gate and to the right, the boys saw their exciting scooter course. It would carry them down several blocks and empty into bustling traffic and businesses, split by the streetcar tracks. The metal courtyard gate had been pinned open. Sam took the invitation and rolled on the scooter through the open threshold to the edge of the street. He stopped at the curb and cranked his head over his shoulder to grin at Josh.

The world was open to the best friends. Neither boy owned a watch or thought of time, and they began to take turns gliding down the tapered hill. The morning was Sam's best day, but he couldn't comprehend that the rest of his childhood would never arrive.

"How was it?" asked Josh, heavily panting after chasing Sam's glide path.

"Wow," answered Sam, "I was flying."

He could feel the scooter accelerate while shooting down the street with the wind blowing his hair back like a bird's wings. The sounds of the steel bearings and wheels clicking on the road reminded him that he was moving faster than he had ever gone before. He practiced swiveling the handles so he could steer in the direction he wanted.

Sam knew his father was clever to have assembled such a magical ride for him. Sam scraped one foot against the cement to slow down to a stop before the main intersection, because the ever-growing crowds of pedestrians blocked the road. And he knew that the scooter wheels could become caught in the streetcar rails anyway, if he wasn't struck by another vehicle.

As they stood facing the gleaming tracks cut into the Zarnenhofa Street, the boys noticed that the street noise had grown much louder. Open-mouthed, Sam and Josh stood watching the mix of pedestrians darting in between the moving vehicles. Suddenly, the boys realized that their smooth ride had taken them blocks from home and to the edge of the non-Jewish neighborhood. They unconsciously took two steps back from the street in an effort to be invisible.

"We shouldn't be here," said Josh. A heavily bearded man with thick sideburns was pushing a cart filled with brown shoes hanging from laces, each hooked over protruding nails sticking out of board. He grunted as he leaned the cart backward to tilt and plant the front wheel onto the crowded sidewalk.

At the intersection, the man was surprised by a street police officer, who abruptly sidestepped the cart and pulled his club from his belt, while yelling at the man. He gestured with the club for the peddler to get back in the jammed street, but the man ignored the officer and scurried past the boys, giving them a sideways frown, almost as a foreboding warning to not enter.

"We don't belong here," Sam said, "and we'd better go before they see us."

He grabbed the handlebars and turned the scooter around for the uphill jaunt. "Josh, I'll push it up and you can take a turn from the top."

A smile briefly returned to Josh's face as he pulled up his coat collar to block the cool morning breeze. Sam struggled to push the scooter up the street. He decided to lift it above the blowing trash debris covering the path with ripped papers, box flaps, and loose stones from decaying walls. Sam saw that their courtyard gate was only a few uphill blocks away, and carrying the scooter slowed the climb.

As Sam and Josh approached the first corner, they heard a metal scraping sound and Sam shuddered with the thought of shredding skin. A metal bar was rasping along the stone blocks of the wall; it was coming toward them from around the corner. Sam gulped; *Were they going to be caught against their parents' warnings?*

Four teenage boys were walking toward them. They moved as one, pressed together shoulder to shoulder. The street gang stepped from the corner and confronted Sam and Josh, who stood there, stunned, with nowhere to run.

Twice as old as Sam and Josh, the boys were still too young to shave and their clothing looked newer than Sam's play clothes, but their jackets were well-worn at the elbows. Each wore a wool cap with a wide visor, seemingly bent as an extension of their posture.

The tallest boy had a long, rectangular nose and wore his cap puffed up like a dome, his large ears protruding beyond the cap brim. He yanked on the lapels of his worn suit jacket, displaying the slashes in the sleeves and turned up cuffs, perhaps tossed away by his father.

Sam quickly learned the leader's name—Andrzej—because the others spoke his name for permission.

Even though there were few trees in this part of Warsaw, two of the boys carried sticks. These weren't branches snapped from a tree, but grayed and long pieces of wood with cut edges.

Sam's downward gaze raced across the sidewalk cracks and spotted the rusted metal rod being tapped against the cement. *Why*, he wondered? The shortest boy was only slightly taller than Sam, but he had pulled his visor down over his eyebrows to cover darting glances. The other two boys covered their ears with the side flaps of their caps and yanked tight their double-knotted, knitted scarves against the chilly wind.

"Look at the rats," said the shortest boy, whose eyes would not meet Sam's. He started nodding his head and stood firm with his legs apart and both thumbs stuck in his belt, posed to block.

Sam's gut filled with a sour taste of their hate, churning like acid in his soul. His mind desperately searched for a gap in the midst of the collapsing moment. He saw the iron sewer grate on the corner near his feet and thought of the escape possibilities, but knew that only real rats could disappear underground through the cross-slits.

"What are you doing out of the sewer?" asked Andrzej.

Sam doubted that he expected an answer. Instead, he focused on an impossible uphill run to the safety of their front gate. Gazing down and avoiding eye contact, Sam heard the sound of more boots shuffling on the sidewalk and sensed that two more boys had appeared from around the same corner. The newcomers had moved behind them. He couldn't see their faces, but he knew they were smiling at the others like a group of hungry wolves that just trapped dinner.

Josh pressed his right shoulder into Sam's left arm, trying to disappear, while Sam tightly clenched the scooter's handlebars. Sam imagined that he was holding his father's hand and that his sudden gigantic appearance would have cleared the corner.

However, Sam knew that his *tateh* was delivering bottles in the midst of tumultuous street chaos. Sam was alone, even though Josh was with him; he hunkered down for impact.

"What are you *schit* doing here?" asked Andrzej. "I told you before that you don't belong here and that if we saw your *schit* faces again, I'd remove the rest of your teeth."

Sam felt the blood drain from his face and a tremor pass through his thin body. He clenched his jaw to keep from reacting. He didn't like being called a dirty Jew and didn't understand the hate, but he knew that when any group would encircle him, it didn't matter what they were saying or why. He knew that not talking was least painful and that he didn't want to wait for another beating.

"What's in your pocket, *schit*?" asked a voice from behind. Sam was punched in the shoulder and kicked in the shin, but didn't go to the ground. That shin was already black and blue, and the additional kick didn't hurt like new.

Sam remembered his mother's words: *"Don't go near those kids. Don't go alone or without an adult."*

Sam knew that he and Josh somehow had to get back to the safety of the courtyard. If they could only cross under the protective arch and be seen by a Jewish adult. *Just get up the stairs.* The street boys were afraid of the protective apartment community, but didn't know why. Sam and Josh had strayed. The two young boys looked at each other with the dreadful realization that they were on their own. Their courtyard was uphill and out of screaming distance. It might as well have been the moon.

Sam lurched forward as his arms were gripped from behind, while the scooter was snatched from his hands. He felt like being forced to watch his father being struck, and he couldn't stop it or look away. Except Sam knew what his father would have done with these older boys, if he had been standing there, and that gave him the confidence to find a move.

"*Leave my tateh alone,*" Sam thought to himself.

The larger boys blocked Josh and Sam from going forward. They were being herded into the side street, pressed against the outer wall of a factory with an iron fence that prevented through-traffic and pedestrian access. Sam and Josh were being moved from any view from the street.

Sam wished that he had listened to his mother and prayed to move time. The surrounding street traffic and noise was noticeably louder. Even the gang of boys paused from their business to look toward the cross street, where they saw an enormous crush of people hustling and running, along with bicycles, trucks, carriages, and some cars pressing to move.

Sam and Josh's world froze, ready to shatter.

Andrzej was holding the scooter handle with his right hand and suddenly swung the scooter high in the air, smashing it against the factory wall. Then clenching the fractured frame, he threw it down hard on the cement sidewalk, shattering the wooden slat and smashing the scooter into a dozen flying pieces.

All of the boys turned away and shielded their eyes from the sharp debris. Sam saw his moment and made his move. The bearings and wheels splintered from the foot slat and came to rest in the middle of the street, where Sam scooped them up in his panicked jolt of speed. Josh was sharp on his heels and sprang after Sam without looking back.

The small Jewish boys disappeared into the tidal wave of pedestrians, hundreds of them flowing down the street as a solid mass. Breathless, they turned into the courtyard, flailing their arms for balance. As one, they sprinted for the wooden stairs, defying gravity by taking two or three steps at a time.

* * * * *

Leah had finished re-chopping leftover vegetables and heaped them in the pot by the stove. She placed her empty burlap market bag on the small side table next to the front door and looked out the kitchen window into the courtyard, wondering where Sam and his scooter had gone. She pressed her lower back with her left hand, then grabbed the rusted handle on the lower wooden window sash with her right hand and gave it an upward yank. The warped window resisted and the glass rattled inside the frame. The varnish was mostly worn to the bare, cracked wood, but she could raise it far enough to stick her head out and scan for her son.

It was still early in the morning, but she could hear the sound of truck horns blaring at each other to clear a path down the narrow Warsaw streets. The initial blast from two trucks suddenly escalated into a screeching chorus of earsplitting honking, followed by the squeal of tires and the crashing sound of glass. Leah was surprised that the collision sound was quickly absorbed into the escalating street clamor. And that is why they had chosen to live on Wolynska, avoiding the clamor from the street car track, and preferring the quiet din of pedestrian traffic.

Where is Sam in the midst of this ruckus? she wondered.

The sound of rattled voices echoed into their courtyard and Leah suddenly felt a burning panic to find Sam. Trying to catch a street angle, she peered down through the courtyard gate and saw a tabby cat with a black collar wander through the courtyard, looking up and down at each door and walkway opening.

The feline didn't belong here and Leah figured that it was searching for its home, but it must have wandered too far, since there were no pets seen in this part of the city. It was too expensive to feed a pet, unless you were wealthy and those people didn't live here.

Leah was relieved to see Sam and Josh suddenly burst through the gate and frantically race toward the back stairs. She unlocked their front door and again leaned out the window for a glimpse of why the boys were running, but only the street rattle followed them. For Sam, the slammed apartment door at his back was a reprieve from the street danger and a serrated end to a period of Jewish existence.

* * * * *

When Leah greeted Sam at the door, she immediately noticed that he was clutching the set of bearings and wheels from the scooter. And nothing else. She spun him around searching, for any cuts or blood, but only saw a torn coat.

"You were lucky," said Leah, as she cradled her stomach. The morning's events seemed more brutal to Sam than the normal street perils. These penetrated his home and in his almost-seven-year-old mind, attacked his family. He was powerless to stop it.

He had not yet heard about Hitler. No one in Warsaw anticipated that morning's dark shadow, which would leave them wondering if the sun would ever shine again.

"What am I going to tell *Tateh* about the scooter?" asked Sam. He gently handled the remnants of the scooter in his hands as if moving the broken limbs of his father, and rested them on the kitchen table. He bowed his head and leaned over them in disbelief.

Leah pulled open a wooden drawer near the kitchen sink and grabbed a tan hand towel.

"You didn't listen to me," said Leah, "did you?" She knew that street boys had something to do with the vanished scooter and Sam's punishment was to tell his father about it.

"Now go to the sink with the bucket and wash yourself up, so we can get ready for Schabes before *Tateh* gets home." She reached over the stove for the silver candlestick holders on the shelf.

"You know, Bobe and Zeyde gave these to us at our wedding." She held one in each hand and looked for any reaction from Sam. Sam rubbed his arm near the coat rip and looked down at his muddied boots, while his mind whirled with thoughts of the street scuffle.

"If you get cleaned up fast, then maybe you'll have a few minutes to ride Ferdek after we leave the baker," Leah said.

Motor vehicles owned the streets, but there was one remaining horse in the courtyard stall, tied next to an old carriage. As a toddler, Sam would refuse to eat dinner until Leah took him to visit Ferdek while the horse ate from its large hay manger. Sam had also insisted that Leah pick him up and let him sit on the horse's bare back. Ferdek had no input on the matter, since he was tied to the large wood stall gate, waiting to pull.

Leah was relieved that the riding distraction still worked, as Sam looked up with a smile wider than the narrow kitchen and snatched the towel from his mother's hand.

"But we must hurry," said Leah, "before he is taken out to pick up crates."

Sam forgot about the lurking street gang and instead, wondered why the horse always resisted carrying empty containers, while his own father was happy hauling heavy, full, soda-water bottles.

* * * * *

The truth was that while Duvid took pride in his height and strength, he simply enjoyed being the only Jew who worked for non-Jews. Since Duvid could write and read the delivery notices, he was useful, despite being a Jew. Duvid's days were extremely long and his route impeded by cobblestones, angled streets, the bitter unemployed, and debris cast down from windows above the street, but he valued each delivery step. Leah had encouraged him to work for his cousin, Mordko the baker, but the money was much less than at the factory.

"That's the way it has always been for us," he would say. "If I just shut up and do my job, then the day goes by without problem." Leah knew that the disrespect from his non-Jewish co-workers was burning him up, but she didn't want trouble for her husband. Each night, she knew that he could return home battered or worse. Duvid prayed and was content knowing that he could read, as well as go to shul and lead the services. It was a cherished distinction that he wished to share with his son.

"Children should do better than the parents," Duvid said to Leah, "so we keep going for them."

"As long as you don't get beaten again," said Leah. One delivery step at a time provided for them, he knew. Small steps counted.

* * * * *

Leah and Sam both turned toward the front door at the sound of someone jiggling the lock and handle. Duvid suddenly burst into the room. He touched the mezuzah on the door frame and spun around to slam the door, just as his son had done moments before.

He tossed his gray work jacket across the back of a kitchen chair and bent over, coughing and gasping from his two-kilometer dash from the factory. Strands of disheveled black hair fell over his sweaty forehead as he bent over to catch his breath.

"What's the matter?" asked Leah, "and why are you home so early? You just left a couple of hours ago. Did you run all the way from work?"

Duvid held up his hand to slow the rapid-fire questions. He stood up straight and stuck out his jaw in a tight clench, then walked to the closed front door and leaned his forehead against the wood. He covered his eyes with one hand and began to mumble a prayer, while rocking forward and back, and ended by pounding his fist into the same wall.

Leah took a step toward him, caressing her protruding stomach, and touched the back of his jacket sleeve. She absorbed the severity of the moment, then lowered herself to one of the chairs next to Duvid. He knew she was with him.

"Anyone else here?" he asked and began to pace the small front room. His eyes quickly darted around the kitchen, looking past Sam and Leah. "They let us go early and said we should be home with our families."

"Why, what happened?"

"Just before sunrise, the Germans crossed the border and attacked Poland," said Duvid. He covered his mouth with his right hand, as if not believing what he said and not wanting to say any more. "I read that they were massing at the border, but hoped it was a bluff."

"The planes this morning," said Leah, pointing to the window.

"The pilots knew something happened," said Duvid, "and they must be moving them to the front. They closed the factory and sent us home, then told us to check in on Monday and see where things stand."

Like a caged lion, Duvid began to pace into the small kitchen, stopping to look out the window at the courtyard and the sky.

"Word must be spreading, because people were frantically scattering and running to the markets for food. It is always crazy on Fridays and this news didn't help."

"What do the Germans want in Poland?" asked Leah. She heard the stories and rumors about Hitler's signing treaties and invading neighbors, and that this would be bad for the Polish people and especially any Jews. And their family was both.

"Everyone at work says it's a land grab by the Germans," answered Duvid. "They will take what they want and then leave."

"Germans?" asked Sam. "Who are the Germans?"

Leah and Duvid exchanged frozen glances, realizing that he had been absorbing the fear in their voices. They had no explanation that Sam could understand.

Panic was still pumping through Sam's mind and now his father was home when he should be at work. He understood that it wasn't time for Schabes because the sun was not setting, and his mother hadn't finished preparing dinner. There was no covered challah waiting on the table and the candle holders were still on the shelf. The weekly anticipation for the calm of Schabes was instantly replaced by a silent dread that Sam could feel tightening in his stomach.

The hectic Friday routine preparing for Schabes was upset and tense, unlike any other Schabes that Sam had ever experienced. Sam also knew that the smashed scooter was no longer his biggest problem, but he also didn't know why and didn't seem to care about it.

"I must get ready for Schabes," said Leah. "We will still have a nice dinner."

Distractedly, Duvid started to thumb through the two remaining pieces of the smashed scooter that were lying on the table. Sam disappeared into his room and quietly closed the door. He was more concerned about disappointing his father than facing the Germans and couldn't bear seeing his *tateh* holding his smashed morning.

A wheel bearing clunked on the table. Duvid imagined what had occurred and knew that a simple fall or crash wouldn't have done this much damage. For some reason, the scooter had been intentionally destroyed. He wondered about the mind of a person who would do that to an innocent child.

"We will talk to Sam about his 'listening' and what happened outside after dinner," said Duvid, "but there is some repair to do before Schabes starts." He went into his bedroom, pulled a box from under the bed, and began to dig for parts.

"I will need some more pieces of wood," said Duvid, "but I can still use the bearings and wheels." Some things could be saved, others not.

"Is it worth it?" asked Leah.

"It's always worth trying," answered Duvid.

He walked into Sam's room and found the boy sitting on the edge of his bed, looking at the ground. "You saved the right pieces, Sam," Duvid said softly, eyeing the spinning wheel movement. "Let me work on fixing it."

Sam stopped frowning and looked at the bearings in his father's large hand. "But let's help Ma get the *cholent* to the baker and we will have a special dinner because I am home early."

"To the market, anyone?" asked Leah, grabbing her coat, scarf, and the full pot.

"Coming," answered Duvid, "I've never seen panicked crowds like this." He grabbed his coat from the chair and gestured for Sam to move. "I think they are hoarding, but too much food will just rot."

He picked up Sam's coat and noticed the new rip, then handed it to his son as they all walked out the door.

"They're not thinking," said Leah, walking along the street against a wall with no windows. The crowd was pressed in on them from all sides and Leah used the wall to protect her protruding belly from being side-swiped. Trudging along, Sam's face was pushed against a woman's long black coat and her left elbow.

"Sam, hold my hand and *Tateh* can walk in front of us so we don't get trampled." It wasn't clear where everyone was going, but they had heard about the German invasion and needed to get somewhere fast. It was a twisted discomfort to know that everyone was dreading the same thing.

"It's barely 10:00 a.m.," said Duvid, looking at his wristwatch, "and as long as we are passing the butcher, let's see if they have any leftover *gorglas* and *pulkis*."

The family couldn't afford real meat, other than bits of kosher chicken, but the bones offered the taste of it in their soup. The butcher knew Duvid from his water-bottle delivery route and would save him some bones with a few meat shards attached, gladly offering it to him as thanks for being in the neighborhood.

The row of Jewish stores adjacent to the butcher shop included two tailors and a seller of Yiddish Judaica books, spelled in Hebrew letters, but pronounced in Yiddish. A man with a long and full gray beard and a black skullcap was holding a wooden cane and calmly sorting through used books and paperbound pages on a cart in front of the store.

Duvid, Leah, and Sam queued up in the line to enter the butcher's store and were quickly squeezed against the windows by the passing street masses. The pushing was more desperate than usual and Duvid began to use his elbows to clear some room for his family. Duvid towered over the crowds and seem to be waving his arms at someone inside the store. As they paused in front of the store window, Sam gazed at the hanging chickens freshly strung up to drain the blood. The smell of butchered meat and blood was raw and made him glad that his father didn't work there.

Sam watched as the crated live chickens were taken off a dirt-covered truck and lowered through a metal hatch in the front of the store. The store worker's blood-stained apron told of their fate. The chickens arrived pecking and peeking through the wooden slated crates, clucking and squawking as their feathers fell to the ground. Sam laughed at the commotion and efforts of the butcher's family to keep them contained in the store after they were removed from the crates, so the boxes could be returned empty to the farm.

The chickens would be mercifully quieted by having their necks quickly twisted, then hung to drain the blood. It was all part of the kosher process, followed by boiling them in water to remove the feathers without tearing off the skin. Slowly, the clucking sounds ceased and their still bodies were hung in the window for viewing by customers.

Duvid caught a brown, paper-wrapped packages tossed high to him and turned, smiling at Leah, since they didn't have to enter the store. After they maneuvered around the corner and down the block, Sam could already smell the bakery on Leszno Street. Elegant pastries were spread on a window tray, next to stacks of bread loaves. Leah and Duvid saw another unnerved mass of people, straining to push into the bakery. *Different people, same elbows,* thought Duvid, as he began to claim his space in the frightened crowd.

"Let's go in and say hello," said Leah, leading Sam by the hand. "Let's follow *Tateh.*"

"I don't like when he pats me on the head," said Sam. "He thinks I am a dog and I'm almost as tall as him." Sam was fascinated with the steel oven doors and watched as the white-aproned baker forced them closed and drew over a steel arm to lock in the heat.

As each woman handed over her cholent pot, the baker pushed it in toward the back of the oven with a long piece of wood. The wooden pusher had a curved end to embrace and move the pots.

"But I'm hungry now," said Sam, who had been savoring the smell of freshly baked bread.

"Be patient," said Leah. Avoiding cooking on the Shabbat took some effort, but both Leah and Duvid relished the peace of that day. Leah tried to rise up onto her toes to see over the stack of warm challah bread loaves filling the window. With the nail of her index finger, she tapped firmly on the front door glass. Leah showed her smiling face and turned sideways to anyone working inside the bakery could recognize her bulging shape pressed against the window. She still grasped Sam's hand close to her side.

Duvid never participated in the weekly routine at his cousin's bakery, but he wasn't shy about getting his expecting wife through the crowd, unpoked.

"Stand aside, ladies," said Duvid, booming his voice over the heads of frantic customers, who were all about the same diminutive height as Leah. "Let her into work." The crowd recoiled, reacting to a male voice thundering over the mayhem. The stern snarl on his face meant business.

"Leah," Rebecca, the cashier, called out and waved her forward to the counter. "I didn't think we would see you so soon, especially with news of the Germans."

"I still want to get our pot in the oven," answered Leah, "before it is full and closed."

Duvid was now carrying the pot with their towels and he placed it on the counter, offering it to Rebecca for the oven placement. She adjusted her white baker's hat, nodded her head, took the pot, and walked back to the oven. All of the other women stared in silence at Duvid's presence at the counter, but said nothing.

"None of this is for the Germans," continued Leah, rubbing Sam's shoulder. Mordko heard Leah and smiled at her comment. He was a young man, not quite old enough to grow a full beard like the elders, but he knew enough to bake the challahs and assisted Aaron on Fridays. Leah could see that the stove and oven were off, but the coals were still lit and would keep the food hot and ready until after services the next day.

Since their apartment had no refrigeration, Leah went to the market each morning, schlepping Sam along. He felt older by being asked to carry a small bag of vegetables and Leah was glad to not have to carry either the bag or Sam. Once back home, the uncut vegetables were cleaned, cut, and cooked that same day. It was always just enough food; there were no scraps to toss out or save for extra meals. At the end of each meal, the plates were almost as clean as when the table had been set.

When the mismatched utensils were set for three, Leah knew it was time and she would place a white scarf on her head, light the candles, cover her eyes, and silently say the blessing. Duvid would swap his hat for his black yarmuka, pour a little wine in his cup, and sing the Kiddish as loud as his voice would carry.

Even when there was little food, Duvid managed to include a piece of challah bread. In the glow of the candles, he sliced it for Leah and Sam, and then chanted the prayer as if it especially needed to be heard by God. Sam stood next to his father with his head covered and absorbed the moment.

Leah knew that while the ingredients might be the same each week, this Schabes meal took extra effort by both parents and marked their determination to follow their traditions, come what may in the morning. The sun was setting earlier and after clearing the table, Leah sat on Sam's bed and gently caressed his tousled, wavy, brown hair, calming his day.

That evening, she felt the baby kick and knew that moments like this may be ending. Leah began to softly sing a lullaby her mother had sung to her about a chimney and fire coming. The words were lost on Sam, but the soft melody rested his day.

Duvid neither smoked or drank, but he knew how to find peace. He rose from the dinner table and moved the lit candles from the table to the stovetop, humming a song welcoming Schabes.

* * * * *

...I have placed my death-head formation in readiness—for the present only in the East—with orders to them to send to death mercilessly and without compassion, men, women, and children of Polish derivation and language.

So habe ich, einstweilen nur im Osten, meine Totenkopfverbände bereitgestellt mit dem Befehl, unbarmherzig und mitleidslos Mann, Weib und Kind polnischer Abstammung und Sprache in den Tod zu schicken.
—Adolf Hitler, Obersalzberg Speech, August 22, 1939

SEPTEMBER 19, 1939

For days, shelling approached the outskirts of Warsaw, then began to strike it.

"When will it stop?" asked Leah. It was difficult to tell what was being bombed, but everyone knew it was the Germans and that they wouldn't stop at the Warsaw outskirts.

Duvid had received word to not return to the factory until he was told to do so. He had walked over to the site two days earlier and found the gates chained and padlocked.

Many Warsaw residents had entered the stream of pedestrians fleeing the city with their overflowing baskets and carts. Duvid presumed that the factory owner had been among the first to run.

Mr. Lechoslaw blamed the Jews for everything that went wrong with his business. He wasn't concerned for his workers' plight, and like his water bottles, he was easily shaken and shattered.

Duvid understood that he would not be able to feed his family. After sunrise, Duvid used the apartment building's ceiling ladder, climbed up the stairs, and stepped out onto the roof. The dive bombing was taking place half the distance of the previous day and seemed unstoppable. With daylight rising at his back, Duvid could see the German planes swoop down on targeted buildings in the city and unload their bombs. They pulled up, revealing the black crosses on the wings, and peeled back to re-group for another run.

Seconds after the bombs fell, pounding thuds could be felt through the ground and up through Duvid's legs. Massive plumes of smoke and debris shot up to the clouds with the force of the ground receiving a massive punch, leaving a rubble-filled crater in place of a building. Duvid climbed down to his apartment, unable to watch the destruction of life, and anxious to embrace his wife and son.

"I think it is time to get Chava over here to stay with Sam," said Leah.

"Chava, now?" asked Duvid.

"My water broke in the bedroom," continued Leah. "We must go to the hospital before the roads are blocked."

"It may be too late for that," said Duvid, "but I will carry you or find a cart if you can't walk. While I run to bring Chava back, put some nightclothes in a bag, and get on your coat and shoes. I just hope she isn't too scared to answer the door. I'll yell up first so she knows it is me."

Leah held the lower part of her stomach and sat back in one of the kitchen chairs.

"That was another contraction," said Leah. "Give me your wristwatch so I can count the minutes in between." He yanked the watch off his wrist and gently handed it to her with a glass of water.

"Just stay still, and I will bring back Chava."

"Don't lose time looking for a cart," Leah said with a sigh. "The baby will be able to walk before you find one. Everyone is on the move and there can't be an unused cart in Warsaw. Run, please run, and come back to us—safe with Chava."

"If Sam thought the scooter was a real surprise," said Duvid, "then this should take his mind off of what happened to it."

In typical Orthodox fashion, Duvid and Leah did not like talking or planning too much about the baby. So much could go wrong for the mother or infant, that tradition dictated avoiding unnecessary discussion about the baby, even with Sam.

"The surprise will be on us if it is a girl," said Leah, "since we only have Sam's hand-me-down clothes for her."

She was bent over the edge of the bed, tightly hugging her pillow. Duvid stopped pacing and turned to look at Leah. "I don't think we should talk about it," said Duvid, "until it is time."

"Shouldn't we tell him why we are going to the hospital and that Chava is coming over," said Leah. "With so much confusion on the street," she said, abruptly stopped by another contraction.

"He sees us and is smarter than you think," said Duvid. "He's been watching your stomach grow and knows that it is not from too much food. When you told him that your belly was too big to pick him up, and he saw you pull out some of his baby clothes," continued Duvid, "he didn't fuss and seemed to know why."

"We need to go to the hospital right now," said Leah. "Grab that blanket for me." She leaned over with one hand against the wall and the other still holding her stomach. "This baby is coming faster than the Germans."

Chapter Two

DITCHES

Life shouldn't be this difficult, Duvid thought. It was jammed. Duvid pulled hard on the outer basement door, scraping it back against the brick shards that had fallen from the impact. The hole blasted in the side of the apartment building rained down floors of bricks, blocking entrances and bombarding people fleeing with their overloaded push carts.

The crowded Warsaw streets lay covered in heaps of rubble and wreckage. He knew there were bodies under the debris. Duvid looked up at the sound of German planes flying westward. *Reloading*, he figured.

The morning light sliced through the cracked-open door and shimmered on the cluster of black-clad men silently standing in the dank basement room. They were shocked to see Duvid walk in and stopped talking amongst themselves.

"I'm surprised to be here, too," said Duvid, dusting crumbling brick dust and mortar from his shirtsleeves.

Suddenly, the outer door was yanked open again and the Rabbi strolled in, holding a cloth-wrapped Torah. He handed it to Isaac, a young man who wanted to go to the Yeshiva the following year. The Rabbi took off his black felt hat and smacked it against his thigh to knock off the dust from falling buildings. He replaced the hat with a black yarmulke he removed from his jacket pocket. Then the Rabbi handed a basket containing a short stack of books to Duvid to distribute to the other men.

The Rabbi's long black jacket, pants, shoes, and yarmulke stood in sharp contrast to his full white beard. He carried himself with a determined frown; he had been through similar turmoil in another time and would get through it again. His response to the current situation was to keep moving, learn, and pray together.

"You saw the hospital?" asked the Rabbi, as he handed another dust-covered book to Duvid, who was still standing near the doorway.

"Yes," answered Duvid, "We went in yesterday morning and Leah is still there this morning. No visitors allowed." He tried to catch the Rabbi's eyes as he continued to hand out the prayer books. "People were lined up carrying bodies crushed by blown-apart buildings," said Duvid. "Doctors could do little and I had to get home to check on Sam and Chava."

Duvid was still stunned that he had to leave Leah in a hospital so throttled with death.

"We didn't expect you to join us, Duvid," said Michael, a farmer with a weathered face and a gentle voice, who worked a vegetable cart in the market six days a week. He pulled his black-striped tallit out of its cloth bag. "And how's Leah?"

"She had the baby late yesterday," said Duvid. Heads turned at the news, followed by a collective gasp. "The hospital staff stayed on the floor through the bombing, even with the ceiling tiles and walls falling in on the beds." He privately wondered if the hospital would be standing when he returned.

"Leah's still with the baby in the hospital," continued Duvid, "but I couldn't get back in after running home earlier this morning, so I came here."

"How many days will Leah stay in the hospital?" asked the Rabbi. "A week?"

"I'm going back now to get her. Everyone is being kicked out this morning to have beds for the wounded." *What should be one of the greatest moments of my life*, thought Duvid, *has become a visceral battle of survival for my family.*

"She has to leave on the same day?" asked the Rabbi.

"The building shook, some walls collapsed, and lights crashed down on the beds," answered Duvid. "Leah didn't want to stay there with the baby once fights broke out among those lining up to get in."

While he certainly had the height and strength to push apart the lines so that he could get back inside the hospital, Duvid had no wish to hurt others who were already hurting. Praying now didn't relieve guilt for not waiting in the maternity ward hallway, but if he had to force his way to retrieve Leah and the baby, he would do it. He knew Leah would agree.

The damp odor of the basement permeated the room and Duvid noticed that portions of the plaster walls had caved in, exposing the wet, crumbling foundation.

As the German bombing leveled Warsaw, Duvid sensed that things would only get worse, so if he could squeeze in one more brief morning service, then he knew what to ask from God. Although his new son's first day on earth was also the infant's worst day, Duvid was determined to ensure that it wouldn't be his last. He wasn't sure how, but he would do it.

As the Rabbi dragged the scattered chairs into several short rows, Duvid watched the Rabbi's movements. Then he turned to another man, Lev, who opened his arms wide in bewilderment. Lev was much older than Duvid and still dressed from work at his carpentry shop, which no longer existed after the last bombing run.

"It's good that you got Leah there early," said the Rabbi, "before they rushed the hospital."

"There are lines of people pushing into the hospital," answered Duvid. "I was told to come back later this afternoon to collect Leah and the baby."

He passed his hand over his unshaven chin and stared at the basket of tattered prayer books. Their cracked black bindings were bound by frayed strings holding the pages together, but the contents were intact. "I'll get back in after services, somehow."

"Incredible," said Michael, who lived in the apartment building next to Duvid. "*Nu*, boy or girl?"

"Sam has a brother," answered Duvid, "and soon they will both run the streets with your boys."

"*Mazel Tov!*" said Lev, who slapped Duvid's back, followed by a series of congratulatory *Mazel Tov* chants from the other men as they shared the only smiles of the day.

A large series of explosions and crashing glass could be heard by the group and they all felt the ground shake beneath their feet. One of the older men fell back into a chair.

"What streets?" asked Michael, gesturing with both hands toward the door. "And this was supposed to be a safe place for services, the basement?"

"As long as the building doesn't collapse on us" said Lev, "we can still pray." Small pieces of plaster rubble fell to the bare cement floor, followed by choking layers of building dust. "See, still holding up," he continued while waving at the dust. "Duvid, you forgot your *tefillin* and *tallit.*"

"Those are the least of my problems," said Duvid, looking down at his empty arms. "I'm still wearing the same clothes from yesterday." He felt out of sync with the world that had changed overnight, but beamed at the thought of a second son.

"Moshe's bags are still sitting on the chair from yesterday," said Lev. "I doubt he'll show up." He grasped the cloth bags and plopped them into Duvid's lap. "They are here to be used."

"We shouldn't wait," said Isaac. "We all need to get back to our families." The flickering light shone on his pale face, long, curling sideburns, and firm jaw. With one hand, Isaac pulled the reading table beneath the single ceiling light. He brushed off the fallen dirt with a backward stroke of his arm and gently laid down the covered scroll.

"Not everyone is here," said Michael.

"We have more than ten and we shouldn't wait," said Hyiam. His point was underscored by the sound of not-so-distant thuds of bombs striking a mark. Hyiam was in his late twenties and respectfully tucked his protruding brown hair further under his cap. He took a prayer book from the basket, sensing that life in Warsaw was finished.

Duvid felt empty without Sam by his side in services, but he knew it would be a fast gathering. In unison, the men took off their jackets, rolled up their left shirt sleeves, and began to unravel their *tefillin*. The dim light bulb illuminated the men's forearms, bonded in the faith of a well-grounded community.

An unfamiliar aura of doom was shared with each gaze in the basement room, punctuated with an earth-shaking blast. Michael's eyes were closed as he rubbed his temples. Duvid sat next to Lev and held a ragged prayer book with the weighty dread of attending his last minyan. He looked down to see Lev pressing and spinning his wedding ring on his finger, while bending forward and back in a deep, rhythmic bow. A private prayer, offered before the morning prayers.

As he waited for the Rabbi to start chanting the Hebrew prayers with his Yiddish intonation, Duvid held the eight strings from one of the four corner fringes of the borrowed *tallit*. He looped them together in a full circle around his forefinger and squeezed the strings as if holding tight to a child's hand. When he read about the words of God being inscribed on the doorpost of his home, he wondered if the building was standing. Those words would have to travel with his family to a safer place.

"After he chants the Kaddish," whispered Duvid to Lev, "I have to run back for Leah and the baby." Services began with half of the regulars missing and ended with the memorial prayer that would silently include a new population.

"If she can walk slowly, we're leaving from the hospital."

"With a one-day-old baby?" asked Lev. "You look like you haven't slept."

"Has anyone?" asked Duvid. "The streets are packed with everyone leaving."

"Is the baby fine?" asked Lev.

Duvid nodded. "Thank God."

He reached over and arranged the cloth covering over the Torah resting on the table. "Maybe it's not safe to leave with a baby during the bombing. Give it time."

For Duvid, the birth of his child outweighed watching the world collapse. As he continued to wrap his left arm, Duvid knew there was a reason Leah had delivered their second child at the very brink of obliteration, and it wasn't to be crushed in Warsaw.

"It's simple," said Duvid. "Stay to be blown apart or get out and live."

Books were carefully opened and the men began to silently rock in place, back and forth. Each man worshiped with similar rituals and the deepest outpouring of personal prayers.

"Let us begin," said the Rabbi.

* * * * *

Duvid had said nothing about breakfast when he stopped by the apartment before services to check on Chava and Sam. He had left Leah resting with the baby at the hospital and ran through rubble-strewn streets to see if they had a home. When he arrived home at 5:00 a.m., Duvid touched the mezuzah on the doorpost and found his sister-in-law covering the front windows with sheets to buffer broken glass and flying debris from the bombing.

"Sam was rattled," said Chava, "and finally just fell asleep in his shaking bed." Chava had wielded her teenage determination to deal with the blasts and not show any fear. She had watched her older sister, Leah, survive two childbirths and wanted to show that she was also ready for responsibility. Protecting Sam from the German onslaught was enough proof.

"Good work. Stay inside with Sam," said Duvid, "and stay away from the outer walls."

"Are you leaving already?" asked Chava. She pulled her long, wavy, brunette hair together and twisted it into a bun, then pinned it under a gray head cloth.

"Leah is resting at the hospital," said Duvid. "I have to go back to get her." He explained to Chava about the easier birth of their second son, and how they were told to vacate the hospital by noon to make room for wounded soldiers and civilians. "They didn't ask. We were told to leave." Then he scooped up the bashed scooter bearings still sitting on the kitchen counter and placed them in a corner drawer. "Another time," Duvid mumbled.

"Where should we go until you get back?" asked Chava.

Duvid strode into the bedroom and grabbed a couple of cloth bags that had been put away in the closet.

"Please stay here with Sam until we return with the baby," answered Duvid. "It should be no longer than a few hours."

An explosion shook the building like a major earthquake and sent them to the floor for cover. A door flew open and Sam ran out and into the arms of his prone father. Without breaking the embrace, Duvid rose and continued with his instructions.

"Stuff any food you can find into those bags," said Duvid, who pointed at the pile of cloth and burlap bags on the floor.

"What food?" asked Chava.

"Leah keeps vegetables and chunks of bread from the bakery wrapped in the upper cupboard," answered Duvid, pointing at the far kitchen cabinet. "You and Sam can eat something and put what's left in the bag. Sam can show you the string to tie it tight for the road."

She immediately began searching the cupboards for any food items.

"I'll take care of Sam," said Chava.

Duvid leaned to the side to put Sam down, who then leaped into Chava's embrace, barely touching the ground.

"Then pack some clothes for both of you and I will be right back with Ma." He paused and turned toward them.

"Stay away from the windows," continued Duvid. "Listen to when any whistling sound stops and then stand in a doorway." He grabbed one empty bag to take to the hospital and turned toward Chava and Sam. He hugged them both and said in a solemn voice, "We're leaving when I get back."

As he quickly headed out the front door, Duvid carefully stepped over the play characters that Chava had cut from the pile of newspapers. The flat families and animals lay in a lifeless heap. The front door closed with a bang.

"When is Ma coming home?" asked Sam. "I'm hungry."

When Sam had stumbled out of his room, he was barefoot and wearing the same clothes in which he had fallen asleep a few hours before sunrise.

The continuous sound of German planes indiscriminately dropping their loads on the quiet Jewish neighborhood alarmed Sam with the fear of being swallowed by the earth.

"Let's put on your boots and extra socks," said Chava. "Watch for the broken glass." She pointed at the floor and kicked some larger fragments to the wall. "We'll get ready to leave."

"Did *Tateh* go to services without me?" he asked in a confused voice. He slowly recalled the previous morning and Leah's words as his parents rapidly departed for the hospital.

"When we return home with the baby," Leah had said to Sam, "you'll have someone to play with and take care of."

The scooter will have to be fixed first before the baby could use it, Sam thought.

* * * * *

Duvid walked down the inner courtyard steps and out the building's front door into a thick haze of smoke, blended with pulverized stucco and brick dust. He coughed out the destruction and rubbed his face to clear his burning eyes. The corner apartment building had been leveled and its debris field poured into the street.

People had already started picking through the pile of distorted beams, smashed glass, wall chunks, and personal property items as a quiet search for bodies and survivors began. Duvid turned and started weaving through the fractured streets toward the hospital, hopefully cutting a safe corridor that could lead him to his wife and newborn son.

German bombers swarmed over the city like deadly gnats and it was impossible to discern if they had a specific target. The residential areas were being decimated and people were unsure of where to run, except to follow any road that headed out of Warsaw and away from the ground thunder and falling city. Duvid struggled against the exiting flow of humanity, climbing over crumbled brick piles of fallen buildings, choking through flaming wreckage, and pushing past the shaken masses.

Piece by piece, blast after blast, the Gingold family's neighborhood was being dissembled in a mortar mix of horror and annihilation. Returning home safely with Leah and the baby would be a small miracle. Since a number of the roads were blocked by collapsed structures, Duvid decided to get back to the hospital by following the twisting reverse route of those fleeing, hoping the massive population left a carved path. His street survival instincts and sense of timing were in high gear.

Duvid pushed past bloodied families struggling to move carts full of possessions and elude dive bombers. He stared in wonder, trying to understand where people thought they were going dragging furniture and beds. Overweight and abandoned objects clogged the streets.

"You're crazy!" yelled a man dressed in a business suit and pushing one of his family's carts. "You're heading toward the shelling!" Duvid ignored the warning. Getting through the street commotion of an entire city population fleeing was like running against the rip tide of a tsunami pummeling the shore of a war. Block after block, he was reminded that it was never worth dying for any personal possession. Shadowed screams of relatives crying over blown-apart limbs of relatives confirmed this fact.

Duvid traversed a zigzag kilometer to the hospital. It was like crossing a moving mountain range. At the hospital, the ground floor walls had imploded onto slick, waxed floors and ceiling lights dangled by their electrical cords. People trampled across broken wedges of wall and ducked past the lifeless lights and twisted ceiling tiles. Medical help was wretched in the dying Jewish hospital.

Before he had left earlier that morning, Duvid had arranged to be let in the guarded back door normally reserved for departures. The disinfectant odor of the hospital now blended with the blast dust that hung in the air. Clear air in Warsaw was scarce.

Searching frantically, Duvid discovered Leah in the front lobby hall, sitting on the floor, tightly holding a swathed newborn. It was a tremendous sight and filled Duvid with an eternity of relief.

"The last time with Sam," said Leah in a weak voice. "I stayed here a week."

Swarms of medical professionals, patients, and family members scurried down the hall and stepped over Leah's protruding legs and brushed against the wrapped baby.

"Let's get out of here," said Duvid. "The ceiling is collapsing." Collective panic wouldn't hold up the building and Duvid hoisted Leah up by her elbows, while she clasped the bundle against her chest.

"Anything else?" asked Duvid. "We're not coming back?"

Leah shook her head. "The nurse gave me some bandages and pads for bleeding. She told me to walk with small steps and if I feed myself, then the baby will be fine with nursing."

Leah didn't feel ready, but they needed to get out now.

"Let's go home and see Sam," she continued. "This is no place for a baby." She began shuffling down the wreckage filled hall and toward the front door. Leah didn't grunt, groan, or complain, though Duvid knew she must be in pain. Her lovely face clenched as she walked forward with their baby.

"I should go in front of you," said Duvid. He took the bag filled with bandages and a few hospital vegetables, and moved in front of her to clear a passage toward an exit. He looked down at the covered baby and realized that they were taking home a baby with no name. *There will be a time for that*, prayed Duvid.

For Leah, carrying a new baby fueled her resolve to continue, and there was no point to do otherwise. As they left the crumbling hospital, Leah's courage was irrepressible and the Germans were not going to change that fact.

* * * * *

"That's the new baby?" asked Sam, trying to peek between the tightly wrapped edges of the soft blanket. Chava peered in as well.

Leah had to catch her breath after traversing the disintegrating city with the baby and walking up the flights of the courtyard stairs into the besieged apartment.

"Yes, he is still sleeping," answered Leah. "Such a quiet baby." As she bent over to provide a better view of the infant's forehead and messy black hair, Leah glanced at the covered windows and glass fragments against the wall. With the baby still in her arms, she went to the closet and pulled out a straw whisk broom to gather the scattered glass bits. It was a waste of time to complain about the new conditions.

"Now we'll have two strong boys," said Duvid, grinning wider than the room.

"Can I go out now and play with Josh in the courtyard?" asked Sam, as he looked at Leah for permission. Leah smiled at his anxious plea to return to the daily routine, but she knew that courtyard playtime had ended.

"Not today," she answered. "We will find another courtyard for you and Josh." Leah had already seen Josh and his family moving a small wagon of belongings down the street, joining a streaming exodus from the Jewish community. Josh's father had waved from a distance, noticing the bundle in Leah's arms. Between the falling whistles of destruction, that was all that could be spared for a good-bye.

"Was it hard getting back here?" asked Chava, some trepidation coloring her young voice.

"Not really," answered Leah, "except for the streets." Her sarcasm had a serious tone.

"We were not able to come directly," said Duvid, "but we did stop by your parents' place so they could see the baby before we leave."

"Looks like you had a difficult night, too. Thank you for staying with Sam," said Leah, as she gently hugged Chava, the baby still in her arms.

Hearing a noise, Leah was surprised to see her older sister, Rivka, walk out of the kitchen with her coat still on. She was slightly taller than Leah and had pinned her long hair under a head scarf. She tended to stand with her shoulders back in a more assertive stance, appearing to be ready for action.

"And when did you get here?" asked Leah.

"I went to see if I could find some food for Ma and Pa," answered Rivka, "and decided to run here to see if your building was standing." She looked at the blown-out windows and shook her head. "Chava said you were coming with the baby, so I stayed a moment, but I'd better get back now or they'll imagine something fell on me." She quickly embraced Sam and her sisters, kissed the baby, and then swiftly went out the door, waving at Duvid.

"And we just saw them, too," said Leah. "We begged them to go with us, but they think the bombing won't last." As she continued to speak to Chava, Leah went to Sam's bedroom and grabbed a second shirt and pair of pants and started to put them on him, over the clothes he was wearing. "Froim was also coming here to see if I had the baby, so he should be here soon."

"We can't wait," said Chava.

The baby started to fuss and Leah pulled out a chair. Unbuttoning her thin blouse, she began nursing him and stared out the blackened window at the murky sky.

"Can I hold him?" asked Sam, who had followed Leah into the kitchen.

The next blast seemed closer and they all heard the sounds of bricks raining down into the street. The plume of dust rose from the fresh rubble and blew in through the smashed windows.

"Not right now, Sammy," answered Leah, "he's hungry." She hugged the infant closer to her breast and silently wished that she could hold Sam, too. As the building trembled, Leah feared that Sam was about to grow up very quickly. She knew that a lost childhood could never be replaced.

"That was too close," said Duvid. "I don't have a good feeling about staying here." Leah stood and began gently burping the newborn over her shoulder, as if saying, *"We're ready."*

"Let's get out of the city," continued Duvid, "and into the open areas where there are no targets.

The apartment door suddenly swung open and Froim stood in the doorway, poised as if ready to leave. He stayed in the door frame and quick scanned the room. Leah's younger brother could instantly see that Leah was thoroughly exhausted from just standing. While she struggled to move, her spirit was steeped in concern about the next few moments.

Froim would gladly follow her lead and they could both turn to Duvid for direction.

"Got my clothes," said Froim, "and from what I just saw, we'd better leave."

Froim Weintal was handsome with a stocky build and the same diminutive size as his sister, but six years younger. His disheveled clothes looked as though he had been roughed up while traversing the city streets to the apartment, but he was still on his feet and clutching his bag.

"Word is that the Germans are pushing into the city," said Froim.

Duvid and Leah exchanged quick, desperate glances and scooped up the bags near the door. Communication in the city was cut and everyone was on the run after urgent departure embraces.

* * * * *

Rivka Weintal ran as quickly as she could to their parents' apartment. In her heart, she knew they wouldn't leave their home. It would be another quick goodbye, then she too would flee for her life, hoping to find her boyfriend in the dash from the city. She wondered if anyone she loved would be alive at the end of the day.

* * * * *

"Sam and I stuffed a change of clothes for everyone in those bags," said Chava. She pointed at the tied sacks in the pile next to the front door. "The top one has your vegetables, Leah."

Froim looked down at the bags near his feet. "If we don't go now," he said, "then the Germans will never let us out and we will be buried.

"That's it," Duvid said. "Grab those and let's get out of here."

The building trembled and Duvid looked down at the wooden floor. Although the Weintal and Gingold families had fostered numerous generations and traditions in Warsaw, many of them had never ventured outside the Jewish quarter of the city.

* * * * *

In the early 1930s, Duvid Gingold and six prosperous brothers, including one named Jacob, lived in Warsaw. When the Germans invaded Poland in 1939, they each faced a decision to either escape Warsaw or face certain death. Duvid never thought about the sudden nature of turning off a light switch, but in a purposeful instant, he realized that the Germans could effectively turn off the lights of both families in Warsaw.

If Duvid left with his young family, he knew he would never see his parents or brothers again. The light was extinguished and the memory of the family glow was suddenly erased.

* * * * *

There was a deafening crash and everyone ran to the kitchen window to see layers of the building's inner brick walls falling into the courtyard.

"Run from door frame to door frame," shouted Duvid. "Run!" They could hear people shrieking in the hallway and heading toward the steel courtyard stairs. With bags in arms, Duvid and his family quickly followed the downward spiral, out the courtyard arch, and into the panic-blanketed streets.

There was a heavy hum of engines flying overhead and a high-pitched downward whistling sound. Blast after ear-puncturing blast could be heard and felt underfoot.

Duvid, Leah, and their extended family ran through the arches and into the street as the buildings on their block were being struck. Their building frontage was wood-framed and covered with dirty gray stucco. It took a direct hit and had its guts blown out onto the street packed with fleeing residents. Bricks tangled with blackened frames from the roof crashed into the open courtyard, burying the stairway with no clear path for anyone left in the building. People were trapped, shrieking, buried dead and alive.

Leah clutched the baby and wouldn't let go of Sam's arm as they followed Duvid, Chava, and Froim into the mass flood of neighbors fleeing East down the road. Screams rose from the streets and echoed over the heads of the panicked population. The jostled and crushing march out of the neighborhood lurched at each explosive impact, pressing the crowd and their belongings into the funnels of people struggling to escape Warsaw.

Duvid and Sam turned to see another direct hit to the front of their apartment building, separating the façade from the structure and sending it crashing down on the street and on top of the throng of shoulder-to-shoulder civilians. Through the choking dust cloud, they could hear the walls of bricks crashing on people and the cobblestones. No one was able to evade the falling debris and many were pummeled to the pavement. There was nowhere to run for cover; only heaped bodies and belongings remained to scramble over.

Leah was surprised that the baby stayed quiet through re-sounding explosions carpeting the city. He was warm and protected in Leah's arms, buffered by layers of oversized clothes and wrapped blankets. Everything in his brief life was collapsing all around him and Leah prayed that it would not be his last day. Life was ending everywhere, smashed beyond hope.

"Hold on, Sam," shouted Chava, who had grasped Sam's other arm as they were pressed forward in the throng of people. "Grab my arm and don't let go."

Through the visible gaps between moving shoulders, Sam caught glimpses of the injured and dying. Though he didn't realize it at the time, it would be the last he would see of their neighborhood. For an instant, Sam recalled his smashed scooter and presumed he was next.

"Stay together," yelled Duvid, trying to keep one hand on Leah's shoulder and pulling Chava and Sam with the other. "Don't wander." It would have been easy for his family to disappear into the chaos of people pulling wagons overloaded with personal belongings, moving slowly under the weight of obliteration.

Block after block, the small family marched past emptied stores and indiscriminately leveled buildings still smoldering from the German bombardment. They seem to endlessly follow the crowds from corner to corner with no open space in sight. Sandwiched in a moving mass of people, Sam felt swallowed by the thickness of it and struggled to breathe beneath the coats stuffed with extra layers of clothes.

Eventually, Sam didn't see any faces, even the individuals who had began the neighborhood march with them. When he felt a gentle tug by Chava and firm yank from his father to keep moving, he was still connected. No one told him where he was going or why their home had been destroyed by airplanes, much less why this was happening to everyone. There was no simple explanation and he trusted that his parents would keep him and his new baby brother alive.

As hundreds and hundreds of people slowly approached and crossed the cable car rails, an unspoken hush spread through the crowd. Yarmulkes were removed or covered by larger caps. Another migrating crowd of thousands of people was moving along the tracks toward the East, also hoping to get out of the city and away from the bombing. Sam could sense that the larger crowd was different and he could hear the Polish language being spoken and shouted, while his group fell silent, except for an occasional whispered Yiddish murmur.

"Where are we going?" asked Chava.

"The Germans are marching in from that way," answered Duvid, in a muffled whisper and pointing West. "So we are going there," continued Duvid, waving his hand in an easterly direction, "to get away from the city."

The segregated populations of Warsaw, Jew and gentile, blended into one slow-moving mass of desperate humanity. It was a dire hornet's nest of commotion and massacre. Even though the groups were in the same predicament, the Jews were concerned about being blamed for the German onslaught.

Considering the explosive death they encountered, Sam was confused when he saw his father bow his head and make a "shhh" gesture with his finger pressed against his lips. Although the street was wider, the merger of the crowds was not welcome or tranquil. While similar bombing fragments covered the departing citizens and forced diverse communities to flee together, it didn't erase generations of distrust and anti-Semitic mindsets.

Froim got wedged by the crowd and separated from his family, losing sight of Duvid's tall frame. In the midst of the bombing, he forgot the community in which he found himself.

"Duvid," yelled Froim, waving his arm above the crowd, "Duvid!" The one name, loudly pronounced with his young Yiddish accent, floated above the whispering mob, revealing that a Jew was in the fleeing mass.

It happened quickly, covered by a scuffling motion in the midst of the terrified horde. Froim was beaten to the ground and his duffle bag of clothes yanked from his hands. No one stopped the melee as the endless line silently walked toward the edge of the city.

Duvid pushed through to where he had seen Froim go down in the crowd. He grabbed his brother-in-law's arm and helped him to his feet without speaking. Froim had a red scuff mark on his cheek and a torn shirt collar, but otherwise seemed fine. He cracked a sideways grin as if acknowledging his verbal mistake. Duvid shook his head at Froim and pulled him back in the direction of the rest of the family.

Even though Leah was only able to walk a tight shuffle as the surrounding horde streamed around the huddled family, she pushed against the crowd to open space for her brother. After several more hours of trudging along with the crowd, Duvid tapped Leah and pointed forward.

Through the distant city buildings, he could see the woods, flanking the road as it branched ahead. Chava and Froim looked back over their shoulders to see that the bombing continued over a city of rising smoke pillars. It seemed to be behind them, along with the burning ash smell of their lives. With few targets in the country-side, they hoped to be safe from bombing.

"Froim, Chava?" asked Leah. Every fifteen minutes or so, she whispered their names in a hoarse voice. Walking slowly next to Duvid and Sam, immersed in the multitude of former Warsaw residents, she couldn't always see her siblings. She marched on and waited for the sound of her own name called out by her siblings. There was no longer a reaction to the calling of names and many others did the same to track their roaming family members. It didn't matter who was nearby, since they all shared the same desperate road.

Throughout their departure from the city, the baby had remained quiet in the cloistered swathing and embrace of Leah, gently swaying with the rhythm of the trek. The only sound was the group's scuffling footsteps against the cement-paved streets. The hypnotic pace was jolted by a pattern of bombs blasts behind the moving line, but it didn't slow their pace or direction.

"Look at that good junk," said Froim. He could see forward and back through the fragmenting line of people, revealing a trail of thousands of pieces of discarded furniture, dishes, beds, and boxes dropped in place on the road, creating an obstacle course of past lives.

"Where did they think they were going?" asked Chava.

"Not across town," answered Leah. Leah was slowing down, weaving around the piles and beginning to drag one of her feet. Fatigue caught up to her fast, for she was trying to nurse the baby as they walked, but there was no stopping her.

"Do you need to change the diaper again?" asked Chava.

"Not yet," answered Leah, "but I need to fix this blanket so I can feed him." As they slowly drifted toward the middle of the exodus, they pushed and pulled each other along, like a train without rails moving across a rock slide.

After several hours, the northeastern migration took them from their cratered and burning neighborhood to the edge of the city. The city streets abruptly changed from pavement to dirt and splintered off in various directions near farm structures. At each juncture, the masses that escaped Warsaw began to separate and drift. What had started as a line of thousands now broke into clusters of hundreds of refugees following each other, lumbering into the countryside and dodging horse-drawn wagons. The bustle of the overcrowded city streets was now flooding and spreading into the countryside.

"Where are we going?" asked Sam.

"Outside the city," answered Duvid, "and further away from the bombing."

"They don't bomb trees and farms," said Froim. As far as Sam could see, there were people walking, some still pulling wagons and pushing carts carrying their few precious belongings. There were no private vehicles on the streets, except a few people with bicycles strapped with bags.

"There's nowhere to move," said Chava, elbowing back against the immense crowd.

"Keep going," said Leah, "we're right behind you." Nodding her head toward her bundle, she said, "He's the only one who likes the marching." The baby was content with the fall air that wafted over the slight opening in the binding blankets. Leah hadn't ever seen such crowds, except to retrieve *cholent* at the end of the *Schabes*.

As the gutters of the city streets gave way to open and expansive ditches, people walked wider on the road and filled the space exiting the city.

"Do we know all these people?" asked Sam. Duvid quickly put his hand to his mouth with a firm "shhh" gesture. Sam had seen what had happened to Froim and decided to be quiet and watch the world on the move. It was a very steady mingling of people from the city who had never interacted with one another prior to that day. People followed other people, not knowing where they were going or if anyone was leading the procession.

Families streamed in from the side roads as they left Warsaw, presuming that others knew where they were going. It was one massive and long convoy of the city's population heading out, anywhere.

Leah carried the baby and stayed behind Duvid, who had strung several satchels of clothing around his shoulders. Froim, Chava, and Sam each held armfuls of duffle bags and sacks filled with food items, ripped-up cloths for diapers, and blankets. Everyone in the departing swarm was in the same position. There was no help.

"Sam, if it gets too heavy," said Duvid, "let Froim combine the best stuff and toss the rest."

"We can't be slowed down," said Froim. "Just toss it."

As they slowly walked over and around other people's discarded belongings, Froim pulled some shirts out of Sam's bag and tossed them down. They all struggled to stay together as the throng of strangers marched without end.

"We need to stop for a few minutes," said Leah, "so I can feed and change him." Duvid immediately pushed sideways to carve a path for them to stop in a ditch. Halting in the midst of the crowd meant that you would be run over by the momentum of the multitude.

After lowering herself gently to the ground, it took Leah a few moments to prepare to nurse, unwrapping the coats and sweaters she had piled on. It was cool enough, so they wore everything possible, rather than carrying the clothing the distance. The other members of the family encircled Leah, offering what privacy and protection they could, as well as a few moments of respite.

"This way," said Duvid. When Leah had finished, Duvid extended his arm and pointed toward the East. After jostling his bags, he took Sam's arm and continued walking. "Away from the Germans," he said. No one disagreed.

Sam noticed the lines of tall willow trees reaching over the road and lining the vast fields of harvested cornstalks. The only trees he had seen near his courtyard were in a park far away from his neighborhood. He wasn't allowed to play in that park, but there were more trees out here.

"Whose trees are those?" asked Sam.

"Maybe a farmer's or nobody's," answered Duvid, perplexed at the question. "The full branches are good for shade."

By late afternoon, Sam was still trying to keep up with his pulled arm. He noticed that the sides of the long thoroughfare were no longer lined with trucks and carts, but covered in tall, grassy weeds protruding from mud-filled ditches along the well-traveled road.

Suddenly Duvid stopped and stood up tall in his tracks. Something had caught his ear and he spun around. Fixing his gaze on the distant smoke-filled sky, he saw the city of Warsaw lying in ruins like a collapsed mountain range, but he looked beyond the unimaginable demolition that they left behind. The columns of fleeing Warsaw residents behind them extended out of sight.

Duvid squinted at a distant sight and his eyes opened wide with terror. The remote, low drone of the bombers had been replaced by a high-pitched whistle that raced down toward them.

"Run for cover," yelled Duvid, "into those trees."

The new planes were smaller than the bombers and seemed faster and closer to the ground. The cutting echo of guttural screaming spun down the road toward them. Duvid could see the first two planes come in low toward the long procession and begin firing directly into the lines of pedestrians. The shells struck like sprayed lightning strikes, hitting in a rapid-fire row with a popping sound, moving forward with the direction of the plane. The bullets came too fast for anyone to leap out of the way at the last second.

Frozen in place and struggling to inhale, Sam witnessed the shredding of souls who hadn't made it in time. Those who could run quickly had scattered away from the road and into the fields.

Dozens of elderly and infirm individuals were struck from behind and fell in place with their belongings still in hand. The speed of the incoming shells was as instant as light cuts through the air and caught many off guard. They died, their bodies bleeding on the road, while others lay wounded and calling for help.

Since there was no medical care for the injured, Duvid wondered if the lucky ones were those who had been killed instantly, rather than left to writhe in pain and eventually die in front of relatives.

The dirt road reached out of Warsaw like a bloody arm, strewn with dropped bodies and belongings. Duvid felt that they witnessed a mass execution. There was no time to grieve. Since the gray, weathered farm buildings were far from the road, concealment from the pilots was the only option to prevent being shot.

The first plane pulled up as the second plane came in to take its turn. Duvid let fall a large gunny sack of their clothes tied over his shoulder and dropped the bag he had been carrying under his arm. He grabbed Sam's hand with his free hand and pulled him toward the ditch.

"Faster, faster!" yelled Duvid, "drop the bags and run." He turned to see Froim and Chava dump their loads and break into a run for the trees.

"I can't carry you, too. Sammy, run!" Duvid couldn't let go of Sam in the midst of the German onslaught, but wasn't able to tug him fast enough to get out of the line of fire.

"I'm trying," said Sam. Whether he was being pulled or dragged, Sam's shorter six-year-old legs couldn't match his father's long stride to avoid being cut down. Sam's feet would occasionally leave the ground as he was yanked by his father's breakneck speed to toss him into the road's ditch.

Duvid turned back and grabbed Leah around her back, scooping her up with the baby, and landing them with a thud next to Sam in the ditch. He flung a handful of leaves and branches over them and dove into the mud.

"I hear whistling," said Sam. Duvid pulled Sam's head next to his in the ditch and gripped Leah and the baby with his other arm. He could hear the baby begin to fuss under the swathing blankets and felt that noise from an infant was a good thing. They held a collective breath during the approach of the loud clacking sound of incoming bullets.

Sam peered up through the branches and could see the guns mounted on the plane, flashes bursting from their muzzles as bullets rained down on the mass of humanity. Duvid braced himself against being hit and held tight to cover his family.

Sam's ankle had twisted in a mud hole in the road as they had sprinted into the ditches. His arm was too sore to reach down and rub his ankle during the strafing. There was a curious moment of silence.

Duvid looked up and saw Froim and Chava stick their heads out from a clump of nearby trees. He didn't know if they could see him and certainly didn't want to wave.

As the roar of the airplane engine faded into the distance, Duvid rose and helped Leah to her feet. Sam stood on his own. Froim and Chava came running toward them. There was no time for celebration, and they all continued to walk on the road close to Leah, while Chava brushed dirt and leaves off of her sister's clothing.

After the planes finished their strafing runs, the injured cried out, unable to move. At first, people returned to wounded relatives, but when Sam was unable to spot anyone who had been hit later join the march, his stomach felt sour.

"*Kic niche, kim, schell!!*" said Duvid. "Don't look back. Let's hurry." He often repeated these words to Sam, who wanted to see who was calling and if there was anything to do for them. Duvid didn't want Sam to see what gunfire did to a body and how bleeding was everywhere.

"Their family is there with them," said Leah, who also wanted to protect Sam from seeing those who had been shot and were dying. There was nothing to do for them.

"Keep going," said Froim. "I'll go back for the food bag and whatever I can find." He started running back up the road, dodging discarded items and bodies, looking for their bags. He found the bag with vegetables and scrounged for the other sacks. When he caught up to his family, he handed out the recovered bags.

Sam pulled at his father's hand to run, but they kept walking at Leah's pace with no running.

"It's too far to run the whole way," said Duvid. "We'll keep going until dark, but Ma can't run. Just remember to always carry your bag."

Sam kicked some larger stones into the ditch and looked up at his father.

Duvid couldn't pray hard enough for another near-miss. Timing was everything, for he knew the Germans were not done. Although the planes started miles away, he could first hear a distant engine rumbling toward them, then the whistling. It started low and from the West, then changed to a high pitch as the planes started to dive. One after another, the planes flew over the crowds, then paused for people to appear. It was an intentional sequence to deceive people into believing that it was safe to come back onto the open road.

Hmmmmmm..... They all heard the distant whine as the planes arced and turned back to continue the shooting.

"Get into the ditch!" yelled Duvid, who heard the low roar and whistle. Froim and Duvid firmly held Leah's elbows and pulled her off the road and down into another ditch, while she held the swaddled baby. She knew that extra blankets wouldn't stop a bullet and scuttled as fast as she could move. They were the target.

"Look at that," said Sam, pointing at the incoming planes. The street hoodlums in his neighborhood had been replaced by something more menacing.

"Get down and lie down!" said Duvid. "Don't move until I say so!!" They learned the routine, but Duvid remained on edge. Quiet was the sign of all clear, then climb out, brush off, and find their dropped bags. Anything too heavy to carry or push was abandoned. Bicycles loaded with baskets and furniture had been left dumped in the ditch.

"What do they want from us?" asked Leah, arching her back and curling her body over the baby. There had been no request to surrender or demands of the civilians, just die immediately.

Ditches offered no real protection against the bullets, but the weeds were a soft pad against the stones striking your knees as you leapt into the dirt. As Sam stretched out with his back against the earth, Froim dove into the ditch and motioned for him to roll over and cover his head.

"Don't get comfortable," said Froim.

As the planes approached, they could hear the whistle from the plane wings and mounted guns, coming in low to strafe the line of people on the road and hiding in nearby ditches. One plane at a time came down, taking turns and then turning back for more.

"What is the black mark under the wings?" asked Sam with his face now planted under the leaves.

"It's the sign of the Germans, a swastika," answered Froim. Sam held back any other questions.

The choking scent of gun smoke and engine fumes coating the road penetrated the crisp fall air.

Clack, clack, clack, clack...fired the planes.

The sound of the bullets hitting the ground was only interrupted by the tortured screams of those who had been directly hit. There were no soldiers or military vehicles in the lines, just civilians—those who weren't fast enough lay dead on the road. Their families had no choice but to run and leave the bodies where they hit the ground. No good-byes. Those fleeing had to look out for themselves and their families. This road was the only way to leave Warsaw, dead or alive.

After burying themselves in another deep ditch, Duvid and his family covered themselves with dry leaves, corn stalk rubbish, and mud. Only when the last engine rumble was gone and the firing paused did they climb out and return to the unpaved road.

"We'll have to move along," said Duvid, "one ditch at a time."

Hmmmmmm.... They all heard the whine from the rapidly approaching aircraft.

"Run for it!" yelled Duvid. "Lie flat and cover your heads. Dig under the leaves." He yelled the family instructions for each jump, roll, and slip into another four-foot-deep ditch. The dirt road was a few feet higher than the land and it was a quick tumble into the ditches, which were now filled with scattered weeds, rocks, and tall grass. Leah quickly learned to brace her clasp on the baby and go in sideways with both elbows supported by Duvid or her siblings .

Hmmmmmm.....

When each aerial attack was finished, there were fewer live people to shoot. There was less and less screaming. As dusk set in, the attack planes ceased the massacre for the day. Survivors retreated for the night under any brush or tree line near the dirt road. The darkness meant that there would be another day to walk further. They all knew what to expect when the sun rose and people started to walk on the road again. For now, some branches and leaves spread over soft mud would be their bedding.

The evening was quiet, in sharp contrast to the day's destruction. Froim wrestled with their forced decision to leave Warsaw. He scraped more leaves over his legs to hold in any body heat during the cool evening.

"What are our choices? Be overrun by the Nazis," said Froim, "or run to the Communists in the East?"

Chava looked at Leah and Duvid for an answer, but there was no response. Neither choice had a clear answer, except that only one side had attacked.

"We can't sort this out," said Duvid. "We just need to live until things do." It was not a political decision. Duvid pulled out a blanket from one of the recovered bags and draped it over Sam and Chava.

"All we can do is keep moving until it stops," said Duvid. "We can't plan much further."

Duvid recalled the Rabbi's sermon about the Israelites and how he had questioned their thinking about whether to return to slavery in Egypt or face the abyss of the desert.

"What could be worse than the slavery in the mud pits of Egypt?" the Rabbi had asked. "Of course, they had to have faith in God to allow them to survive in the wilderness."

Is that any different than having warplanes strafing my family? Duvid wondered.

"I think Sam and Chava are finally asleep," said Duvid. "We'll figure out a direction in the morning."

Froim looked around the encampment, nodded his head, and rolled over into his leaf nest. The light crunching sound blended into the evening breeze dancing through the trees, scattering more cover leaves. Instinctively, the adults knew there was no going back, and that they must keep moving away from death.

* * * * *

"When do we go home?" asked Sam. He got up from his burrow, standing at the early morning sound of his father's voice talking with Froim as the two men walked back to the family. Leah was sitting up and nursing the baby, while quietly talking to Chava about the bits of food left in the bag.

With her free hand, Leah brushed off the shoulders of her leaf-covered child and gestured for Sam to sit back down.

"I think we should stick with that group," said Duvid, pointing at crowd of about a hundred refugees who were up and slowly heading East. "Yesterday, we were lucky. I don't think we would get past another day of the planes. Not on the open road."

"Let me finish with this diaper," said Leah, "and we'll join them." When she had quickly re-swaddled the baby, they grabbed their few bags and headed into thicker woods with the still-stunned crowd of refugees.

"I can't walk much faster than yesterday." Leah was determined to keep up with the eastward movement, even though no one was sure of the outcome.

Like most of the escaping Warsaw residents, Duvid and his family had never been this far out of the city. The easterly direction would take them across fields and disappear into overgrown woods.

"There's no road that way," said Froim.

"Follow those families who are pushing through the brush," said Duvid, pointing ahead at a larger group of refugees meandering eastward. Branches crossed each other, blocking any direct path as the protruding sharp needles cut into the layers of clothing, like numerous hands with pointed nails grabbing and holding one back.

"Froim," said Duvid, "walk next to me so we can stamp down the underbrush so Leah and the others can walk more easily."

He waved Chava and Sam to walk behind them and in front of Leah until they reached a clearer space in the woods.

"Are the planes shooting again?" asked Chava, looking up at the canopy of leaves blocking the morning sky.

"I hear the whistling." Duvid knew he had made the right decision to not follow the bulk of Warsaw residents who chose to stay near the roads. Those routes may have been less obstructed by nature and easier to move carts, but were certainly more deadly for those headed toward outlying villages. The hum of the German planes and rat-tat-tat of their machine guns were behind them, targeted at unfortunate stragglers.

The trees had started to drop their September leaves, but were still full enough to block the Germans' view from the air.

"The Russian border can't be more than another day or two of walking," said Froim.

"You make that sound easy," said Leah.

"It is still faster than moving between ditches," said Duvid.

Leah nodded her head in agreement, happy that the baby was still dozing in her arms. Duvid presumed that the Germans had quickly overrun the city, since the bombing had stopped. There was no going home.

"His first days have been tough," said Leah, looking at the infant and stomping down on the dried branches at her feet. "We'll walk to the Russians."

By the end of the third day of walking out of Warsaw, the refugees pressing through the dense woods had spread out in disconnected lines. Although their direction was concealed from the German planes by the trees, they didn't want to be pinned into one narrow path.

"Stop here," said Duvid, holding his arms outstretched like a blockade. He waved his fingers inward, indicating that the family should quietly huddle together. Other families within sight had suddenly dropped down out of sight. The woods suddenly seemed too quiet. Leah carefully bent down to change another diaper and Duvid gently placed his hand on her shoulder.

"Not right now," he whispered. "The others heard something out there."

As the sun began to set on another day in the woods, Duvid could see ahead where the trees briefly cleared, revealing very high grasses, abruptly ending in a thin clump of woods.

"There's something over there," said Duvid. "Do you see that shiny reflection through those trees?"

"I don't see anything," answered Froim, "but I'll scout it out before we move. The grass is tall."

"Keep your head down," said Duvid, "and don't call out."

Froim dropped to his knees, tossed his bags at Chava's feet and turned to smile at Duvid.

"Wait here until I get back," said Froim. As he began crawling out of the woods and into the high grass, the cap on his head slowly submerged in the gently waving weeds. Duvid thought he saw his head briefly pop up in the opposite woods, and then quickly vanish again. Chava, Leah, and Sam silently looked at Duvid for any reaction to seeing a sign of Froim. Nothing.

After an hour of cramped sitting on fallen twigs, they heard cracking sounds.

"Pssst," said Froim. His head stuck out of a nearby clump of brush. Duvid quickly scurried over to Froim, who slowly stood against the trunk of a larger tree and began to stretch out his legs.

"I ran into one of our forest friends also trying to get a peek," said Froim. Duvid impatiently lurched open his hands with an "*out with it*" look on his face. "We got to the other side of those trees and could see long lines of trucks and soldiers everywhere."

"So fast," said Duvid, shaking his head and fearing that the Germans had outflanked them.

"Then I saw their big, furry hats," continued Froim. "It's the Russians."

CHAPTER THREE

BLESSING

—————————————————————

"They're not moving," said Froim, "and they probably don't care what happens to us." The Russian army was at the border with Poland, and while they made no overt threat to the refugees who were collecting at the fringe of the woods, the soldiers were not welcoming.

Bam, bam...bam. Duvid and his family all flinched at the sound of distant Russian Mosin–Nagant rifle shots.

"No screaming," said Duvid. "It sounds like a warning. Froim, did you see how many are posted and can we get around them?"

Shielded by the woods, Froim walked with Duvid to the rest of the family, who were all resting in a thicket of fallen logs. Leah was looking through the food bag to see what was left to share for the evening.

"We had better find more food for tomorrow," said Leah, "since this is empty." She tossed the empty duffel bag at her feet and began to rock with the baby.

"We can't get through," answered Froim. "They knew we would be coming and brought enough men to guard the Russian border for kilometers in either direction. The line of trucks, tents, and guns goes out of sight."

Duvid shook his head in frustration, but did not look away from the border.

"Let's go see," said Duvid. Froim led him through the tall grass to his prior observation point in the outer cluster of trees. The two men watched as a group of two dozen refugees came out of the woods and approached the defended line, carrying only their bags of belongings. An arc of Russian soldiers came forward to meet them and stop their movement toward the reinforced border.

"Do you hear all of that?" whispered Froim. There was an outburst of Polish and Russian hollering, including female voices.

"I hear what they're asking the guards," answered Duvid. "Food and to cross the border. I don't speak Russian, but the answer to both demands was *nyet*."

The shouted exchange boiled over when a few of the families tried to rush and run around the wires laid across the fields. Rifles were cocked and the soldiers forcefully shoved the Polish people back toward the trees. Some were hauled by their collars, while others were cajoled with bayonets and rifle butts. Shots were fired over the heads of the retreating refugees, sending the children and parents running back, and ensuring that others did not emerge. No admission.

"But watch this," said Froim, pointing at a man who slowly approached a point at which the wires crossed. He was met by a single soldier wearing a large, furry hat with a bold star on the front, perhaps an officer. The two met face to face and talked quietly. The man pulled something from his pocket and handed it to the Russian. The soldier turned toward the gate and yelled at the guards to pull open the wire fencing and let the man pass through.

After clearing the border, the man ran across a field and out of sight.

"You don't have to speak Russian to know what just happened," said Duvid. He watched another man approach the wires in the same manner and repeat the same crossing process.

"We have nothing to give for us to get across," said Duvid. He slapped Froim on the back and they rejoined their family for another cool night in the woods.

As darkness fell, it was clear that the Russians were only there to guard the border and nothing else.

"Since we're walking back through the grass," said Duvid, "let's stay there tonight and get out of here in the morning."

"As long as it is softer than branches," said Leah.

They were all hungry, but it seemed safer to be sleeping in the tall reeds. As Froim showed Sam how to make knots from the grassy reeds, Duvid listened to the murmur echo of numerous other families also settling down for the night.

Leah reached deep into her coat pocket and pulled out a small bag of bread fragments. She had always liked to tuck away a small portion for later and that was now.

"I was holding on to these from the hospital until we were desperate," said Leah, "but who knows about tomorrow."

Chava took the bag and pulled back the opening, revealing several dried crusts and sectioned rolls.

"It's not much," continued Leah, "but eat it all, because we're not getting anything from the Russians."

In a moment, the bag was empty.

As dusk approached to end another day in the woods, Duvid stood between Leah and Sam, and could see a group of several hundred refugees exiting the woods with their belongings and moving toward the border.

"Duvid," asked Leah, "what do you see now?"

As the pack of families approached the Russians, they began to push against the line of soldiers. Soldiers had their rifles in hand, but with children in the jumble, there was no resistance to their firm border.

"They are yelling in Polish and Yiddish for everyone to get out of the woods," said Duvid, "and come to the trucks." Backed by Russian guns, the hollering to immediately approach the trucks lining the wires reverberated up and down the edge of the woods. Maybe people thought they would be fed or taken somewhere safe, but it seemed that everyone who had camped in the woods, after surviving the bombing and strafing, were ready to leave.

The shouting did not promise anything or even offer food, just instructions to get into the trucks.

"The trucks can't go into the woods," said Froim, "so we have to go to them."

Duvid had a distrusting frown on his face as he watched people emerge from the woods and cross the open grasses toward the trucks.

"Everyone is going," said Froim.

"And we can't stay out here with a baby and nothing to eat," said Chava.

With no alternative in sight, Duvid nodded his head. They grabbed their meager belongings and joined the other families to march the few hundred yards into the lines pressing for a truck. The hollering was overpowered by families yelling names in their group to keep together through the pushing. As hundreds—or perhaps thousands—of evacuees flocked toward the trucks, soldiers flashed their rifles to contain and move the masses onto waiting trucks.

It was a complicated and dubious truce, but it became sharply clear what the Russians were doing. They weren't acting alone.

"Look at the trucks," said Chava. They were a mixture of commandeered private vehicles and Polish army trucks with the symbolic bird on the doors.

The sounds of the day suddenly changed. As they approached their assigned truck, Duvid realized that he was hearing a language similar to Yiddish.

Before that morning, Sam had never seen a German.

Over the past few days, he had been told that German planes had bombed his home and shot at his family on the road out of Warsaw. And now each truck was driven by a civilian, forced to drive by the German soldiers on board, overseeing the Russian guards to shepherd his Jewish family onto a Polish army truck. It was complicated, but obvious.

"Do you know where we are going?" asked Duvid. The German soldier understood him and responded with a smug grin and a shrug of his shoulders. He knew and pointed to the truck. Sam wondered why the German soldiers' helmets had a slot cut away above their eyes, but he decided not to ask.

"*Schnell, macht schnell,*" yelled the German soldiers, urging the refugees to speed up. It wasn't clear whether they were shouting orders at the Russians or the Jews, but the soldiers knew that when the Jews were gone, then the Germans would be, too.

As each seized truck was stuffed with the migrant families, Sam found himself sitting on his father's lap, pressed between Leah with his infant brother and Froim. Chava stood on the bench, holding onto Leah. They wore their bags like articles of clothing. Sam could see other kids crammed together on the floor of the truck under adult legs and being held by their parents. They were loaded fast and moved out, traveling West.

"The scuff on your face is almost gone," said Leah, brushing her free hand against Froim's cheekbone. "I wish you wouldn't fight so much."

"When the fight comes to me," Froim said, "what's the best way to resist?" He didn't like being admonished by his older sister, but he knew that he'd have to answer his own question.

"Where are we going?" asked Sam. It was getting dark and the truck sped along a series of side roads with no traffic.

"We don't know yet," answered Froim, unable to see beyond the herded group. There were no stops for bathrooms or food, and no room for conversation. People seemed in shock from the bombardment, shooting, lack of food, and no chance to rest.

"Maybe somewhere with a roof," said Chava.

"Let's see what happens when we get there," answered Duvid. The open sides of the truck allowed the poised German soldiers to watch the driver and guard the passengers stuffed inside. Although they were already overloaded at the border, the Germans paused to force Jews wandering on the road into the trucks. Sam noticed that everyone on the truck spoke Yiddish and started to whisper their concerns about the trip.

"How do they know they're grabbing Warsaw Jews?" asked Chava.

"The farmers hold tools," answered Duvid. "Jews dress like the city and are carrying luggage."

"They're taking every back road," said Froim, "because they shot up the main streets." They were in the middle of a pack of trucks destined for an evening assignment.

"Where are they taking us?" asked Leah.

"Back to Warsaw," answered Duvid.

* * * * *

The ride back to the city was solemn.

"Why were they shooting at us in the first place," asked Leah, "if they want us back in Warsaw?"

Within a few hours, they left the dirt road and entered the formerly vibrant city that now lay in ruins.

"I can't see the front or the end of this convoy," said Froim, leaning over the side of the truck. Their guarded truck was in a long line of trucks filled with gathered Jewish refugees, not the first or last. The children on board were dozing in their parents' laps or on the floor, including both of Duvid's boys. Even some of the adults had dozed off and were peacefully snoring when they were interrupted by jolts from the cratered city streets.

"Don't look," said Leah. She bowed her head in the baby's blankets, prompting Chava to do the same. It wasn't a friendly return and the targets of the German planes still lined the shelled streets where they had fallen dead days earlier.

As the truckloads of human cargo made their way back to a dead city, the view confirmed the nightmare. The truck ran over a chunk of blasted street and its ricochet against the bottom of the truck jostled everyone.

"Are we here?" asked Sam. Sam's excitement to go home was dashed by the darkness of the city. The power was still out, but it was easy to see the outlines of former buildings now in various sized piles of wreckage. Nothing looked the same as they were driven to an area in the northwest side of the city.

Their truck line stopped on a long street that had been cleared of rubble. Most of its three-story apartment buildings were still standing. Dozens of German soldiers marched down the street, dispersing guards at each building. Soldiers came out of each building, shouting a number at the truck guards. With rifles over their shoulders and clipboards in hand, guards from each building approached, pointed, and emptied every truck, ordering the passengers out and into an assigned building. Sam's truck pulled up to a three-story townhouse building with a tan stucco façade.

"Zwanzig," said the guard at the door. The guards used their rifles as truncheons to force the requested twenty families out of the trucks, including Leah, Duvid, and their family. Additional soldiers came out of the building to hustle the families and their bags into the building. The soldiers were organized and had occupancy numbers determined for each room unit in an apartment on the block. Families weren't divided, but overcrowded into single-unit rooms.

"This building is made better than our old apartment," said Duvid, pointing to the wooden stairs and railing. "Not as creaky or warped." His booming voice echoed off the bare tile floors in the front hallway and carried into the darkness. "Fortunately, this area wasn't heavily bombed."

Sam was so excited to be indoors that he grabbed a few bags and struggled to go down the four steps to their assigned garden-level apartment. The front door of the building had been removed from its hinges, along with the individual apartment and unit doors.

"They must want easy access," said Froim, "and I don't like it." He stepped into the assigned room, followed by Duvid. "What was that guard saying to you?"

"We have to share the apartment bathroom and kitchen," said Duvid, "with four other families." The other rooms were down a main hall in the unit, which were filled with other people from the line of trucks. The sound of Yiddish could be heard echoing down the unlit inner hall.

"He said there might be a food station in the morning," continued Duvid, "one man per unit."

Leah entered their room and looked for a chair to rest on with the baby. The electricity and gas had not been restored and with the exception of flashlights used by the guards, it was dark and difficult to sort out the edges of the room. Truck lights on the street reflected in through the windows provided a dim view of the new home. Other than a mattress tossed on the floor, the room was empty.

"From what I can see, the wood floors and trim on the room are nice," said Froim, "but I'll rip it off and burn it for heat if we don't get coal or something." He ran his hand across the darkly stained window frames and floor molding. The basement room was the size of a small bedroom and smelled musty. As their eyes adjusted to the shadows, Froim startled Leah by pushing the mattress against the far wall.

"We don't want to trip over you," said Froim. "You're safer near a wall."

"Look," said Chava, "the nails are still in the wall where they hung pictures." She gently touched the dusty outlines of the picture frames rubbed into the plaster walls.

"It was ransacked before we got here," said Froim, "and I doubt the kitchen will ever be used for food."

They turned toward the screeching sound of more trucks stopping on their street to unload, followed by a couple of fired shots. Sam jumped up and ran to the set of front windows, which were partially sunken below the ground level, but provided an easy spy view of the street.

"How long are we going to live here?" asked Sam. There was no answer in the room.

"At least we're all together," said Chava.

Duvid gently guided Leah and the baby to lie down on the mattress. As they dropped the bedraggled bags, they heard the emptiness echoing in the room.

* * * * *

"Where are you going so early?" asked Leah, as she tried to find a comfortable corner of the mattress to nurse the fussy baby. The crack of daylight offered her a first glimpse at the sparse room.

"It's becoming difficult to feed him, so see if you can find anything to eat or drink. Anything," she said in a quiet voice.

"You both need to be strong for the *bris*," said Duvid.

"Can we still do that?" asked Leah.

The confident look in Duvid's raised eyebrows told her not to worry about the details of the ritual. Before anyone else woke up, Duvid had buttoned his coat and was down the hall, up the stairs, and out of their building on Konarskiego Street. As he walked out of the building, Duvid briefly turned to get a first daylight view of the building and could see the top of their garden-view windows, as well as the three upper floors. The few buildings on the block looked similar with smooth stucco facades, trimmed with bricks and large extending eaves.

Down the street, he could see the burned-out skeleton of a similar building that must have been hit in the bombing. The charring of the fire covered the walls of the adjacent apartment buildings. This residential area was nicer than the courtyard apartment neighborhood, where they had lived for years, but the bombs didn't care. Duvid looked at the street with random piles of rubble pushed against the curb and imagined the devastation that had rained down.

When he almost collided with one of the pairs of German soldiers marching down the street, one of them pointed for him to turn at the corner. Duvid was joined by two other men who came out of the next building and were headed to the same corner. They were both unshaven and as tattered as Duvid, but held empty bags in their hands.

"There's food up that street," said one of the men holding a bag, "but you've got to get there early. We learned yesterday that when they run out, that's it for the day."

Almost in unison, other men began to emerge from buildings on the street. "Did you come in last night?"

"Very late," answered Duvid. He pulled an empty bag out of his pocket and as they turned the corner, he picked up his long walking pace. For an instant, he felt that he was back in the old neighborhood market, surrounded by Yiddish. With only one male adult allowed to represent each apartment unit, few people knew the others competing in a dense throng of men. The hungry crowd pushed against the tables, manned by soldiers armed with submachine guns strapped around their shoulders. The raising of guns immediately eased the shoving, but the guns were not fired. The Germans had an ulterior motive for the feeding.

With his long reach, Duvid was able to grab a few apples, a loaf of bread and a few containers of milk. As he stuffed it all in his bag, the soldiers closed the line that extended behind him. That was it for the day. Duvid knew that while he had lucky timing that morning, they couldn't depend on the Germans to provide enough food. As a family, they would need to self-ration, but favor Leah so she could stay strong for nursing. It would be a difficult balance.

The German soldiers sitting at the tables looked more like clerks, rather than the soldiers standing behind them. To walk away with the food, each male had to register all the individuals in his family and their ages, especially the children. They sensed that something was not right, but they desperately needed the food.

At the registration table, Duvid looked at the German soldier's uniform and noted an eagle clasping a swastika above the right shirt pocket. A leather belt went over his shoulder and across his chest, holding extra gun clips and a single hand-grenade. The soldiers near the table were being supervised by officers, Duvid presumed, wearing all black uniforms. The Nazis had conquered Poland.

* * * * *

"Did you have to give them anything?" asked Leah, as she took stock of the rations in the bag.

"Information about us," answered Duvid. "We all had to do the same thing. From what I saw, everyone here is a Jew." Duvid looked down at the crunching sound of Sam devouring a small apple and felt it was a better morning. Leah had finished some powdered milk and held tightly to their one-week-old son.

"This should help," said Leah, looking down at the dozing baby in her arms. "Sam, save some apple in your pocket for later," continued Leah, "because there may not be more."

"It's hard to save anything when you haven't eaten for days," said Froim. "I feel like one of your flat paper people, Chava."

"Can I go outside?" asked Sam.

"No," answered Duvid, "it's not safe yet. Buildings are still crumbling." Other than the run for morning rations, only German soldiers marched on the streets.

"I wish we had some magazines or papers that I could cut up with him," said Chava.

"The Germans seem uncomfortable with people outside," said Duvid, "so I will look around in the morning. There is so much trash, so maybe there's an old newspaper, too."

* * * * *

Early each morning, the Germans watched Duvid and the other men arrive with empty bags, although the residents purposefully walked different routes to check-out the neighborhood.

"Can I go with you?" asked Sam. Duvid was surprised to see his older son already sitting up on the mattress before the sun appeared, but he realized it was difficult to keep a street-wise child amused with newspaper cuttings, especially when there was a neighborhood to explore. Trucks with soldiers had been trolling the streets and seizing people for work crews, but Duvid thought that a bit of watchful fresh air was healthy.

"When I come back," answered Duvid, "we can take a short walk on the street." Sam had not ventured outside the apartment since being placed in the building several days ago. The bombing had stopped, but the street was empty of people. "You should be fine, as long as you stay near the front door."

"I think we all need some air," said Chava, "other than tossing out the diapers and the garbage."

"We'll always go in pairs," said Froim. "I want to see where they have put us."

"It seems north of where we used to live," said Duvid, "and near the edge of the city. When I walk in the morning," continued Duvid, gesturing toward the East, "I can hear the train station over there and see a cemetery the other way."

"Never alone, Sam," said Leah, pointing her finger at him. "I mean it."

Later, when Duvid returned with their food rations, he took Sam outside. They noticed other people milling around the street looking at the buildings and pointing out directions. Sam enjoyed holding his father's hand without being dragged into a ditch.

Before he knew it, they were several blocks away from their building and headed toward something that Duvid wanted to see. People were cleaning up the bombed rubble and clearing the streets. They passed by men dressed in work clothes and suits and ties, shoveling away the debris. Whatever the soldiers told them to do, they did without argument. The Germans wanted the roads opened.

"Let's stop here," said Duvid, pausing with Sam behind the edge of a building near a corner. "Cross the street slowly so I can get a look down the street, and then we'll go back to Ma."

As they stepped off the curb and glanced to the right, they saw that the street led to a barbed-wired gate, guarded on one side by Polish soldiers wearing their pointed square helmets. The Germans controlled the gate and were posted on both sides of the wires, monitoring the line of trucks going through the armed crossing.

The Germans were ordering the Polish soldiers to speak to the Jews, who were unloading the rations inside the wires.

Abruptly, Duvid and Sam turned around.

* * * * *

"From the opposite curb," said Duvid, "we could see through the fencing to the other side, where it looked like just another business day for non-Jews."

"We saw white trucks, too," said Sam.

"Ambulances were taking out sick and probably contagious people," said Duvid. They could see the nurses wearing white hats with crosses, along with doctors wearing white shirts and coats, opening the rear hatches so the guards could inspect who was lying inside.

"The Germans didn't want to get too close and ordered them out the gate."

"We had visitors while you were gone," said Leah.

It had been the first knock on the door frame since they had settled into their room several days earlier. A Polish nurse stood at the door with a Kapo. The Kapo stayed out of the apartment; the nurse entered and politely knocked on the door frames of each room. Eventually, she walked into where Leah was sitting with the baby.

* * * * *

Although the Kapos were the Jewish police, organized by the Germans to enforce the ghetto rules and watch the population, they also walked on the knife's edge. Their uniforms typically consisted of brown or black coats, hats with visors, leather belts, and boots. Often, they had wooden clubs hitched around their waist belts, but were not allowed to carry guns. Their armbands, emblazoned with the yellow, six-pointed Star of David, confirmed that they were Jewish and comprised the ghetto police, rather being members of the official City of Warsaw police.

* * * * *

Froim and Chava also listened to the exchange.

"We can take both of your sons out of the area, especially the baby," the nurse had said in Polish, scanning her clipboard of families and apartment numbers. "If we say the children are ill, the guards will let them out for treatment. One of our doctors will say they have a fever and need to be isolated."

Leah was not interested and offended by the request. "*No, yick vill niche avec gaben nem!!*" said Leah, vehemently opposed to the suggestion. The nurse understood that it would be difficult for any mother to give up a newborn, but she would nevertheless stop by every few days to check on them and repeated the ugly question. The conversation never changed and Leah's answer was always the same. "No."

Leah was furious about being questioned again and again.

Then just the baby?" the nurse had asked.

"I won't give him up," answered Leah. "I will not say he is sick and let you take him. Stop coming here."

"You had better leave," said Froim, who stood by the entrance, waiting for the nurse to exit.

"Don't even let her inside," said Duvid. That became difficult with the doors removed. There was no privacy or hiding when the Germans or the Kapos wanted to find someone. With only tattered sheets hanging between rooms, there was no need for soldiers to knock.

"What's that yelling?" asked Sam. He was trying to peek out their garden window to catch a glimpse of the afternoon street noise. Disturbances were a regular occurrence.

"They're taking someone, again," answered Froim. "Don't let them see you looking at them or they'll take you, too."

Sam stepped to the corner of the window frame to watch the event unfold.

"Where do they go?" asked Sam.

"All I know is they don't return," answered Froim, "and don't ask questions."

Arrests were a regular event. The Germans kept records of who was in each building unit and Sam would watch a few soldiers show up with an officer dressed in a black uniform. They would send in Kapos to bring a specific individual out of the building. There would be a scuffle and yelling, followed by the screaming of the relatives of the person being dragged away. It was never good when the Kapos arrived, because they were told to do something horrible by the Germans.

As time went on, more families were being pulled apart and the shrieking could be heard up the halls and down the street.

"I'm not sure what they were looking for," continued Froim, "but they have a list of names." He bent down and looked directly into Sam's eyes. "When you see them coming, don't go outside, because you might be grabbed, too."

Although the bombing had stopped, Warsaw's air was far from quiet.

"It's not even winter and they're running out of rations," said Duvid, "and they only had this mush in cups."

Duvid handed Leah the container of a pasty mash with an oatmeal-like consistency. No more apples or bread.

"And I keep seeing trucks on our street unloading more people," said Chava. "Where are they going to sleep and who is going to feed them?"

"Many are Hungarian Jews," said Duvid. "I hear their Yiddish in the morning lines complaining about being grabbed by the Germans and dumped in here."

"They're calling this the Jewish ghetto," said Froim.

"With this many Jewish families crammed into each room," said Duvid, "it feels like the Germans are storing Jews. As long as the Nazis move forward and collect more Jews, it will only get worse for us."

Each of the rooms in the apartment was already full with a family and their extended relatives. For Leah, Duvid, Chava, Froim, Sam, and the baby, one small room was definitely tight. When they lay down at night, they positioned themselves like a set of spoons, all facing the same direction. One could only turn if they all turned together. Since the baby needed to be wrapped, there was only one other blanket to pass and share. If the baby cried, then no one in the room slept.

"Hope he likes cold milk," said Leah. "The stove is gone."

When they had enough wood or coal to burn on the stove, Leah would warm up milk for the baby, but when people were moved into the one shared kitchen of the apartment, there was no stove access. More and more people were brought to the ghetto, overcrowding non-existent space. There was no heat in the apartment and the one fireplace became useless when there was nothing left to burn.

"Well, finally something good came with this last group," said Duvid. "We now have a *mohel*. He's Polish and came in from a sweep in the western part of the country."

"A *bris* may be a month or so late," said Froim, "but at least it's happening." The circumcision would be late, but not further delayed.

"We will do the ceremony tomorrow in the basement," said Duvid, "after the men return from getting the rations. I put out word that we need a *minyan*."

"It's easier next door," said Leah, "but we have no food to offer."

"I also asked everyone to bring something to share," said Duvid. "They'll understand."

"Can I go too?" asked Sam. "Can I help and what's a *mohel*?"

"Of course, you have to be there." answered Chava. "You're the big brother. The rest your father can answer."

She cut a smile to Duvid, who was sitting in the corner, looking forward to his entertaining explanation of the ceremony. Sam jumped into his father's lap and looked up at him, as if waiting for a good story. Duvid looked at the other adults in the room and then Sam.

"All Jewish boys get circumcised soon after they are born, within days," said Duvid. He explained how being an observant Jew, even when things are difficult, is very important to the family and God. "A *mohel* is a man trained to perform the circumcision, or *bris*."

Leah, Froim, and Chava listened intently, as if it were the first time they had heard the ritual explained. "It is just a piece of useless, extra skin that will be cut off," continued Duvid. "It won't hurt him, because we will give him a little wine and he will be sleepy. Just a quick prick."

Sam bit his lip and looked at the baby, not wanting anything to hurt his little brother.

"We did the same for you after you were born," said Leah.

Sam's eyes burst wide open and then shot a glance at his mother. Leah nodded her head confirming Duvid's description, then continued rocking the baby. "Then we'll give him his name." Sam didn't hear any more.

When the visiting nurse stopped by in the afternoon, she left Leah with gauze and a dropper for the procedure.

"What's that for?" asked Sam.

"There may be a little blood," answered Leah, "and a drop of wine calms the baby."

Sam spun around looking for anyone who was also concerned. There was no reaction and the next day, the *mohel* arrived with about twenty people for the ceremony in the basement room. Sam hid at his father's side and tried not to watch. Leah stood near, but remained with the other women in the room.

Froim held the baby while the *mohel* opened a *tallit* and began to recite prayers, as everyone in the basement room remained standing. Sam couldn't read Hebrew, but he heard the Yiddish words for *covenant, God,* and *blessing,* but it wasn't referring to a specific prayer. The room was silent as the *mohel* leaned over the baby.

"Is he alright?" asked Sam. He clutched his father's thigh, reacting to the sudden, sharp cry of the baby boy. "You said it wouldn't hurt."

"Don't worry, Sammy. He will be asleep right away," said Leah.

"This is his first real cry since birth, like it's his first day."

Sam watched as the dropper was removed from a small cup of wine and the precious drops given to the baby. His brother was quiet again.

This was a more celebratory crowd than Sam had experienced during normal services he had attended with his father. Sam remembered morning services before the war and standing between thirty black hats, full beards, and tallit fringes. No women had been in that room, and for a young boy, there had not been much to see or say. For the weekly Saturday morning service, he wore pants with suspenders, a white shirt, and a cap with a visor to wear when he took off his yarmulke in public. Drawing attention to being a Jew had never been a good thing then and especially now.

The bris was a brief ceremony, but significant to everyone in attendance. People were laughing aloud in the room. The found wine for the baby was shared and one of the women had brought a few sweets she had traded for at the wire. Everyone grabbed something.

"Cie gusunt!" everyone said to the family, wishing the best of health, ignoring the reality. *"Osta chine kint.* What a lovely baby." Sam had nothing to measure the beauty of a baby against, but the fact that he existed was enough.

Sam noticed that his brother seemed content with all of the new faces looking at him.

"I missed it," said Sam. "What's the baby's name?

"Baruch," answered Duvid. He knew his son was in name and literally, a blessing.

"It's a perfect name, because every baby is a blessing," said Chava.

"See, Sam," said Leah, "people are smiling and happy for him."

She gently placed Baruch down on a table and began to change the gauze under the watchful stare of his brother.

"Nothing happened to him," Leah continued. "It didn't really hurt and it made people happy."

No gifts had been brought to the ceremony. Living was the gift, and everyone felt it. The *bris* was a ritual that affirmed the past, while facing the unknown. It was the only time Sam and his family would smile in the Warsaw ghetto and the last time they would be happy in Poland.

*****

While the Germans allowed a heavily guarded open market to exist near the food station, Duvid had nothing to trade. He walked past the hurried exchanges of goods and Yiddish taking place under the watchful eyes of the Kapos and Germans. Every morning, he waited to receive the poured mush and occasionally, stood for hours in a bread line. The rough part was fairly dividing the meager portions with his family, while also providing for Leah's sustenance of Baruch. There was never enough even for one meal a day for one person. With infrequent scraps, it was a slow death through starvation.

In addition to the scraps recovered at the morning food station, Duvid and Froim brought back rations they occasionally received from their slave-like efforts on a local work crew, assigned to clear the streets for the German vehicles. It seemed best to connect with a work detail, seven days a week, rather than risk being plucked and taken somewhere unknown. The simplicity of the work wouldn't last for either of them.

During the long winter and into the summer of 1940, the open market withered with the paltry food station allotments. People were running out of anything useful to exchange, leaving only carts of old books and ragged bits of clothing and linens. The black marketers were active, but trading there was too risky and high-priced for even basic commodities.

The Kapos came around each morning to gather the number of workers required by the Germans. They yelled in the street and used their wooden clubs to beat on the door frames of the building and ask for the quota.

"We need five men," said the Kapo. "Able-bodied men." The stocky Jewish collaborator waited, pressing the front of his brown coat with his hands to flatten creases. He banged the club again, this time louder.

"If I don't get volunteers," he continued, "then I will pick some with the help of soldiers."

* * * * *

Beyond speculation, no one understood what was happening or what they should do, other than not to be noticed by the Germans. There was a constant fear of being stopped and dragged off for work and never returning. Resisting meant a beating or being shot dead by the Germans, and they did not ask first.

"Whether they are killing the Jews in the street, in the woods and fields, or taking them places to work," said Froim, "they are never seen again."

"Stop it," said Leah, "you're scaring Sam and it's time for sleep."

When there was no food and the late November sky was dark early, it was best to go the sleep in the dark building.

"What did you hear today?" asked Duvid, trying to speak in a quiet tone.

"The father and son were picked up yesterday and haven't returned," answered Froim. He was pointing at the next room, inhabited by one of the families who had been brought in with them on the same truck.

"That sounded like Freda screaming yesterday morning," said Duvid. "I heard the truck pull up when I got back from the station."

"Sometimes they don't wait to go to a building with a list," said Froim.

"Now you are scaring me, too," said Chava.

"You need to stay inside with Leah and Baruch," said Froim. "I've seen them beat people into military trucks. Families on this block talk about relatives never being seen again and the mistake of interfering."

"I hear the same thing," said Duvid. "Turn the other way or be pulled into the truck."

The conversation drifted off in the darkness, but continued in the morning before Duvid left.

"The Nazis shoot people in place," said Duvid. "so everyone can see the bodies on the street."

The Germans made examples of those who resisted being pulled onto the unfed work crews.

Leah covered her face with her hand, not wanting to visualize what Duvid had seen.

"And we're starving," said Froim. "We can't survive on a piece of something once a day. Now they have even turned off the water."

"It's the same everywhere," said Duvid. "They are trading for water in the market. Warm water over a small fire costs more. I think we need to look at other ways."

Froim smiled at the suggestion he had been waiting to hear.

"They have no interest in our continuing to live," said Chava.

Everything happened in the one room, including conversations of desperation.

"Sam, why don't you see if any of your new friends are outside yet," said Duvid.

"Stay in front of the building," said Leah, "and run inside if you see any trucks coming down the street."

Chava and Leah frequently checked on him, but by the end of November, Sam was busting to get outside the one-room existence and explore the street. With no books or magazines to read, even Chava was unable to keep the boredom from the room. Printed material was more valuable as fuel to burn for heat—and any paper or combustible things had long since been used.

Leah knew that the street was dangerous, but it would soon be covered with snow. It was difficult to look forward to spring.

"I'll be careful," said Sam.

"That's what you said last time," said Froim, "and they almost caught you."

"You don't want to find out what happens," said Chava, "if they catch you. You may not see your seventh birthday."

Leah frowned at Chava's blunt warning, but added nothing to soften the message.

"You need to stay near our building," said Duvid, "and away from the gate area. Nothing good happens there and you shouldn't be near it."

Sam understood the warnings and promised to keep a bit of distance from the gate, but wasn't prepared for what he would see.

He was delighted to step outside and meet up with other boys who were settled into their row of apartment buildings. Many of the newer boys spoke Hungarian, but they understood how to toss stones against a brick wall in the alley. Sam missed Josh and their courtyard games, but he was happy to have Gerek as a companion when he was outside.

Gerek was a Polish boy who spoke Yiddish, and whose family had been brought in by the Germans from outside the city. He was a bit taller and leaner than Sam, and wore an oversized cap that covered his forehead. Sam imagined that it had belonged to an older brother who wasn't around anymore.

The boys tossed stones like bocce balls against the side of the building, measuring the winning lob with the closest hand spread. They later moved up to using old, worthless coins and shiny bottle shards. The bombed-out structure across the street provided plenty of items for play.

Duvid had warned Sam and his friends about the possibility of shattered building frames collapsing on top of them if they played near the exposed brick walls. All the boys saw were the right-sized, charred wooden rafters, used to knock brick pieces back and forth between them.

One morning, they found a few inches of snow on the street for them to toss and kick around. For an instant, with a blanket of fresh, white snow, Sam could forget about how his life had turned to black and gray.

"Let's go to the gate," said Gerek. Boredom is a powerful fuel for the curiosity of a child. "We can watch the guards marching."

Sam knew that it was beyond the agreed-upon play distance, but he had already been down to the gate with his father. *We'll just stay out of sight*, he rationalized.

Cutting through the row house alleys, Sam and Gerek ran across the tracks in front of the Muranow line streetcar, prominently displaying a Jewish star. The street car did not leave the ghetto area and seemed to be the only mode of transportation for Jews other than walking.

The boys felt comfortable walking near the gate where a group of Kapos were gathering.

"Here, take this," said one of the Kapos. He looked both ways and pulled out a small piece of bread from an inside coat pocket and gave it to Sam. "Hide it and eat it out of sight."

Sam looked at the meal and shoved it into his front trouser pocket.

The Kapo pulled his hat firmly down on his head and cut Sam a smile, twitching his pencil mustache. If it seemed that Kapos knew everything, then they also knew when to look the other way.

The friendlier Kapos disappeared after a few months and were replaced by others who would firmly prod and strike people in a watchful, Gestapo-endorsed manner. Under the view of the Gestapo, the new Kapos chased the boys away from the gate and the wires. The boys suddenly realized that they were closer to the gate than promised.

Neither Gerek nor Sam understood German, but they heard the screaming and understood the stiff Gestapo arms gesturing to the Kapos to keep the gate area clear. If the Kapos didn't respond fast enough, then the Gestapo would ruthlessly beat them unconscious. The other guards stood by without showing any emotion. The boys quickly hid in a ruined stairwell. They looked at each other with their mouths open, aghast at the brutality.

The German soldiers selected one Kapo and began to hit him. Then they beat him down with their batons, followed by swift kicks in the gut. As the Kapo lay on the ground, a rifle butt and a boot heel bashed his head until he was rolled up in a helpless, bloody ball. The Kapo did not fight back, just did his best to block the blows to protect himself until it was too late.

It was the first time Sam had seen a skull cracked open. The sadistic Gestapo officers practiced public humiliation and beating techniques on Kapos or random Jews when they didn't think the soldiers were hard enough on the people. It was difficult for Sam to ignore what had become a common sight.

Sam was almost seven years old, and death was fresh in his mind. He had seen the Germans use bombs, inflicting immense destruction on the residents of Warsaw. Sam had witnessed planes target and intentionally strike down rows of fleeing people: men, women, grandparents, and children. He knew hunger and that people were starving, but this was different and personal.

The Gestapo soldiers were face to face with the victim and the violence was severe and unforgiving. There was no explanation and Sam was concerned about sharing what he saw with his parents. He wasn't supposed to be there.

Each morning, several dozen Kapos gathered in a formation near the gate and stood at attention, while being addressed by the Gestapo and German guards. The hierarchy was clear. While the soldiers could be seen driving trucks, cars, and motorcycles, Kapos walked or bicycled everywhere. The Gestapo had dark uniforms and hardly ever passed through the streets. Instead, they gave orders at the gate for the guards to deal harshly with the Jews, including the Kapos.

During the first days of Warsaw's occupation, the Germans had smiled at the boys. That brief veneer of kindness was quickly dispelled, revealing a street terror that left the boys running scared. Sam and Gerek knew to duck out of sight and not be caught watching any German actions.

"They're coming again," said Gerek. "Listen." He pointed behind them and up the street. The boys could hear the guards marching and the shallow echo of their boots clinking on the bricks. The soldiers were returning to the gate with individuals they had seized during raids. Their prisoners were to be turned over to the Gestapo. The Jews would not be seen again.

"My *tateh* told us that they are taking smart people," said Sam.

"And they just grab anyone if several people are talking in a group," whispered Gerek.

It was a new level of fear the boys didn't understand, a methodical horror that was causing people to disappear. The boys had seen enough and at the next distraction near the gate, they sprinted back to their street.

When he returned to the apartment later that day, Duvid saw a lost and distant stare on Sam's face, reflecting what was happening at the gate. The winter snow was not able to cover the brutal conditions and deteriorating life in the caged community.

Duvid looked down at Leah and baby Baruch. They were sitting quietly on the mattress. He felt the gaze of Chava and Froim on his shoulders.

"At last night's meeting," said Duvid, "we agreed on a plan." They all knew what he was talking about and that he could easily be killed for the desperate action. For weeks, Duvid had been slipping out of the building in the middle of the night in a prearranged manner to meet unnamed men at an unspoken location during an agreed time.

Duvid's idea to save his family had countless risks for all of them.

CHAPTER FOUR

BEING NEXT

"**N**o more dozing," said Duvid. "Ours is the next stop."

Froim's head jerked up, ending the only restful moment of his day.

Their daylight hours were spent on an ice-covered work detail; shoveling snow-covered building debris to be bulldozed, clearing the roads for German army vehicles. Looking backwards as their German army truck rumbled through the demolished roads, Duvid could see that there was no private motorized traffic in the ghetto, only swastikas. Their small, open truck, tightly packed with thirty half-frozen workers, lurched to a stop near the gate, allowing cross traffic to enter the blockaded streets.

"We stopped so they can let more in?" asked Froim. "Endless and every day."

The Kapos were nowhere in sight, as the German guards on both sides of the wire fencing opened the heavily guarded gate to let in another line of trucks.

"Look, they're just dumping more people in here," said Duvid.

Each truck barely stopped, pushing out the families through the back hatch and tossing their belongings to the pavement, enveloping the desperate women, children, and men in choking exhaust fumes. One by one, each snow-encrusted truck rolled back out the gate, Duvid presumed, to return with more Jewish inhabitants for the ghetto.

Wherever they came from, these families had bundled for winter when they were forced to travel. A line of guards emerged through the gate and quick-stepped to the corner, where the refugees gathered. While the setting sun reflected off the metal edges of the guards' machine guns, the sound of their black boots marching on the cleared pavement echoed against nearby buildings. The stomping rhythm vanished under shouted orders, corralling the few hundred exhausted people along the street gutter.

All Duvid could do was watch, waiting with Froim in their halted truck.

"*Wie biste gekomen?*" called out a worker on Duvid's truck. Some of the people responded, calling out the names of the small, unknown communities from which they had been taken.

"They're not Polish," said Duvid, stomping the icy mud off of his boots onto the gritty truck bed. "Possibly from Romania or Hungary, but I only hear Yiddish."

"All of them are Jews?" asked Froim.

Duvid nodded his head.

The newcomers were scared and beyond tired from their journeys from God only knew where. Duvid knew the Warsaw Jews would greet Jews from other countries with friendly words; the German welcome was a blunt challenge to their survival.

Duvid had seen as block after block and day after day, the families quickly walked through the gauntlet of shouting soldiers screaming at them to move faster to their assigned buildings. Families scurried as well as they could, following signs to posted guards who ordered them into specific apartments. The children were always covered in road dirt and openly talked in their home languages, while their parents were silent, stone-faced, and unsure of their fate.

The waiting trucks, crammed with forced laborers, Froim and Duvid among them, drove off.

* * * * *

New ghetto residents quickly learned that the one lifeline offered by the Germans was thin and sporadic. Food stations were dispersed from an early-morning food truck run by the Germans. It was a one-time and limited supply of mash poured out at a certain time and location to one member of the family.

Nothing was wasted. Sometimes, the meager rations were later traded for shares of food, clothes, or medicine.

The truck was brought in by the Germans, but Kapos handed out the food under the watchful eyes of the guards. The frozen Warsaw wind held the exhaust from the truck aloft, mixing it with the exhaled steam breaths of the men in line. The promise of a family scoop of mash extended the shuffling column down the block and over the snow banks.

"Why did the soldier hit that Kapo?" asked Sam. He had gone to the morning food truck with his father and waited until the Germans were out of sight before asking the question.

"We were next in line behind that man and have the same kind of kettle," Sam murmured as they walked.

Sam tugged on his gloves, which fit loosely over the cloth wrapped around his hands.

"He thought the Kapo gave too much to the man," answered Duvid. "It was the same amount, but sometimes the Germans beat on people just to show they can."

Sam felt like he was in a race trying to keep up with his father's stride.

Duvid rubbed Sam's head. "It doesn't have to be fair or make sense; it's just the way it is and everyone knows it."

Duvid held the full kettle with both hands and doubled his pace. "Ma will like this if it's still a little warm."

"Don't spill," said Sam.

"My hand is on the cover," said Duvid. "This will be a surprise for Ma and Chava."

Earlier that morning, when the food truck pulled up to its curbside location, a large vat had been sitting in the back. The half-filled container of watery potato soup was left over and still warm from the early delivery at the labor camp.

"If we don't eat this quickly," continued Duvid, "it will taste like street slush."

"Can I go with you tonight?" asked Sam, panting from the swiftness of the walk.

Duvid whipped a look back at him. Wide-eyed and tight lipped, Duvid gave his silent answer. Sam got the message. He was still curious about where his father had been going after dark, but only knew that he returned after Sam was safe in his dreams.

This was their first winter living in the confined Jewish area and Sam's family concentrated on trading for food, rather than extra clothing. When they had fled during the bombing, they all left with two sets of clothes, layering both to avoid carrying too much while running. While cloth wears out and boys quickly outgrow boots, the items would have to last indefinitely.

Before the war, Sam's coat and boots had been deliberately bought two sizes too big, giving him room to grow. The coat was made of heavy, scratchy wool that reached to his knees and the boots were clunky, but durable for a few seasons. As the winter set in, no one took off his or her coat, preferring to sleep in it.

"If you put your coat on second, then you'll be able to bend down and tie your boots," said Leah every morning.

Considering how much attention she had been giving to Baruch, Leah was happy to do the tying for Sam, whether or not he could do it himself.

"You won't trip on the laces and fall down," said Leah, "if I tie them." She knew he might have to quickly run away from something or someone, and couldn't afford to trip on loose laces. She was practical when Sam went outside, always watching the street and reminding him to look out for trouble.

"*Gey vek fin dort!*" Leah admonished. She knew that the boys liked to go near the gate and watch the guards, but she couldn't go with them and be seen outside with Baruch. All she could do was firmly tell Sam to stay away.

"Don't worry," answered Sam, "I'll stay with Gerek." He knew that they were faster than the adults, but understood that a child on the street was a prime target to be tossed in a truck. Disappearing never had an explanation.

"First go upstairs to Miriam," said Leah. "She has some extra clothes we can trade for food."

Before he met up with friends, Sam knew he had to exchange something to help take care of Baruch's needs, like getting ripped clothes and sheets for diapers.

Other families in the building often saw Leah walking the halls for fresh air with Baruch, and frequently offered to give her items to trade, especially when a family member had disappeared or died.

"Don't forget the sack." Sam cinched the opening of the empty cloth bag and tied it tight over his shoulder, because occasionally vegetable pieces "for the boys" would be placed in it. Even starving people reached out to help children.

"*Nem das far der mamen,*" said Miriam, standing in her doorway and stuffing items in Sam's bag until it overflowed. She and her husband, Joseph, were in their forties and had been forced to travel from Hungary, only taking their love of family. Without explanation, she wiped her tear-filled eyes with her sleeve and gently rubbed the side of Sam's face.

"I'll tell her it's from you," said Sam, "and come right back for the rest." Upon his return, she filled the bag with clothing from their teenage son. It would have been nice to play with other boys in the building, but Sam noticed that Miriam and Joseph didn't have anyone living with them, and decided to not ask why.

* * * * *

Although Leah had stopped following the religious days, she often inquired about the day of the week to catch Friday night. Before the war, that special evening had been one of the happy moments of the week, when everyone in the family, including Froim and Chava, was there and Leah covered her head with a scarf and said a blessing. There was bread cut by Duvid, standing and reciting the prayer.

Friday had become just another night in the ghetto. Without the rituals, it was difficult to connect. Even in secret *minyans*, where rabbinic students with beards and books gathered, people slowly disappeared and only part of a service would be done. It was never a happy moment and when the service ended, no one talked and people quickly left, not wanting to be caught observing any Judaism.

The Germans tried to strangle faith out of the people, but Leah kept Shabbes in her heart, imagining when she should be lighting the candles and listening to Duvid say the blessing over the wine.

Most evenings, instead of resting after hours of laboring in the cold, Duvid slipped out into the darkness. He often returned with muddy boots and his pants, jacket, and hair steeped in dirt.

In their room, they referred to his absences as "a meeting." Duvid was able to squeeze in several hours of sleep before departing with the morning work truck, where the grime from the street and the grime from his clothes blended together.

"How long are you going to do this?" asked Leah, as she scraped dried mud chunks off Duvid's jacket elbows. The darkness made it difficult for him to see the accumulated pile of dirt, hand-swept every morning by Chava into the street. Leah didn't question why and adjusted the one blanket over the boys.

"We should be done before spring," said Duvid. "It's slow work and only a little bit can be done at a time without being discovered."

"Baruch and Sam are asleep," said Leah. "Lie on the mattress with them and get a few hours of sleep before the truck comes."

There was no argument as the bone-tired man lay down hard on the edge of the mattress.

* * * * *

Duvid and Froim returned home at the end of every winter day stiff from the cold, their faces red and raw from the icy winds that had gripped the city. There was no Sabbath from the slave work, harsh weather, or hunger.

As Chava helped her brother free his feet from his frozen, mud-caked boots, she looked up at Duvid's slight smile.

"See if you can get some wood for the stove and warm these up," said Duvid.

With one hand, he pointed down the hall at the unit with the communal stove, and with the other hand, he pulled several small potatoes from his pocket.

The room seemed to light up with the prospect of tasting a morsel of food other than the daily mush from the German food truck.

"Where did you get them?" whispered Leah.

"The Kapo, Noah, slipped them in my coat," answered Duvid. "He said it's to help with the boys."

"Why can't we have more food?" asked Sam, who was sitting on the mattress next to Baruch. He watched as the baby struggled to roll over beneath the pile of swaddled cloth.

"The Germans don't like us," answered Duvid, "because we're Jews." Sam was afraid to ask why. Duvid knew that Sam had seen how the Jews in Warsaw were treated, and there was no easy explanation for a young boy who was forced to step over blood spatters in the street.

* * * * *

When Sam was finished playing with Gerek and the other boys, he would run up the three floors of his building to look out a back window on the upper stairwell. He would pull himself up on the frame and see between apartment buildings and over the guarded fence. On the other side of the barrier, Polish life seemed like he remembered. Those children were wearing clean clothes and walking with friends or playing soccer in the street. There were no Jews over there and he wondered whether they could see inside his prison.

From his window lookout, Sam could also see the Gestapo and German soldiers patrolling the gate and beating down Jewish workers and people in the street. He now understood why his parents told him repeatedly to stay nearby, where they could watch and protect him.

All Sam knew was that he was always hungry and his play space was becoming narrower and narrower.

* * * * *

"Do you still have that pin?" Leah asked Chava.

"Sure," answered the younger sister," but I'll have to take this apart." She had pinned together junk pieces of cloth to fabricate people and toys for Sam to occupy his time, but Leah needed the pin.

"You're getting so tall, Sam," said Leah, "that you are growing right out of these pants."

Getting taller wasn't a reason that the pants needed to be taken in, but no one in the room questioned the explanation. Leah tightened the waistline on Sam's pants and cinched it together with the safety pin.

"Sit down, Sammy," she continued, "I have a story to tell you." Baruch was sleeping on the mattress, so she was able to pull Sam into her lap. He smiled and rubbed against her shoulder. It had been a while since he had been able to snuggle with her. She couldn't give Sam either the nourishment or attention he craved, but Leah could still take his mind away from their ghetto. Chava sometimes read from a newspaper that Froim found in his work truck, but Leah wanted to take Sam further.

"When I was a young girl," Leah began, "my parents took me to see some gypsies who camped near the city." She explained how the gypsy children wore bright, shiny clothes and danced in fast, rotating circles. They spun as they moved around, causing their baggy shirts and pants to billow, while the adults threw down firecrackers, making the dancers jump in unison. Sam's eyes lit up with the vision of the carnival gathering.

"After the dancing was done," continued Leah, "people would toss coins in a hat so the gypsies could buy food for their families."

Sam gave his mother a bright-eyed, "tell me more" expression. Leah noticed that Chava, Froim, and Duvid were also waiting with anticipation.

"The evenings were quiet when the gypsy caravan moved on, so my *tateh* took us to a movie that was showing at the Jewish theatre." Leah told about the Yiddish movie they had seen, called *The Dybbuk,* about a nasty ghost. As she began to explain the story of the dead person, she saw the blank expressions on the faces of the adults, all sitting on the floor. She suddenly realized the story was hitting too close to their reality. Leah paused and turned to her sister.

Chava took the cue and re-focused Sam's attention on the found newspaper to rip into shapes for improvised cars, horses, and people.

"Where's Ferdek?" asked Sam, holding the rough paper shape of an animal. Leah knew the horse had probably met its demise in the bombing of their old neighborhood, but she knew that Sam had already seen too much death.

"He's probably pulling a wagon somewhere," answered Leah. "And soon when this is all over," she continued, "he'll have a nicer place to live, too. We just have to stay together!"

Duvid, who had been quietly listening to the stories, nodded his head and smiled at his family. Living seemed in vain, but his silent actions were hope.

* * * * *

"When do I get to come to the meeting?" asked Sam, stirred awake by his father's clandestine departure.

"Soon enough," answered Duvid, "but only if you don't tell anyone and I mean, anyone."

He held his finger up to Sam's forehead, as if making a firm explanation point.

"Until then," Duvid continued, "you need to take care of Ma, Baruch, and Chava, and remember to run when you hear trucks."

Sam understood, especially the trucks part. Early that morning, he had watched out the front window as his father and Froim climbed into the German army labor truck. The men in the truck were much older than he recalled from earlier in the week. Then he remembered his father's comments about many of the younger men not coming back to the truck for the return ride. It didn't make sense to Sam, combined with the workers in the hall telling about the men being shot and killed, but he knew they disappeared. Sam never heard a reason; he just saw the reality.

When the German soldiers showed up with their trucks, Sam watched them grab Jewish men from the street or pulling them out of buildings. Using their rifles, the Germans rounded up men, often knocking them semi-conscious, and shoved them into the trucks.

In the earlier days, the soldiers had lists with names and the Kapos knocked on doors to get people for the truck, as required by the Gestapo. Eventually the list didn't matter and Sam peered out the window, seeing men struck by the Germans. Sometimes even women got brutally thrashed when they insisted on holding onto the men. Anyone who interfered with the Germans' action would be struck and dragged into the truck for a one-way trip. It was a daily routine.

"Don't step in the red snow," said Leah, pointing toward the front pavement. The bloody token of the German morning was a caution sign for Sam to mind his parents' warnings to stay on edge and keep his eyes open while playing stones with the other boys.

Chava and Leah watched them play near their building and prayed for Sam's watchful eyes. Everyone understood the need to get outside, but there was no safe place. Other than the second-hand market, no movement was allowed in the bombed out and occupied city.

Early evening winter darkness covered the deteriorating ghetto, entangling it with the fear of the strict German curfew. When all activities were supposed to end, it was time for Duvid and several trusted cohorts to continue their real work.

One evening, Sam had already fallen asleep, only to be awakened by the sound of his parents in the midst of a passionate conversation. The room was black, but shadows of his family were cast on the walls by the headlights of army trucks passing on the street. Duvid did his best thinking on his feet and Sam could see his father standing near the window next to Leah.

Chava and Sam were resting on the mattress, near Baruch, who was sleeping under a blanket. Froim remained seated on the floor and listened carefully from a corner of the room.

"We need food. You need food," said Duvid. "We have to work harder for it."

"But what happened to the younger boy?" asked Leah.

"He disappeared and no one knows what happened," answered Duvid. "Not even his family talks about it."

Leah looked to her siblings for their sense of doing the right thing, but they knew what was at stake.

"We never have enough to trade," continued Duvid, "so we have to be more involved to get any food."

It was impossible to plan for the future, but he knew that only hard decisions would get them to the next day. Leah picked up the bag for extra clothes and reached inside to see if there were any items that could be traded.

"Doesn't anyone have older children to do this?" asked Leah.

"They are either too old and slow," answered Duvid, "or tall and sickly. I've asked around, but there's no one left."

The room was black again and Sam perched on his elbow, trying to stay awake to listen to the hushed voices. He didn't need the light to see.

"We need food to live," said Duvid, "and the Germans don't want us to have enough."

As Warsaw froze solid through the winter, even fewer white coats of visiting nurses or doctors were allowed through the gates. The void of basic medication and care was intentional. Death from untreated illnesses and starvation was becoming commonplace for the very old and very young. At times, the streets resembled an open morgue with stiff bodies waiting to be collected.

Duvid attended "the meeting" almost every night and as things got worse and more desperate, he would be gone for longer periods. Duvid abhorred the feeling of waiting for his family to die.

"Sam, as long as you're awake and sitting up," said Duvid, "do you want to come with me to the meeting?"

In the gloom, Sam looked at his mother for confirmation, and as she nodded her head, he rolled off the mattress and jumped to his feet.

"You must promise to follow what *Tateh* tells you," said Leah. "The streets are more dangerous in the middle of the night."

Leah leaned forward to embrace each of them, while Chava reached out to touch Sam's hand and Froim firmly patted his shoulder.

"When we walk outside of this room," said Duvid, "don't even whisper to me. We must be quiet, understood?"

Sam silently shook his head, as if demonstrating his readiness. Walking softly through the halls, they exited their building through a rear door into the cold blackness. As they walked a couple blocks through back alleys, Duvid tried to step on dry spots in the snow and avoid loose rubble and prevent a crunching sound.

Without speaking a word, Sam tried to mimic the movements of the long strides. He watched carefully as his father occasionally stopped and with a bare knuckle, tapped on a frozen pipe attached to a wall. Sam heard tapping from another pipe down the alley. He didn't understand what was happening, but followed his father's zig-zag trail through the backstreets. Duvid had obviously done this many times and seemed to be guided by sound and unseen hints, rather than blind luck.

Sam felt they were sneaking up on a building and thought he could detect others moving in the shadows. After they entered the basement through a delivery door, they were suddenly joined in the hallway by men who seemed to come out of nowhere, all silently walking to the same room. There were no greetings or handshakes. Stealth meant survival.

Duvid led Sam down a series of dank halls and directly into the meeting room. Even though it was well after midnight, people were quietly waiting in the room. The one dim ceiling light glowed against the darkness, exposing the sharp edges of the dismantled humanity in the room. The twenty men stood or perched on crumbled walls collapsed on a dirt floor. They gently kicked at the scattered broken bricks and cobblestones. Duvid introduced his son to cool greetings and stern looks.

"He's the perfect size," said Hiram, "but can he do it?" Hiram was younger than Duvid, but shorter and a bit emaciated.

"We've lost a lot of time since Abram disappeared."

Amidst soul-searching and staring at the dirt, they all understood.

"He's seven years old," said Duvid, "and he'll listen to Yankle."

"Is this the right thing to do?" asked Schlomo, who stroked his long and narrow black beard. He had two children younger than Sam.

"We have to get food," answered Duvid, "and can't wait until it gets worse."

There was a murmur of agreements among the men.

"I agree with Duvid," said Uri. "We can't stop now." He stood up, re-fit his cap over his unkempt hair, and crossed his arms across his brawny chest. Uri tried to catch the shadowed eyes of the others in the room. He was still wearing his work apron and he knew that his word carried some weight. The Germans had commandeered the hearse from the funeral home where Uri worked; he and his co-workers were ordered to collect bodies on the street.

"They're killing us," said Uri. "You've seen the pavement. Those people did not die from old age."

Sam figured that his father wanted him to hear this discussion, especially if he was being asked to help get food. He heard two men in the back of the room discussing a neighbor "who never re-turned."

"We'll never get enough weapons to fight," said Ruben, "but let's not starve to death."

"I think we should ask Yankle," said Duvid. "I've spoken to Sam and he knows what's involved, the rules, and the risk."

Sam nodded his head for everyone to see. All eyes turned to Yankle, a fifteen-year-old boy and the longest surviving member of the men who contacted and traded with the Polish black market. His skin was pale, made starker by the beginning curls of black sideburns. He was short for his age, but still taller than Sam. The stoic look on his face told Sam that Yankle was dead serious about the task and resigned to make sure that Sam was the same.

Without speaking, Yankle had a manner of looking around the room and watching the men without moving his head. Sam felt he could trust the older boy.

Duvid's expression froze, staring at an exposed wall, trying to think of another way through it all. Over-thinking meant being caught and hesitation could mean death.

"Give him a few nights to start," said Duvid, "so we can practice. Gather the list and collect the items. He'll be ready on the next run."

Duvid had seen Sam outrun neighborhood bullies, Kapos, and German guards, but this would be more difficult and perilous than all three at the same time. The fate and trust of every man in the room, as well as that of their families, depended on a boy.

Over the next few nights, Sam learned to enter through different buildings that were adjacent to where the clandestine meeting took place.

Later he would learn that the members of the meeting climbed through holes in busted-out walls leading to dug-out channels, joining underground passageways, building to building, and then yet to another building. They climbed through dark, dirty, and twisting tunnels, emerging through an opening covered by the clutter of old and busted furniture, brick, stone, and wall debris.

The pre-arranged route for each man was never the same twice, especially when the meeting needed to be moved to a safer location.

"What do we trade?" asked Sam, once he and Duvid returned to their apartment unit. It was almost dawn, but Leah and her siblings were wide awake, sitting up and listening intently.

"Everyone pools their items to trade for food and medicine," answered Duvid. "You bring back the things we asked for on a list during the last trade." An uncomfortable trust existed with the black marketers.

Sam looked at Leah and nodded once, after the swapping notion had sunk in.

"But it has to fit in the bags, so we both can scuttle through the passages," Sam said in a wise voice.

"Can you trust everyone in the room?" asked Froim.

All the men at the meeting were familiar to Sam, since they either lived in their building or on the block, but he never knew they were in the night group.

"They're hand-picked relatives," answered Duvid. "No strangers or friends."

Sam smiled, realizing that even his friends wouldn't know.

"You have got to sneak out with the older boy, quickly trade," said Duvid, "and sneak back in with the items."

"Who is this other boy?" asked Leah.

"I can't say his name," answered Duvid, "but he's older and has been doing this longer than anyone." Duvid skipped the reasons.

Leah looked into Sam's face for a gut reaction and he beamed with the pride of being paired with an older boy.

Sam knew that this version of street games was more serious than the above-ground one, and that much was riding on his success. It was life and death, and Sam looked certain about completing this task.

"I will show him the route tomorrow night," said Duvid.

Sam would have to quickly learn the smuggling route. Only Yankle knew it and he would show Sam what was not openly discussed with the group. The secret entrance was limited to a need–to–know basis.

"I can't draw it or write it down," said Duvid. "You're just going to have to remember what you see, without talking about it."

Sam nodded again.

Later that night, Sam was stirred from sleep when Duvid said, "Let's go."

Without a word spoken between them, they snuck out of the apartment building, as they had the other nights. Duvid would never let him go out at night alone, but he wanted Sam to absorb the covertness of the nocturnal ghetto movement.

For months, Duvid had experienced the operations, while Leah and Chava organized items to trade for food. Duvid held Sam's gloved hand as they wove through frigid and dark back streets and alleys. Occasionally, he would suddenly pause, squeeze Sam's shoulder, and point at a sound or direction, as if cleared to move on.

After a long and quiet march to the location, they went behind the building and entered through a back door out of plain sight. Sam was startled by two young men with black, scraggly beards, wearing long dark jackets, silently standing inside the door's shadows.

Duvid and the men instantly recognized each other, and then froze, listening to the street. One of the men tapped Duvid's arm and pointed inside. They were posted so one could run with word to the group if they needed to disappear. If the location of the meeting had changed, then they would say something at the door. The lookouts were always in their twenties, never older. They needed good eyesight, hearing, and speed to alert the meeting.

Sam and his father began the descent down many flights of stairs. Sam exhaled at the bottom, suddenly realizing he had been holding his breath.

These door guards controlled how many people could advance down the street and toward the building, moving from one hidden arch or doorway to another. They each had to listen for the signal, a tap or click, waiting for the patrolling Kapos to be out of sight and earshot. The movement was quick and without hesitation, while always watching and listening for a signal to stop and hide. Anyone else moving on the street was never a good thing and a reason to run for your life.

"When we paused, did you see the chain of lookouts posted on the street," asked Duvid, "signaling to move forward?"

As they walked down the hall toward the door, he wanted to make sure Sam saw everything. "They control from across the street," he continued, "when to cross and then signaling again when to move further."

No words were spoken outside. Although the city remained unrepaired from the invasion and many standing buildings were damaged or near collapse, echoes of a whisper were magnified in the guarded silence of the night. Everyone understood the meaning of the tapping signals and how the slightest noise could tip off the Kapos, ending the meeting before it began. It was a slow and cautious process to move the men in the dark, but it ensured the secrecy.

"Last week," said Duvid, pausing again before they entered the meeting room, "one of the lookouts heard a truck filled with guards and followed by Kapos."

Before the meeting ended, the lookout relayed an alert about an approaching patrol.

The hallway was dimly illuminated by the light seeping through the crack in the door and Sam looked up and into his father's eyes.

"There are many holes to disperse to other attached buildings," continued Duvid, "but it only works if the lookouts warn us."

Duvid showed Sam the furniture to move, revealing one of the holes to climb through to gain access to the neighboring building. Soon, Sam would learn to disappear under the streets and hide the entrance in one swift move.

The punched hole led into a crawl space, which connected to a series of more punched-out holes and hand-dug shafts, leading to other holes. The connections were muddy and cold, ending in adjacent buildings. It was all too dark to see, unless you knew where to go. Duvid grabbed Sam's hand to follow connecting paths to an exit. Sam was in another world.

Scuttling through on my knees will ruin my pants, thought Sam, *but now these will be my work clothes.* He owned a second pair of pants, but they were now too big.

There were many holes and hidden exits, and Duvid was interested to see if Sam caught on to the plan. The design was for the men to appear to be exiting from different buildings, and never together. If one was apprehended, he was alone and not to return.

* * * * *

"Before they left tonight," said Leah, "Duvid said money was best for trading when the list is sent around tomorrow."

The list had been circulated, recording the desperate needs from the families in the building. The weekly record of items to trade for medicine and food was at first paid for with money and jewelry. When people ran out, they offered what they had left in forms of cloth items, personal objects, and things they couldn't afford to part with, but did.

"We can't trade these," said Leah, "and trust that they will be fair or deliver anything." She held her fist tight and reluctantly handed over the items. "But if you can get money for them in the market tomorrow, after you get back," she continued, "then we can ration the money for specific items."

She offered her handful to Froim, carefully placing a piece of cloth in his hands. "I can't believe it has come to this, but dead people don't need rings."

"I'll see what I can get," said Froim, "but people are dumping anything and everything."

"I thought we would have these forever," said Leah. She saw that others had put their watches, earrings, necklaces, and other jewelry on the list to trade, but she never thought grasping for life would come to this so soon.

When Leah and Duvid were married less than a decade ago, starving under German rule in a ghetto had never been contemplated for the "better or worse" reference in the marital vows. This is where it stood.

"I couldn't even afford a wedding dress," said Leah, "so my friend sewed it for me."

"I remember that dress," said Froim, "and all the fittings with Reina and her pins."

"We sold everything to pay for these wedding bands," said Leah, "and now we have to sell them for food."

She released the two wedding bands into Froim's open palm. The money received from the sale would be spread as far as it could go to buy what was available to smuggle. While they initially received some bruised apples, most of the incoming food was canned and powered milk to mix with water for babies. Leah added things to the list for Baruch, practical things such as bandages, creams, and aspirins for fevers.

In return, there would be a rock-hard loaf of bread, which could have been stolen or found in the garbage, but there were no questions. Occasionally, broken candles were tossed in with the food and quickly used for a bit of heat or light. What couldn't be used might be traded again in the market. Items went around until the supply dried up or was turned off.

No longer were people surprised at changes and in fact, waited for the inevitable downturn. At first, there had been running water in the building and laundry drying on lines. When the water slowed, there was less laundry and then none. Drinking water was then only available in a public area. It was not to wash anything, just drink.

The food supply was strangled, rotten, and preciously scrounged. Like turning down a dimmer switch, life seemed to be getting darker. Even though families were responsible for their own needs and never seemed to have enough to keep everyone warm, safe, and fed, they still shared.

Like Leah, mothers who were nursing received bits of food from everyone, trying to equalize life in the building community. Sharing and trading were vital, especially where the goal was to survive to the end of the day. The Germans didn't permit long-term planning.

During the day, Miriam went door to door gathering things to trade. In the early evenings, Duvid attended small meetings in their building with Sam to receive the list of names and needed materials. Miriam could read the list and lay out the items to see if they were worth including in the load.

"Let's see what we can get for this," said Miriam, holding up a white lace tablecloth.

"Put it in the bag," said Duvid, "and we will see. It takes up space in the bag, but it's light."

Duvid smiled at Sam, who was quietly listening to what he and Yankle would carry that night. Everyone in the building who contributed items would receive a specific item in return, or share in the contents of the burlap bag, returned with medication and cans of food. Everything had to fit in the bags with cinching strings crudely sewn into the openings, since the boys would be crawling through the tunnels on their hands and knees.

"Be right back," said Sam, as he tossed a handful of pebbles into his coat pocket. There was some light left in the day and Sam thought he would see if Gerek was outside to pitch stones.

"It will get dark soon," said Leah, "so stay on the block. We can't go looking for you."

She knew it would be a sleepless night for Sam, and thought that seeing his friend would be a good distraction from what was on everyone's mind. But the street was empty, except for a blanketed shadow sitting on the corner. With the massive amount of refuges being gathered and forced into the ghetto by the Germans, it was not unusual to see people compelled to live on the streets. Ripped from their homelands and unsettled, they were street residents.

"Sammy," said the man, beckoning to Sam. "*Komme her.*" Sam ran toward the voice, which seemed to emerge from a snow pile near the curb.

"Hello, Mr. Hofmann," said Sam.

"We've been through this a thousand times, Sammy," said Mr. Hofmann. "Only the Germans call me by my last name. You call me Daniel."

Sam knew Daniel had taught in a Jewish school in another country and was able to understand the old man's Yiddish through his thick Hungarian accent. The Germans had scooped up the Jews from Daniel's village and dumped them in the Warsaw ghetto with no place to stay. It had been a harsh winter, especially on the street with no shelter other than a narrow overhang from the adjacent building. Daniel was an educated man and felt compelled to share his knowledge, despite having a harsh outdoor classroom.

"There's room for a story," said Daniel. He was not tall and as he slowly tried to push his ravaged body to a seated position, he patted a spot on his threadbare blanket.

Sam could see that Daniel was stiff and frail from exposure to the winter elements. He survived by people giving him a share of their rations from the Germans. There was little else to eat and he was too old and weak to join a work crew. His shabby, white beard barely covered his gaunt face and cracked, trembling lips.

"I have time," said Sam, who quickly sat down on the brittle blanket.

"Good. If I read, it will keep your mind busy." The distraction would be especially useful that night. Daniel's only possession was a book of stories that he pulled out of his pocket. The old man would read about people living in a big city with lights and horses.

Twice a week, Sam stopped by to see Daniel on the street and listened to him read about far-away countries and how people dressed and acted. The stories were about places that were safe.

Listening to Daniel's stories kept up Sam's spirit, which he had lost. Daniel often stood up as if he were more comfortable reading while on his feet, and then the old man started to cough. After choking through a page, he interrupted the story.

"Give me a minute," said Daniel. He pulled out a big, tattered handkerchief from an inner pocket in his mud-gray coat, and began to hack a series of coughs into it. Day after day, the coughing lasted longer and longer, leaving him gasping for a breath of air that his lungs would not hold. Each time, he remained polite and excused the pause until he could read again.

"Today, Sammy, your gaze is here," said Daniel, "but your mind is somewhere else. Anything you want to talk about?"

"No," answered Sam, "just hungry."

Daniel felt that something was different about Sam's demeanor and the way he intensely watched passing German patrols, but Daniel didn't ask him about it. Sam was somewhere else.

"Then we will finish the story tomorrow, when my cough is gone and your attention is back."

The cough would not get better and Sam's mind would focus on another world.

* * * * *

"Maybe get an older boy to do it," said Leah. "Tell them tonight."

"We have been through this," said Duvid, "and he is ready."

Sam was changing into his scuffed up and torn pants, getting ready to go to the meeting.

"They started with men, who were not as agile or fast enough. Those men started to disappear," Duvid continued, "so they brought in smaller boys."

"That doesn't make me feel better," said Leah. She wanted to believe that this made sense, but as a mother of two sons, it didn't feel right. There was nothing fair about the ghetto or what was decided as necessary. She kissed Baruch and Sam, so it didn't seem like a goodbye to anyone. For the first time as a mother, Leah felt numb.

"We need kids," said Duvid, "or the food stops."

Leah watched Sam re-tie his boots and walk to the door. She told herself, "The worst thing that could happen is that he won't bring back anything. If there is danger, he knows to run to avoid capture."

They all knew that being caught meant never being seen again. Others in the meetings would confirm that they had younger brothers or sons who never came back. Relatives didn't want to ask the Germans and draw attention to the fact that they were related to someone who was taken. It was the constant fear of being next.

After midnight, several men gathered with the collected items and lists in the dark basement near one of the hidden wall openings.

"You will be fine with him," said Duvid, "since Yankle has done this many times." He embraced Sam and gave him a kiss on his forehead. "If there's any problem, you can't ask for help," Sam's father continued. "Drop everything, run fast, and don't look back."

The dim basement light covered Duvid's deep frown and pressed lips as he turned his eyes away.

"And don't give any openings away," instructed Yankle. "Just run ten feet away and hide."

Even though he was only a teenager, Yankle walked with the experience of someone twice his age and spoke with the calm of having done this his whole life.

"You will always be with someone who knows the ropes of how to move and stay hidden." Yankle looked deeply into Sam's eyes and spoke intensely about his role and what he must not do.

"*In kim nisht meyer,*" said Yankle. Once they started in the tunnel, he didn't want to be bothered or hear anything from Sam.

"*Za shtil.*" Not a word. "*Red nisht mit mir. Ikh vel redn tsi dir.*" Yankle made it clear that only he would be doing any talking and that silence was vital. Sam blinked in agreement.

"Do exactly what he tells you and stay quiet," said Duvid. Sam noticed that most of the others in the room had suddenly disappeared, leaving him with Duvid, Yankle, and one other man. It was critical to keep the secret knowledge about the entrance to a minimum. There was a concern that if the Germans took someone away who knew the secrets, names, hidden places, and activities, it would expose all the people in the building and neighborhood to collective Gestapo punishment.

Sam felt a hand on the side of his head. A man with a puffy, dark beard and sideburns knelt down in front of him.

"Hold still so I can get this on you," whispered the deep voice. The cold mud covered Sam's face, hands, and nails, while his dark clothes hid any exposed skin that might reflect light. The man pulled down Sam's black knit cap to cover his neck and ears. As he turned in the tunnel opening and grasped the bags and lists, Sam noticed his father silently wipe his eyes. Yankle tapped his shoulder and pointed to the wall.

Envelopes of money and valuable items were given to Yankle, along with the list of what was needed by each family. The list always included payment in advance for an unsure return delivery.

Yankle stuffed everything into his inside coat pockets and asked Duvid to strap the bags over his shoulders and lash them to his legs, so his hands were free. Lighter satchels were similarly attached to Sam's back and legs, so he could still move quickly.

"These items are to trade for medicine," said Duvid, as he placed the strap around Sam's shoulders. The bags held softly wrapped items and were easy to carry on his back. A mud-covered Yankle moved a dresser aside, revealing a hole in the wall. Sam was puzzled, for the hole was filled with dirt.

This was the first time Sam had seen the undisclosed hole that led out of the building. He didn't know where it went, but Sam realized that he was going to see what very few others had ever experienced. Without a word, he followed Yankle's lead and began digging out the dirt cover by hand. When there was enough space, Yankle disappeared through the hole bearing two full satchels, followed quickly by Sam and his bags. As the dry dirt ran up his sleeves and into his socks, Sam knew that his mother would not be happy with any dirt brought back to the apartment. He blindly crawled behind Yankle, bumping into the heels of the older boy's boots with his forehead or fingers.

Catching a mouthful of kicked-up dirt mixed with stifled air, Sam felt the bags scrape against the pebbly walls and understood why adults couldn't get through the tunnel. He was the perfect size to quickly wiggle his way through the narrow shaft. Sam had learned from his father to not waste time waiting for the world to cave in and instead, he thought about what was all around him as he moved forward through the earth.

When Sam brushed against a piece of wood used as a support beam, he braced for a cave-in. After thirty minutes of inching through the pitch-black dirt tunnel, Sam felt the touch of cold air against his face. This chamber had been deliberately burrowed crooked with a few twisting turns, each covered by loose dirt.

Wherever it was soft enough to dig, Yankle scraped aside the dirt into a gap, revealing an open space in the tunnel. Sam could hear Yankle grunt as he pushed the dirt over and reached back to tap Sam to advance. They crawled over each pile and into another sharp bend, followed by another pile to move. Slowly inching toward the unknown outside darkness, Sam wished he were invisible.

Yankle paused and tilted his head back over his shoulder toward Sam. *"Kim mit mir,"* said Yankle. He wanted Sam to stay close as possible and not get lost in the dark. Yankle whispered that when they were out of the hole, they must move very quickly.

"Makh es shnel, shnel!"

Sam understood and silently agreed.

Sam still couldn't see anything, but he sensed that Yankle had turned upward and was pushing something heavy out of the way. At first, he thought it could be a large rock covering an opening, but then could see a square outline against the dark, clouded sky.

The cement bench crudely slid on snow-cleared pavement, exposing the secret entrance. Yankle lifted himself out of the hole and reached back to yank Sam onto the frozen ground. Sam had followed Yankle into the exit shaft and now stood on a base of rocks, where he was pulled up and out by his arm.

Sam looked up and was startled by the ghostly outline of a woman reaching toward him. He swallowed a gasp and looked around for Yankle. He saw that they were surrounded by large, square-edged rocks. Headstones, statues, and crosses seemed to guard the underground access into the cemetery.

Sam didn't know what the stone woman was trying to reach, but he wasn't interested. Behind her was a large stone entrance to a small building with a chained gate and door. The daunting mausoleum was edged with polished stones and two narrow sidewalks led away in opposite directions.

Sam suddenly realized how fortunate he was to not have surfaced inside a grave or one of the many mausoleums. Either way, he knew his mother would understand why he was in a Christian cemetery. Sam was as dark and dirty as the tunnel. He sat in the snow next to a family plot of four stones in the midst of a collection of other headstones and trees. No one could have told him he would be emerging from his underground journey in the cemetery, and now he had to lie still in a graveyard, surrounded by dead bodies.

Being quiet took on a new meaning for Sam and he chose to not think about his deceased companions. He needed to calm his thoughts and body, and not cough or sneeze. Lie still and he might be able to leave the cemetery.

He could see Yankle pulling the cement bench back in place to cover the hole. When he realized the hole was no longer an easy escape, Sam remembered his father's advice—if there was a problem, he should immediately run and hide.

After months of secret digging, it was important that the opening not be found. *Cover the hole and run*, Sam repeated to himself. Neither Yankle nor Sam spoke a word and when Yankle crawled off to sit behind some other stones, Sam just followed him as previously told. They lay on their stomachs behind a fresh mound of dirt from a freshly dug grave and waited for something to happen.

Sam didn't know what else to do other than be silent and lie motionless. He could see a road carving a path through the cemetery grounds and exiting toward an open street outside the ghetto. Sam knew it was not open for him, especially when he saw German military trucks packed with soldiers driving back and forth.

After thirty minutes of lying flat in the chilling dirt, the boys heard the sound of a stone knock. Yankle answered with one knock against a headstone to show where they were waiting. He started to crawl between the headstones, followed closely by Sam, who felt dried mud cracking on his forehead. Yankle would be cautious about connecting with the smugglers, since they were hiding behind stones, too.

For what seemed to Sam like hours, there was no physical movement, tapping, or other noise. The extended silence was

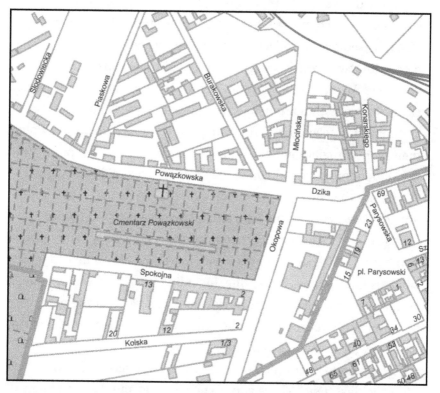

PARTIAL MAP OF WARSAW GHETTO SHOWING THE LOCATION OF THE CEMETERY
(SOURCE: POLISH CENTER FOR HOLOCAUST RESEARCH, WWW.GHETTO.PL)

mutually understood to expose any third party. Once in the cemetery, everyone involved knew that the location of the rendez-vous would be far away from the tunnel.

Yankle and Sam had to go toward the sound of the other tapping sound, which did not move. Their signal was to show that everything was clear and that it was more or less safe to move toward the source. If it seemed confused, interrupted, or exposed, then Yankle had said to run through the graves without being seen and get back into the hole without leading anyone to it. Sam listened to Yankle's breathing and waited to crawl or run.

With the series of rock taps, they slowly approached the tap response and connected behind a large statue figure wearing a cloak, poised over a collection of headstones near the fencing. They met with two Polish men, Sam thought perhaps in their late twenties. As well as Sam could see in the darkness, both looked clean shaven with buzzed haircuts, almost military. They wore dark clothing that seemed too fine for graveyard crawling. The Polish men were so confident that none of their skin was exposed that they stood up, looking down when speaking to Yankle and Sam.

Before they had left the meeting place, Yankle had told Sam that it wasn't always the same men and no one ever offered names.

"This is it," said the taller man with a raspy voice. They placed two bags on the ground in front of Yankle's head and picked up the satchels the boys were carrying, including the list of items request-ed for next time. Even in the dark, Sam could see that the men were as he remembered—people when they were fed, clean, and healthy. Sam thought he could smell soap.

"We couldn't get much of your list, so stop asking for what you didn't get last time." There was no negotiation and the boys knew it.

"People are paying you," said Yankle, muttering under his breath. He was insistent, yet cautious. The whole evening was filled with secrecy and fear. Yankle understood there was no second chance to do it right. He also knew they couldn't trust anyone, especially since the last boys who traded for the group hadn't returned and were never seen again.

Yankle couldn't argue in the cemetery; there was a constant fear of either being killed by smuggler gangs or the Germans. And he had promised Duvid that he would bring Sam back safely.

One of the men said in a quiet voice, "Don't write down fruit anymore. We can't get that for you. We will be here at the same time next Wednesday."

Yankle knew that sometimes the Polish men would be there, and other times not. There was no explanation when they didn't show, leaving a burning concern that the evening was a trap.

The exchange of words and bags only took a moment. Yankle was concerned about being spotted and caught, and was uncomfortable staying in one place with the Polish smugglers for more than an instant. It was time to leave without a sound.

Yankle grabbed the swapped bags left by the smugglers and gestured for Sam to get behind him. It was back to silence as they crawled between monuments and the few trees to conceal their way back to the hidden hole. They frequently paused to hide behind one of the larger monuments, where they listened for any other movement. Sam could only see the looming shadows of large crosses and motherly figures with their hands outstretched. Sam wanted to ask a question about the grave sculptures, but knew to control his curiosity and stay alert.

There was more unknown about the evening than known, but Sam realized that the tall iron fence was on the street side facing where the Jews lived. He wondered if his family was awake and if they knew what he had done. It was the first time he had been out of the ghetto since being brought back to Warsaw by the Germans.

Sam also figured that the cemetery was as far as he was going, but relished the thought of being counted on to help his family, just like Chava and Froim. He imagined that Leah would be relieved to see him, and hoped his father would just be proud.

Yankle didn't dare to stand and look around, but eventually spotted the immense vault near the hole. After navigating on hands and knees back through the snow and numerous headstones, he

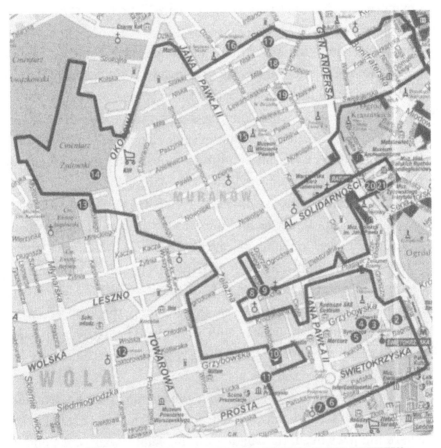

MAP OF WARSAW GHETTO SHOWING THE LOCATION OF THE CEMETERY
DARKER LINE INDICATES GHETTO BOUNDARY.
(SOURCE: POLISH CENTER FOR HOLOCAUST RESEARCH, WWW.GHETTO.PL)

found the cement bench. The crawl was slowed by Yankle turning to erase their marks in the snow. Looking and feeling more like frozen mud rats, the boys checked that the bags were secured on their backs before dropping back into the hole. They didn't realize how much light was reflected by the snow, even at night, until they dove back into total darkness and covered the opening.

Sam went first and felt his way through the blackness and although it was the same mud in the tunnel, the path was awkward and slower because Yankle had to stop and re-cover the turns with soft dirt.

"When you feel the table covering the other opening into the basement," whispered Yankle, "tap on the wood covering the hole. Only one tap." Sam began to crawl faster in anticipation of getting home. After several minutes, he was able to softly tap a knuckle against the wood. In one smooth movement, his father yanked away the table.

Exhausted and completely covered with fresh dirt and mud, the boys scrambled out of the hole with their bags into the embrace and shoulder slapping of Duvid and the man who was waiting with him. Looking at his son, Duvid was unable to hide the pride in his heart and the relief on his face.

"Was everything OK?" asked Duvid. "Did it go as planned? Are you all right?"

Sam didn't know how to respond to the rapid-fire questions and smiled at the sound of normal conversation. Duvid untied the bags from Sam's legs and removed a layer of mud-caked clothes from Sam's trembling body. With gentle hands, Duvid tried to brush off the dirt in his son's hair. When Sam was dusted off as well as possible, Duvid asked Yankle to escort Sam home.

"He was brave," said Yankle. "I'll go again with Sam, maybe next week."

"*Sam, gay tsi der mamen*," said Duvid. "*Gay ahaym yetst.* Go home now." He knew that Leah was not asleep at home, but waiting to see Sam walk in the door.

"*Ikh'l kimen shpeyter*," continued Duvid. He would return home too, but first had to fill in the tunnel opening, remove and disperse the scattered dirt, then clean away any tracks in the room.

"Yes, *Tateh*," said Sam, "I'll tell her you're coming soon."

* * * * *

Leah was wide awake and despite his unearthed appearance, Leah grabbed onto her mud child and gently swayed with him in their apartment doorway.

"*Ya, s'geveyn in ordenung?*" asked Leah.

"Yes," answered Sam. "It was fine and we got the trade bags."

Sam thought that he could now go to sleep for a few hours, but there were more rapid questions.

"*Vash dikh un*," said Leah. "*Ikh'l dir geybn epes tsi esn un gay tsi shlip.*"

He did as instructed and washed as well as he could. Yes, he was hungry, and then wanted to go to sleep. She didn't need to ask him twice, and Leah began to help him change out of the dirty clothes.

* * * * *

Sam had developed a tight, invisible bond with older neighborhood Jews. He now realized what his father had been doing at night for the past several months, and understood that the secrets he carried were not for his street friends or open for discussion at home. The adults knew better than to ask for information. There was safety in the silence.

As Sam immersed himself in new fears of tunnels collapsing, capture, disappearing, and being killed, he slowly stopped thinking about lost relatives and past courtyard play with friends. All of his memories were replaced with the purpose of surviving another day.

"Ma, can I go outside for a bit?" asked Sam.

Leah realized that he might need some daylight and fresh air. "Just stay on our street," she answered.

After his first foray, Sam found himself bursting with pride over the evening's activities and almost skipping out the building's front door. He turned at the sound of his named being called.

It was Daniel, still sitting on the street corner.

"Sam," said Daniel. "*Rulik, kim aheyr. Zug mir vus host getin hant.*" Daniel wanted to know what he had been up to. Caught! It was an innocent question, but Sam couldn't tell him what he had been doing that day. Sam froze in his steps.

"*Ikh hob gurnisht gemakht,*" answered Sam. "Nothing at all," continued Sam in a nervous chattering manner. "*Ikh kim aros.*" He would be right over.

"*Kim aheyr,*" said Daniel, gesturing to the boy.

What did the old man want? Why did he want Sam to come to his side? Sam wondered.

"*Di vilst ikh zol dikh epes laynen?*" Daniel asked.

"Of course," answered Sam, who exhaled with relief. "I have time to hear a story."

* * * * *

MAY 1940

"Does this make sense for Sam anymore?" asked Leah. "He's done more than enough and it's time to let others do this."

"He's been so lucky," said Duvid, "but ever since we lost Yankle, it's more risky and we seem to get less and less in trade."

"For the last trade, we had nothing left to exchange," said Leah. "And we agreed that when it's not worth it, then he should stop."

Duvid had put so much energy and sleepless nights into digging and supporting the underground trading that it felt like walking away from family. Leah's reasoning was inescapable and it was time to find another way. At the last meeting, Duvid recommended that the tunnel entrance be moved to a different location. Trading would now be moved above ground for Duvid and his family.

As residents in their building died from illness, starvation, or age, their relatives often gave the clothes to Duvid.

"Sam, go with Froim to the market," said Duvid, "and trade all of it for whatever food you can find. If they won't take it in trade, then give it to anyone on the street who is worse off."

It seemed that every day, the Germans were bringing more Jews into the ghetto. With the welcome spring weather setting in, they would give extra clothing to Sam so he could secretively trade it through the German wires to people outside the ghetto. Whenever people learned that there were children or a baby living in the area, they would share with the mother and children. It was important that children survived.

"*Gib di mame in di kinder fir,*" Sam would hear from people in the building, telling him to give something to the mother or the children. "*Zay zoln eyrsht esn.*" They should eat first and live.

Sharing became a way to live and Sam had the gutsy skills to walk between the streets as the messenger. He also noticed that he wasn't the only child openly engaged in trading, since most adults were either in a work detail or gone.

"Sam," said Duvid. "*Nem dus tsi, tsi deyr familye . . . Tomer hot emitser epes andersh far indz, breyng es tserik.*" On a daily basis,

Duvid would tell Sam to go to a specific family and trade a certain item with them for something they wanted to pass to Duvid, so he could then trade it for food. It was like fitting the moving puzzle pieces of life together, forming a picture of existence.

Sam's youthful presence was endearing. He would leave with bits of clothing and often come back with food. Sometimes he returned with a vegetable or bread, traded for clothing from the dead that had been given to Duvid by neighbors.

It was a dark and sad market with a diminishing number of items circulated over time. Exchanges were fast and so frequent that people would come home wearing different coats or hats, if they could get a warmer one from someone with an extra. Then they would hand over their coat to someone shivering on the street. Nothing was wasted.

When neighbors got weaker and died, their leftover clothes were also passed on to trade for food to feed the children.

"Go tonight to unit 3B," said Duvid, "and Mrs. Zanski will give you some things that we can use."

"What things?" asked Leah.

"Her husband used to work with me," answered Duvid, "and she still has his things. I saw her in the hall and she asked us to send Sam over to collect it."

"It's too late to trade anything tonight in the market," said Leah.

"Wait until you see what I grabbed from the workers' table today," said Duvid, holding his hand up to ask for a moment. He typically saved any food he was occasionally given during the day and pulled from his pocket chunks of bread and a potato. It was a good day. It was better than the usual daily turnip and they were fortunate to be together and inside.

As the people living on the street became frailer, many of them just collapsed against a curb or wall and did not move again. When their moaning stopped and the eyes no longer sought help, it was time to call for the body wagon.

Life was being cut off. The minimal water supply to be shared in the apartment building was severed. The station faucets in the walls on the streets were run by the Germans and were only to be used at established times during the day.

"That's it for water," said Duvid, "until they shut off those pipes, too."

"They're controlling our every move," said Froim, "so they can watch us."

Water was primarily used for drinking. Some might be carefully poured over hands, then the run-off used to rinse diapers. Chava cut up old shirts for diapers and Leah was lucky to have safety pins, since they were still used to hold torn clothes together. There was no thread, buttons, or needles to repair anything.

When they were tacked together with safety pins, Sam could wear a bigger shirt and pants with the cuffs and extra materials pinned up. No matter what they used an article of clothing for these days, Leah never wanted to know where something had come from and why it wasn't needed anymore.

"I'm very sorry, Sam," said Duvid, "but you need to stay inside from now on, unless you are with one of us. The Germans are desperate for workers and they are grabbing anyone who can walk. They're using children to clear the streets."

"If you are outside," said Leah, "they will take you away."

Every day, Sam overheard conversations about someone from the building who had been thrown into a truck and disappeared. He wasn't going to balk at his parents' warnings.

* * * * *

"No more fences?" asked Leah.

She was holding up Baruch by his tiny hands and trying to get him to stand on the bare floor, while Duvid, Froim, Sam, and Chava watched the balancing act. "He's been crawling around, so walking can't be far off."

Sam stood and playfully mimicked the wobbling in the remaining daylight.

"Good start," said Froim, while pointing at Baruch and chuckling at Sam.

"The Germans are not really removing anything," answered Duvid. "They're adding. I start tomorrow morning when they bring in the brick and mortar by truck. If I'm forced to work all day for the Germans, maybe I'll get some food to bring home."

He had been approached by a brown-capped Kapo as he stepped off the work truck with Froim and was told about the morning re-assignment.

"They want us to build a wall," he continued, "and they'll take others from the building."

"That's it?" asked Chava. "They want another wall?"

Duvid shrugged and clasped his hands together and looked down in deep thought. There was no space to pace in the room.

Shortly before dawn, a German army truck pulled up in front of the apartment building and was met by two unarmed Kapos, who arrived on foot. An officer from the truck spoke to the Kapos, who then ran into Duvid's building. One Kapo was ordered to stand at the front door as the other walked down to Duvid's unit.

Since the front doors of the units had all been removed, the Kapo walked right into the inner hallway leading to the unit door. There were no locks on doors and it was like living outside with constant exposure and no privacy. The Kapo flung open the door, revealing everyone still lying on the floor, except for Duvid, who was standing and ready to go.

"Where are the adults in the building?" asked the Kapo. "They need twenty."

Closing the door behind him, Duvid cajoled the Kapo out of the apartment and walked with him toward the outer hallway.

"If they don't immediately report to the street," said the Kapo, "they'll be dragged out. And the Germans are not kind with their boots, so it is better to come or they will shoot each one dead in front of their families, or worse."

Duvid remembered an elderly neighbor saying that it is better to not fight back and live another day. He still didn't know whether or not he agreed, but it was the best way to avoid getting your head bashed open on the street.

Once he arrived at the work site, much to his surprise, Duvid's group wasn't told to build a wall. He was given a certain number of bricks to be laid in the twelve-hour shift, but it was to be used on an existing building on the perimeter of the ghetto. They were ordered to "brick up" all of the windows and doors, and build walls between adjacent buildings to close the gaps.

The forced laborers only worked from inside and between the buildings, carefully watched by guards with aimed machine guns. A German engineer walked around with blueprints and spoke to a worker in charge. The worker was wearing a colored band on his arm, identifying him as being able to translate the German instructions into Yiddish.

Duvid was pleased that there was a ration for working and when they were told to eat the moldy bread or dried vegetables on the spot, Duvid hid much of it in his pocket to bring it home.

"What did they have you do today?" asked Leah.

"They're closing the walls and windows all the way up to the top," answered Duvid, trying to scrape bits of dried mortar off his fingers. "We'll be closed in and won't see the other side anymore."

"If we can't even trade, how do we eat?" asked Chava.

"The rooftop doors will be sealed, too," continued Duvid, "so there will be no more going up on the roof, Sam. There's now a guard tower by the gate."

The Germans did not like being watched and Duvid sensed that this was the beginning of the end.

* * * * *

FALL 1940

Faith was all that was left in the ghetto. It was like watching a tree being slowly strangled to death, except in the ghetto, there were no trees or parks, gardens or flowers. Nothing green, and Sam wondered if the whole world was dying, too.

Duvid felt it was time to pray and told the men who were joining him for Rosh Hashanah prayers to meet in a basement room down the hall from their apartment.

"We need to do this," said Duvid, "even if they are afraid to come."

"Ask Sam to watch the street for trouble," said Leah.

The solemn prayers were a life anchor to keep everyone confident that there was a future for a new year. When the service was over, the men started to leave. Duvid didn't move.

Sam tugged on his father's coat, while Duvid continued to rock back and forth with his eyes closed.

"*Nocht niche,* " said Duvid. He knew that Sam was waiting by his side. "Not just yet."

The men left the service, slowly moving out of the building. Surviving on crumbs just one time per day, people were moving more slowly and dragging their feet, like sleepwalkers. There were fewer people on the street because it took energy to walk. People began to look like bums who went through hell, unkept, gaunt, *"verblungent,"* lost, and confused of what to do. Only safe within themselves, they sat dreaming with glossy eyes.

The ghetto was starving to death. It was as if each person was held together by a tattered string. When Duvid and Froim returned at the end of the day, there were more people sitting in the street and sidewalks, lying around without conversation or chatter. People were falling dead like leaves unhinging from a tree in winter, dropping dead where they fell.

Clothing was reduced to rags and torn blankets served as hats and coats. Many residents were without shoes, for they had traded footwear for food. Instead of shoes, they wore rags wrapped around feet, flopping on their legs. There were all sorts of dirty-rag fashions, held together by the shredded corners of former garments, once belonging to former people. Frayed strings stretched beyond survival, unable to hold onto a former dignity and meager life. There was no purpose to the indescribable agony of daily life other than the total annihilation of the ghetto residents.

The Gestapo had the only clean coats and shiny black boots in Warsaw. The colors of the world had been stomped out and everything was black.

OCTOBER 1940
Mass deportations into the Warsaw ghetto begin.
400,000 Jews are incarcerated within the brick walls.

CHAPTER FIVE

THE CLINK OF DEATH

In those times there was darkness everywhere. In heaven and on earth, all the gates of compassion seemed to have been closed.

—Elie Wiesel

LATE NOVEMBER, 1941

"I'm back," said Sam. Before he closed the warped front door behind him, Sam tried to kick the fresh snow off his boots in the outer hall by banging his feet against the cracked wooden threshold. Since their one-room "re-settlement" apartment had been stripped bare of its furnishings, Leah cautioned that street dirt and snow were not welcome on the bare floors, where Baruch sat.

Clink.....clink....clink. Leah could hear the snow-muffled sound moving away from their building, but she couldn't stomach looking out the window. Sam made a few additional stomps and walked into the apartment, still wearing his hat and dark gray, tattered coat. The small hat flaps barely covered his ears, leaving his earlobes exposed and frostbitten pink, matching his fingers protruding out of missing finger-tips in his adult-sized gloves. The air in the cloistered apartment was as cold as the outside air, so Sam didn't think to take off his coat inside. The fallen chunks of snow weren't melting.

"They kept you later than yesterday," said Leah. "More loads?"

"I stopped at the corner and talked to Daniel," said Sam. "He wanted to read to me and I really like his stories."

Leah knew that seeing Daniel was the only bright moment in Sam's day. Those pavement lessons were valuable and distracted Sam from the wagon work.

"Can I bring him more cloth to sit on the snow?" asked Sam. "He is coughing more blood and the ground is cold."

Leah nodded her head and went to the closet to find something to bring the old man the next day.

The coat hooks on the back of the front door remained empty, except for some found scraps of dirtied shirt sleeves and jacket pieces with buttons. Attached buttons with thread were useful and easy to reuse when patching an article of clothing and shrinking the size. Little was overlooked or tossed away until it had decayed beyond any semblance of use. People in the ghetto were like that, too.

"Let me get you something to eat," said Leah. "You have had nothing." She knew it would be his first and only bite of food all day.

"I know," said Sam. "I heard the wheels and then they hollered for me, so I ran."

He had left home in the early morning with the hunger that woke him in the middle of the night and each morning. The burning, empty ache doubled him over with racking cramps and followed him into the day as a rolling pain, churning over and over again. The stomach gas produced from the empty burning escaped through burping, which Sam began to ignore as another uncontrollable part of the day. Most other ghetto residents dealt with the same embarrassment and grew tired of excusing it.

Living in the ghetto meant never being full and at best, eating things hardly passable as a food substance. The degrading side-effects felt by the body were common and a sign of its slow and painful demise. Residents competed with rats to find and store tidbits of food—maybe a stale crust of bread or soft bits of browned vegetable scraps, like a carrot fragment that had been stored in a mattress for a couple of days.

One of the best ways to stow a piece of food was to keep it on your person, whether in a pants pocket or hidden between scarves and other clothing corners. Neither stash location made it taste any better.

And if anyone in the family apartment acquired something through a trade, forced labor, or at a ghetto food station, it was split with all family members, along with saving a portion hidden in a chosen mattress. If something was stowed for later, it was a treasured putrefied morsel. Hope was saving a pitifully rotted speck of food for another day.

"Chava just got Baruch to nap," said Leah. "Come sit with us and I will find something for you to eat."

Chava gently waved at Sam to quickly close the door and then held her finger to her lips, gesturing, "Shhhh." The apartment's single room now had three street-stained mattresses on the floor for Froim and Chava, Duvid and Sam, and Leah and the baby. The lone closet held folded piles of traded clothes and mismatched shoes, as well as towel and blanket scraps. One stack of haphazardly folded clothes had been torn as diapers and tossed after some use, since they could not be cleaned.

Next to the closet door was a short, built-in bookcase holding stacks of newspaper sections that Duvid had found during the past few months. He rationed his reading, since seeing an old dated article gave him a brief sense of normalcy, and he didn't want to exhaust the content in one sitting. He couldn't spare money for current news and ignored the stands with German magazines featuring Adolf Hitler on their covers. Word of mouth was more reliable and traveled faster in the ghetto than the German press.

The room's four square walls were bare and void of personal photos, mirrors, or color. The front door frame was empty, too. In the back corner was a wood-burning stove with an ill-fitting vent through the wall. The scent of burning wood was smoky, but a pleasant diversion from the raw and rancid smells of their living space. And on a cold night, the stove gave some warmth with a small amount of scavenged wood.

In another corner was the wide floor grate for bathroom drainage. They couldn't afford privacy and relied upon each other's discretion and care to survive the day. It was the price to avoid participating in open defecation on the street.

If Sam was able to have a piece of foul turnip or carrot, he didn't enjoy it for very long. By late morning, he felt the runs and diarrhea the worst because his eight-year-old system couldn't hold anything and completely digest it. It was a daily drain on his system and eating an old fragment of something was an intestinal gamble. He hoped to get a bit of nutrition from the food nugget before it became waste.

Sam didn't like the forced work of loading the wagon every morning, and his frustration was compounded by needing to duck into alleyways to urgently relieve himself.

"I don't have any extra trousers for you," said Leah, "so go where you can and keep these clean."

It was evident that most ghetto-dwellers, including the other corpse collectors, had the same problem. Wherever people walked without long coats, you could see their torn pants smudged and wet in the tush area. They were gaunt from not being able to find or hold in any food, and frequently didn't have any decent clothes left to change into. The scent of the passersby was putrid and exchanged in silence, no longer earning a comment or look, but the degradation cut deep.

With nothing to do and nowhere to go, the men who weren't picked up for forced labor either walked around slowly or leaned against walls, or collapsed somewhere on the ground. A corner was the prime location to beg, and woman and children frequently joined together with open hands and caps upturned. Emaciated children and adults became beggars, resting their withered limbs on the ground.

When their energy had been starved out, they were no longer able to hold themselves upright. They eventually died. Strangers covered them with papers and box fragments, indicating that they were ready to go. Eventually the corpse collection wagon would roll through the area and the bodies would never be seen again. They often had no family left to mourn their loss.

Unless a person was going to a market to trade or was forced to work, there was less and less reason to be outside. It was safer and expended less energy for families to stay indoors and watch over each other, since people disappeared without notice.

There was nothing of value in their apartment, but Sam and his family members appreciated not being on the street and were glad to feel any evening food going down their throats. They were never full and existed on the shared warmth of returning home at night.

"I'm just glad you're back," said Leah. "Settle in and let me see if there is a piece of bread for you that I can break away from the mold."

Sam followed his mother to the far mattress and had no reaction to the food offer. He smiled at Chava, who was sitting in the only chair, rocking a dozing Baruch wrapped in a yellowed blanket.

"You're home early," said Chava. "Did something happen?"

"The snow was getting higher and the wagon was full and too heavy," answered Sam. "I already had six and the cart was getting stuck, so they sent me home. I might have to go back out, if they can empty it into a passing hearse."

Leah heard Baruch fussing in his blanket and she didn't want to disturb the infant by arguing with the wagon explanation.

"My arms hurt from pushing in the snow," said Sam, rubbing his biceps. "They're stiff. And when I came in the building, some lady downstairs gave me her bread crusts."

"*Host epes tsi esn?* Do you have anything to eat?" the older woman with a wooden cane had asked as they walked into the building together.

"*Host gegesn hant?*" She truly seemed to want to know if he had eaten yet today.

Sam didn't know if he should take food offered by strangers and started to walk away.

"*Vart, khel dir geybn a shtikl vus ikh hob.*" He waited and decided to take the offered bread, smiled at the old woman, and gave the morsel to his mother, since it might be better than what she had in the apartment.

"Since she was from our building, I took it." Sam knew that if his mother didn't like the bits, then they could still be traded or given away, but she would know best.

"Even when they have nothing themselves," said Leah, "people are so kind to you boys. But I still don't like that you have to do this work every day."

She looked over at Chava and Baruch, then turned back to Sam. "It's getting colder and they don't feed you anything. We know you want to be strong like *Tateh*, but you are younger than the other boys, so let them push."

Leah had stated every physical reason she could think of to object to Sam's mandatory participation, but didn't want to mention the obvious mental toll. Her son was being forced to remove dead bodies from the streets. It was important to her that Sam felt his parent's love and support, but she never imagined it for this purpose. To Leah, it seemed that encouragement was all they had left to offer him.

Sam suddenly ran off toward the corner floor drain grate.

"Are you all right?" asked Leah.

"It's hard to hold it," said Sam. "I had to use a side-street a couple of times with gutter papers to clean myself."

Eating anything available wasn't much better than starving. If Sam didn't eat for days and then had something to eat, it would be immediately followed by cramping pain, as if his stomach didn't recognize what was being put into it. His body was refusing to digest it. The cramps were frequent and actually felt worse than just the hunger, he was hesitant to admit. Eating fast and gulping the chunks only would make the cramps worse.

Leah tried to get Sam to slow down as he ate, encouraging him to take small bites and save some for later. "*Es bloyz a klayne shtik,*" said Leah, "*in shpeyter esti nokh a bisl.*" Whether it was to stretch out the scrap of food or make it more digestible, Sam learned to slow down despite his ravaging hunger.

At night, hunger was an empty feeling for everyone that they masked from each other. Why complain that you are physically sick, when everyone you see is also suffering. Sam had developed a cough from spending all day outside, compounded by sleeping in the cold apartment. His hoarse cough burned in the sour pain of his empty stomach, cramping on the emptiness. There was no medication available to his parents, but Leah would do her best.

"*Zets dikh avek a bisl in trink a bisl vaser,*" said Leah. "*Nish kan sakh; bloyz a bisl in zets dikh avek.*" It was difficult for Sam to calm his cough and be still, even with a little drink of water, but he understood the need to not make it worse for himself.

"*Za shtil*," she said to calm his breathing, gently stroking his head.

The smaller water bucket now had to be carried for many blocks from a city well, and mindful of the effort, Leah would always save some water for drinking before using it for any other purpose. Not a drop was wasted.

Non-drinkable water was reused later, extra for washing hands and the few dishes or cleaning up after a full diaper. Even to wash dirty floors, it always had other uses in another bucket. Nothing was tossed out until it was replaced by another full bucket. The running water had been shut off before they were re-settled in the building, so the sink with a drain was only for dumping.

They all agreed that it was best for Sam to go in a certain pot, and then Leah or Duvid would dump it down the floor grate with the reusable water used to wash it down. The others were more careful and didn't need the pot.

* * * * *

"Chava, if you want to get some air," said Leah, "then you could take some clothes to trade for food in the market." Leah went to the closet and began to pull out some clothing items worth an exchange. "I'll sit with Baruch and Sam, since you haven't stepped out for days, maybe weeks."

"With the empty bakery and butcher shop," said Chava, "any market food is third-hand, or worse. I'll take the clothes, but it's hard to find anyone who would take hunger over being cold. With each round of trades, there is less and less."

"I agree," said Leah, "but we have to keep trying."

"And why is this going to be different?" asked Chava. "I just hate going out there to see people begging for food that we don't have either." Tears welled up in her eyes.

"You might have seen older relatives die," Leah's younger sister said, "but you never had to watch them starve and freeze to death."

Leah understood the underlying worry and tried to diffuse the moment.

"And that's the only good thing about winter. The street doesn't smell as much," said Leah. "Just ask Sam."

Sam looked up after hearing his name and smirked at the pungent reminder. The ghetto looked like a dug-up graveyard and had the inescapable stench of an open sewer. And Chava knew they were all trapped, dead or alive, including their vanished parents.

"It still smells like death," said Chava, "and we don't even know who is alive."

"I'm worried about them, too," said Leah, as she reached into the closet to re-fold the remaining clothes. It had been more than two years since hearing from their parents, just before their home had been blown to pieces in a bombing run.

"The Nazis are destroying Warsaw and filling it up with every European Jew they can find. It's confusing." Leah carefully straightened the black head covering her mother had given her after Sam was born.

"After the bombings and shootings, do you really believe they're alive?" asked Chava. "I think about them when I see the older people lying on the pavement. I think, that could be our parents."

Leah stopped moving and fixed her stare into the dark closet.

"They didn't want to leave, but at least you and Froim are here with us."

"You know what's happening as well as I do, Leah," said Chava.

They had both heard the same stories from non-Polish Jews who had been forced into the ghetto and then relocated to camps, never to be seen again.

"There's a new place being built near here," said Leah, "a work camp, which will be ready soon. Some of Froim's friends have been taken to work on it, about an hour away by truck. Have you heard of Treblinka?"

"No, but I doubt it's what the Nazis say," answered Chava. "When his friends don't return, then you will know the truth. And we don't need to go to another Nazi ghetto or just take rotten food hand-outs; we need to get out of here. Don't you see? It will never get better here. It's not supposed to."

"Well, leaving is not as easy as walking out the door," said Leah. "First wires and fences, now bricks and walls. Of course, the Kapos only have clubs, but the Gestapo have machine guns."

Even in private, it was never a comfortable conversation shared between relatives.

"Is Duvid still working on walls?"

"Yes," answered Leah, "but it's gotten worse. He said they're sealing up the windows and doors with bricks. When they are done, it will be one giant wall around us."

Chava looked at their one window, which had been covered with a sheet.

"No, we can't just leave." Leah shook her head in dismay.

"I know," said Chava, "but Jews don't live long in here, and we're Jews."

"Don't think that I haven't thought about leaving, but nothing is easy with the boys," said Leah. "Before I had Baruch, I complained about how uncomfortable I was rolling over in bed, and now I'm done complaining."

She looked over at Sam, who was playing with paper cut-out people, and sitting next to Baruch. "I'll talk to Duvid when he gets home."

Chava turned and gave her a curious look, inviting further explanation from Leah. "We're not to speak about it, but Duvid has talked to a few families in the building," said Leah. "I'll see what he figured out."

"Whatever they decide," said Chava, "count me in so we don't die here, too."

She was thinking about their neighbor's husband, Joseph, who had just died. Determined to find some food, Chava firmed her chin and snatched a burlap bag hanging from the closet doorknob and stuffed the sparse clothing pile in it. She was still wearing her long coat and gloves, and wrapped a long scarf twice around her neck. She pulled a blanket over her shoulders and hugged the bag to her chest for additional warmth. Then she walked toward the front door.

"I hate what this is doing to us, especially the boys." She also knew that her sister must eat to continue nursing Baruch, but didn't need to point that out to Leah. Chava heard a gentle tapping at the door and slowly opened it to gaze into the outer hall.

"For the boys," said Miriam, entering the apartment door. They listened carefully to her thick Hungarian accent to pick out the Yiddish words. Miriam reached toward Leah with some potatoes and stale bread wedges.

"And you can trade some of his clothing." She held out a small, gray cloth bag with the top drawn together with a shredded yellow hair ribbon. The woman was nearing forty, but her gaunt and drawn face appeared to be well into the seventies. Her hair had begun to fall out and her eyes drooped from fatigue and were drawn into their sockets.

"Joseph died last night and I don't need as much," Miriam said in a subdued voice.

Sam was trying to peek at who knocked at the door and Leah wondered whether it was he who had handled Joseph during his wagon rounds that morning. Leah extended a hand toward Sam, asking for a moment of privacy. She pointed toward the mattress, and noticed the safety pin on his waistband.

"Thank you," said Leah and reached out to take the food and clothing from Miriam's hands, which were merely bones stretched over with a parchment-thin layer of dried skin. "Let us know if you need anything or want Duvid and Froim for a *shiva minyan,*" a gathering of mourners.

"I will," said Miriam. "Now feed those boys." Her comment echoed like an instruction, rather than the kind-hearted gesture from a woman in deep agony.

Leah remembered seeing Joseph leaving the building a few weeks earlier. His graying beard had been stylishly trimmed and squared off at the bottom, but near death, it appeared as an unshaven, scraggly mess. The women looked into each other's eyes and exchanged an unspoken understanding of what was happening to them.

Miriam accomplished what she most desired—sharing her food—then silently left and returned to her own unit. While the older woman recognized that she might not survive for much longer, the children must make it. Perhaps they would remember those who didn't, sharing what happened here. It was an exchange for hope.

Chava had also heard the conversation between the women and felt compelled to not let death by starvation occur in their apartment, especially not to the boys.

"I'm going," said Chava. "May I borrow your scarf to wrap around my own?" Leah nodded.

"Watch yourself," said Leah, "and don't stay out there too long. If you don't find anything to trade, just run back here and we'll try again tomorrow."

"I've survived German planes shooting at our family and jumping into ditches with you. I'll be fine in the market." Chava kissed Baruch and Sam on their foreheads and darted out the door with the bag of clothing pieces.

"Where did Chava go?" asked Sam, looking up from the paper figures he was playing with.

"She's visiting the families upstairs and then going to the market to trade some clothing for more food," answered Leah. "She'll be home soon."

Leah silently asked God for Chava's safe return and smiled at Sam.

Leah knew the market was surrounded by slow death, but she realized that without Duvid or Froim at home during the day, Chava was the only one who could trade for food scraps. Certainly the weakest, Baruch would never survive if Leah didn't have the minimal sustenance to nurse him. Leah was wracked between the guilt of not feeding the boys and allowing Chava to venture outdoors and face the many dangers on the streets.

* * * * *

Leah's fears were well-founded. Unmarked trucks drove through the ghetto with guards randomly grabbing older children, who disappeared forever. Panicked parents asked other parents if they had seen their son or daughter. Often, these ragtag trucks were commandeered by the Nazis and entered the ghetto to be filled for a one-way mission. Whether young people disappeared for a camp's forced labor detail or otherwise, the trucks returned empty and without explanation.

Chava listened for speeding trucks and focused on reaching the market and losing herself in the tight crowd. The blatant hunting and grabbing of children was frequent, terrifying to witness, and impossible to comprehend. Anything could occur when the trucks entered the ghetto and there was nothing anyone could do about it.

The young woman watched the daylight quickly diminish and decided to pick up her pace, even though she preferred to not be noticed as someone who still had the energy to walk briskly. In her final months as a teenager, she didn't want to be snatched away from her siblings, Duvid, or the boys. She had stayed hidden away in the garden-level apartment and wanted to remain as invisible as possible. She also wanted to help with baby Baruch. Surviving with her starving family members was better than being beaten and snatched onto a truck. She didn't want to disappear.

While she knew it was nearing the end of the year, Chava ignored her twentieth birthday. The year had passed without bathing, Passover, or dressing up with friends and going to the Yiddish theater. With the German invasion, it seemed that life had stopped, or even ended. There were no celebrations with friends, especially since she didn't know if any of them were alive.

She preferred to stay inside with Leah and Baruch, rather than walk through the crushing ghetto streets, filled with people seemingly lost for a direction or place to safely rest. Nothing was clean in the ghetto and even fresh rain water or snow became dirty once it touched down.

The people who lived in the ghetto had begun to look like the grimy ground beneath their feet. Colors disappeared from clothing, food bits, the streets, and markets. People were hollowed shadows of gray dust.

The neighborhood had changed into a mix of Jews violently uprooted from German-occupied lands, thousands thrust into the decaying ghetto every week. In the isolation of the ghetto corners, people freely spoke Hungarian, Czech, Bulgarian, or Polish, but Yiddish was still the common language for sharing information among this forced population of Jews. Common information disappeared and the Yiddish notices and advertising posters that had once plastered exterior walls and back streets fences were torn off to burn for heat, leaving an ever-thickening layer of glue. Their ghostly presence was a shadow of a lost promise.

Chava knew the market was near the ghetto trolley tracks, and realized what she would have to do to get there and back. There was no escape from what was strewn on the pavement and curbs of the street. Holding tightly to her sack of clothes, she darted into the pressed crowd, ignoring the groaning of skeletal adults and children lying collapsed against walls of empty stores, begging for a handout from people with nothing to share.

"Please," said a boy, sitting on a snow pile with two other boys. None of them wore shoes or coats. "Any food, please," he repeated over and again. Chava couldn't look in their direction and bowed her head as she walked to the closing market. The brick and cement building facades along the way were riddled with shrapnel fragments from fallen bombs, tossed grenades, and sprayed machine gun bullets. Missing chunks remained open and crumbling as pieces continued to fall away to the ground.

Both the cold and hunger were excruciating, but when a family had more of one than the other, it was possible to trade. While Chava was determined to trade for any food to feed Leah and the boys, it was late and just moments before the evening curfew when she approached the market street. She would either get a last-minute deal or nothing for the few clothing items in her bag. As she passed a fire in a barrel, a Kapo ran up to it and banged his club on the metal rim, then scurried to another fire.

"Put it out and leave," said the Kapo, as he continued to beat the rim, pounding out hot ashes to the ground. "Immediately. Orders!" He pulled down on the broad brim of his brown uniform cap and looked over his shoulder for approval from those who were giving the orders. Other Kapos in the market began to yell for the fires to be extinguished and for everyone to clear out.

One of the three SS guards standing on the edge of the collection of market carts was just waiting for a reason. He held a submachine gun with one hand on the stock and the other on the trigger, as his eyes twitched over the crowd.

"Douse it now," repeated the Kapo. "Clear the yard."

It was a command to the crowd and an efficiency performance for the guards. "Everyone out!"

While few ghetto residents feared the Jewish Kapos, they understood that orders under the watchful eyes of the Nazis meant kill the fires and scatter like rats—immediately. Although they had the guns, the Nazis seemed uncomfortable with people collecting in the streets, even for the warmth of a corner rubbish fire. The burning of Warsaw, one garbage can at a time, was too slow and disruptive to the Nazis.

As the sky darkened and the crowd pressed to leave, all Chava wanted was to be at home again.

* * * * *

"Hold still," said Leah, "and I can pull these pants a smidge tighter." Without questioning, Sam knew why Leah moved the pins again. Each week, extra material was taken up in his pants and dilapidated coat. He saw everyone in the apartment and on the street do the same thing with pins, cords, strings, and bands.

Pinching their clothes tighter, especially at the ankles and wrist cuffs, looked like a sour fashion to avoid baggy material.

"If your clothes fit snugly," said Leah, "you'll be warmer."

As each layer of his body mass vanished, Sam never felt warmer. Clothes were never let out for more room, only pulled and cinched tighter. Safety pins spearing inches of threadbare garments together was a winter skill, offering no additional warmth for either children or adults, but doing so kept the clothes together.

After Chava left, the apartment was dead quiet. Leah was still sitting on her mattress near Sam with Baruch lying in her lap. She suddenly realized how long it had been since she had been alone with both boys. It felt like never.

"Hello?" said a woman's voice. "Is anyone here?" They were back again.

There was a firm sound of knuckles rapping against the apartment's front door, followed by the repeated sound of the same voice, only quieter.

"Hello, anyone?"

Leah stood and picked up Baruch, then slightly cracked the door open to reveal two middle-aged Polish women standing in the doorway, each wearing a long, gray, winter coat and a white nurse's cap. The taller woman's light brown hair was parted down the middle and neatly combed into braids in the back. She carried a folder with papers and both women seemed out of place, like salesmen in a graveyard.

"Irena," said the shorter nurse to her companion. "No one here wants to talk to us and we have a long list."

Leah pulled the door wide open and looked at the women, who were quietly talking to each other in Polish with a business-like demeanor. Leah understood Polish, even heard through a doorway, but she only spoke in Yiddish.

"Yes," answered Leah, holding Baruch, "we live here. What do you want with us?"

"There may be a chance to save your baby," answered the shorter woman.

Leah was shocked by the answer and turned around to check on Sam, then looked at the cleanly dressed women. She walked into the hallway and closed the door behind her, leaving it slightly ajar. Sam walked over to the door and tried to listen to the conversation through the crack.

"We have heard about you," said Leah. "Why do you do this? You're wearing an armband, but you're not Jewish. I don't understand. You're Polish."

"We have a permit to enter and leave the ghetto, but we also need the Jews to trust us," said the other woman.

"We heard you joined the Zegota," said Leah. "Why would you help the Jewish underground?"

The woman did not reply and looked at her companion.

"I'm not Jewish, but I'm a mother, too, like you."

"Is that why you wear an armband?"

"Maybe, but my father's a doctor and he has helped a lot of Jewish patients, too, especially those who couldn't afford to help themselves. I live near Warsaw and heard about what is happening to the Jews here, so I'm following my father's example."

"What do you want from us?" asked Leah. She knew the answer to the question, re-wrapped the blanket around Baruch, and held him tightly in both arms. Sam peeked out of the doorframe to see who was talking to his mother.

"There are families outside the walls who want to help, even though it is dangerous for them, too." The woman opened her leather folder, pulled out a stack of papers, and began to scan a list with columns. Leah tried to read the information, but it was written in Polish.

"I think it might be best to get the youngest boy out before they close the gate on us."

"Can you do this?" asked Leah.

"We have the help of many people risking everything, and yes, some success. The Nazis have not caught on—yet."

The neatly dressed woman turned around to look at the building's front entrance. "I'm here for the very young children and the babies," said Irena, "your baby. Your other son is too big. There's no time to lose. We know that at any moment the Nazis can stop us from coming into the ghetto."

"How do you get children past the guards?"

"We hide them," answered Irena, "if the ambulance is full. We also get out some very young children, if we give them a Christian name and diagnosis of a disease like TB, there are few questions. The Germans also don't like typhus."

Leah looked at Baruch, held tightly in her arms, and began to shake her head.

"I know it is not perfect or the best solution," said Irena, "but it can save lives." She reached out to caress Baruch's head and Leah pulled away.

"How could I do this?" asked Leah. "Go away."

Both Polish women turned and looked down the vacant apartment hallway toward the sound of footsteps shuffling in a rear doorway.

"I can't stay and talk anymore, but discuss this tonight with your husband and I will stop by tomorrow."

"His answer will be 'no,' too," said Leah.

"It's not safe for either of us if I go to the same place too often," said Irena, "so if you want me to take your baby out of here, tomorrow will be your last chance."

She reached out again to touch Leah's shoulder, but Leah turned around and pulled the threadbare blanket more tightly around Baruch's head.

"Please, just think about it." Irena shuffled her papers back into the leather folder, re-buttoned her long coat, and quickly left the building with her associate.

Leah went back into the apartment and closed the door tight.

"Who was that lady?" asked Sam, clutching the hem of Leah's dress.

"She wants to help us," said Leah to the swaddled Baruch. Thinking of Sam's daily forced duty, she feared this offer was perhaps the only answer to save Baruch and that she was being selfish. They were starving. Leah wondered why they all deserved to die.

* * * * *

Chava walked back from the closing market and saw throngs of gaunt children sitting under vacant store windows, collapsed on snow banks, seemingly unable to stand or walk. They no longer approached her, touching her elbow and asking for food. They remained on the ground with no energy to stand, desperate for another life gasp with an opened hand, soiled in their own clothes, and unable to think of the following morning.

A few boys wore ragged, over-sized coats and hats, which appeared as though they had been dug up and passed along from grave to grave, permeated with the raw stench of bodies that had previously worn the garments. Glancing at the gaping holes in their shredded pant legs and shirts, Chava could see stick-thin legs covered with bits of recently sprouted adolescent hair and bodies with no muscle or mass.

She hurried passed another group of six young boys, almost sitting on top of each other against a building for shelter and warmth, each smiling with a few missing or crooked, yellowed teeth and a hand open for any generosity. Half smiling in anticipation of any outreach, despair was the only warmth for abandoned children.

At the corner was a family with younger and older children huddling together, waiting for anything better. They were as ragged, dirty, and gray as the ghetto itself. New snow in the ghetto didn't remain white for long and was rapidly strewn with human defecation. Even fresh air smelled like old urine—you couldn't walk away from it. The family had nowhere else to go.

Chava was thankful that Sam wasn't a street beggar yet, and felt horribly guilty that she had nothing to offer the outdoor children. She wondered if they would survive the winter with no food or shoes. They appeared to be wearing pants from their earlier years with the shredded cuffs barely at their knees. They were dirtier than street dogs, and their feet had thick blisters from exposure to the ruptured cement shards.

One older boy had cloth scraps wrapped around his feet tied with twine. The holes in the material were filled with snow, occasionally exposing pink-brownish skin with white flakes peeling away. She felt that even her own starved smile was hollow and pointless to them.

Suddenly conscious of her own grimy appearance, Chava reached up to tuck her hair under her head scarf and then realized it wasn't all there. Unable to wash their long hair for many months, Chava and Leah decided to cut it short for easier care and to avoid lice. Months earlier, Froim and Duvid had cut their hair close to the skin and tried to avoid letting their unshaved faces collect too much filth. Duvid kept enough hair on top of his scalp to run his fingers back through it for when he needed to think clearly.

Chava was embarrassed for reaching into the past and doubled her steps to push through the dispersing crowd more quickly. Walking back to the apartment, she clutched herself for warmth and ached with the thought that what she saw on the streets was their unavoidable future. It was the callous and brutal realization that the ghetto could be worse for them, and the horror of admitting it.

Chava had not been outside the apartment building for a month and had been cautioned by Froim to not show her face in public or risk being forced into a work truck. So far, even the Kapos seemed oblivious to her presence in the apartment and they had not called her out to a work crew. Leah was glad to have Chava around as another adult to speak with during the day, and someone who could help with Baruch and keep an eye out for Sam.

While Froim was only a couple of years older than Chava, he echoed their missing father's orthodox advice that she avoid attention, dress conservatively, and be cautious. She never liked hearing her brother's "told-you-so" admonitions, but he was on the mark with warning about the deteriorating street life.

Having lost much of her weight and pinning her clothes tighter and tighter, Chava never would have believed that she was better off than others in the ghetto, but now she saw it. She wouldn't admit it to Froim, but it cast her determination to do more than just survive and would define her without spoken words.

Every day, Froim started early and left the apartment at 5:00 a.m., before anyone else woke up. He ran to a designated corner and was taken away from the ghetto in an unmarked, dirt-covered truck packed with dozens of other slave laborers, and carrying well-armed guards. At dusk, Froim returned on the same truck to the ghetto entrance gate at the guarded Leszno and Zelazna intersection. Other than the dirty clothes on his back, he took nothing with him when he reported at dawn and returned to the guarded gate with nothing at the end of the slave labor day.

He spoke to Duvid about what he did, but never shared details about digging the deep trenches. Froim closely followed Chava's path home through the market's edge, passing many of the same squalid street beggars who had no place to go. He kept his head down and avoided eye contact with anyone, focused on the hidden contents in his right coat pocket.

"It's not much," said Froim, as he entered the apartment and tried to shake off the day's cough. Leah walked to the water bucket and poured a sip of water for her brother. Froim pulled his hand out and opened it to reveal a small, dried-out roll wrapped in his tatty handkerchief.

"It fell off the guards' lunch table and landed near our ditch, then I kicked some snow over it. When they weren't watching," he continued, "I grabbed it." Leah smiled at her brother's skill. "Just dampen it to get the grit off and break it in pieces."

Leah took the battered roll from his hand, grabbed a cloth, and walked to the water bucket.

"I heard it was Friday and thought this might get us closer to *Schabes*."

"Thank you," said Leah, "but getting your head bashed would be your last *Schabes*."

"They kick and search us every night as we come back through the gate, and I was lucky tonight," said Froim.

"And how is being kicked lucky?" asked Leah.

"As our truck pulled away, I saw one of the men in line get hit with a rifle butt. When he went down, another guard started to kick and scream at him."

"I'm waiting for the lucky part," said Leah.

"They treat their dogs better and I almost tossed the roll to one of them," said Froim, "and then an officer pulled the guard back and when I got in line, they seemed in a rush to be done with us. I think they were cold, too, and tired of standing in the snow all day. So I kept the roll and they let me through."

The front door opened again and Duvid entered, still brushing the snow off of his shoulders and shaking it down from the hair on his head.

"Leave that out there or Baruch will scoop it up," said Leah.

Duvid bent down and with his large hand, swept the fallen snow into the outer hallway, then nodded in agreement.

"You're both a bit early today. Chava went to the market to trade for food."

They embraced near the door and Leah swept more snow off of Duvid's back and shoulders. While lack of personal hygiene and privacy had ended casual kissing, it never severed their warm embrace.

"The mortar was not holding against the snow," said Duvid, "so they let us go and told us to start earlier tomorrow. I think the German engineer with the warm coat, gloves, and black attaché case was too cold in the snow to tell us how to stack bricks."

"When the sun is going down and the guards are frozen, too," said Froim, "then they will think about us."

"It is getting dark earlier and this place never seems to warm up," said Leah, "unless we get this old stove going."

She squinted to focus in the evening shadows. She adjusted the shabby towels wrapped around Baruch and pulled down a tan, woven hat over his forehead. With her free arm, Leah struggled to re-drape a partially shredded blanket over her own shoulders. She tucked its ends together under Baruch's chin.

"Were you able to bring home any wood?"

"Yes," answered Duvid, "and I left it inside the front door."

He walked down the short hall to retrieve the wood and slightly raised his voice to be heard.

"The building we're closing up had a lot of twisted, blown-out door frames and windows still hanging from the outer walls. We had to finish ripping it out of the openings, before we could tap in the bricks, and then burned most of it in a barrel to keep our hands warm. At the end of the shift, I grabbed some of the smaller wood pieces and stuffed them under my coat. Good thing the guards were too cold from standing in the snow to care to search us before we got back on the truck."

"See," said Froim.

"Like I told him," said Leah, "wood chips aren't worth another beating for you, too."

"I saw the Kapos," said Duvid, "and waited until they looked away. But I'm so sick of asking to breathe."

He grabbed the band on his right arm and pulled it down off his coat sleeve. Then he whipped it to the floor. Leah and Froim looked down and saw the Jewish star starring back at them. Duvid quickly picked up the band and tossed it on an empty coat hook.

"*Tateh*," cried Sam, launching himself into his father's dusty arms. With Sam hanging onto his shoulder, Duvid walked over to the mattress where Baruch was spinning out of his blankets, and collapsed next to the toddler.

"You should be the only thing around my arm," said Duvid, referring to Sam, who still didn't want to touch the ground. "And we don't have to be reminded we're Jewish."

Duvid looked at the adults in the room wearing the required arm bands with a Jewish star and realized that if his boys remained in the ghetto, they wouldn't live long enough for the edict of wearing the mandatory yellow star to apply to them. It was a dying option.

The door opened again as Chava seemed to run into the apartment. She quickly closed the door behind her.

"A little warmer in here without the wind," said Chava, as she began to unravel the scarf layers circled around her face. Leah, Duvid, and Froim looked with deep anticipation at the empty clothes bag hanging out of her coat pocket.

"What did you get for the clothes?" asked Leah.

Chava hung her head, flopping her shortened hair forward to shake out the static and snow.

"Not much worth looking at to eat," answered Chava. "Maybe it was too late in the day, but people have nothing to trade. There were carts of books, baskets of worn sheets and towels, but no food. There was one woman selling cups of water that she was warming over a fire."

Leah looked at the boys and then Duvid.

"She was melting snow and that was it!"

"But I found a familiar face, an old neighbor of yours, Mr. Trushinsky," continued Chava.

Leah looked up at the fond memory.

"He and his wife and her parents are sharing a room with another family, but he didn't complain. He asked about both of you and the boys, and then gave me a few of these from his handkerchief."

She reached into her trouser pocket and pulled out three small turnips layered in ground dirt. "I didn't ask where he got them, but said he would take the cloth items to fill shoe holes against the snow."

"I once heard the Rabbi talking about Cain and Abel and some lesson about not getting blood from a turnip," said Froim, "but I think we're getting close."

"Well," said Leah, "we also have a couple of carrot pieces." She gestured for Duvid to roll off their mattress.

"So before you have to go out, let's divide it all up and nosh."

"There's no meeting tonight," said Duvid. "With the amount of snow, they decided it would be too difficult to stay hidden with the reflection and footprint trail. Tomorrow is safer. Sam will have to continue collecting, until I can talk to them."

"Tomorrow?" asked Leah, "How can we let this go on? I hoped someday he would go to school, but he is being forced to dig bodies out of the snow."

Chava called Sam over to her mattress and pulled out from underneath her browned pad the familiar collection of colorful magazine paper silhouettes they had cut out days before. *Flat people need nothing*, she would say. Although Froim did not "play," he understood the diversion and sat down to give Sam some separation from his parents' conversation.

"I will bring it up tomorrow night," said Duvid.

"You meet with them almost every night," said Leah, "and they decide to not decide anything."

Duvid slowly nodded his head and then looked at the hooks in the hall and their hanging bits of fabrics.

"They see what we see," said Duvid, "but leaving must be done carefully and with extreme secrecy. It protects those who leave and those who stay."

"I don't care if they agree," said Leah, "but my eight-year-old son is done collecting the street dead. How can everyone think this is normal for a boy to be starving and walking the streets to fill a wagon with bodies? Who do you meet with that agrees and when are they going to expect Baruch to help, now that he is walking?"

The question was blunt and its truth harsh, but the reality for Duvid's family was gruesome and inescapable.

"And what's this man's name?" asked Chava, as she held up the short paper form of a walking man. Sam held the cut-out in his hand and examined the flat body in the diminishing light.

"Let's call him Izzy and put him to bed, too." Sam gently laid the form flat on his mattress and covered him with the edge of the frayed cover. The adults all exchanged glances, absorbing Sam's caring gesture to the flat body.

Duvid's family, along with everyone else in the ghetto, was starving to death, and he realized that soon there wouldn't be anyone alive to collect their bodies. It was also clear to him that it must have been the Nazis' plan from the beginning. He understood that doing nothing meant slow and certain death.

"It hurts to watch him," whispered Duvid, "and it feels like we are being forced to dig our own graves and crawl in."

He ran his scratched and bloodied, mortar-covered fingers down his patchy beard stubble. "We need to get out."

He started to slowly rock forward and back, as if he were praying. "Half want to leave and the others want to stay, but it is hard to talk and know who to trust at the same time."

"I don't like Sam digging through the graveyard to trade or collecting bodies, and I can't believe I'm saying this," said Leah, "but isn't that better than trying to escape and getting shot by the guards?"

"We may not have a choice," answered Duvid, "without first starving."

Leah and Sam looked at each other, neither of them knowing where the conversation was leading.

"We need to get out now. It will only get worse," said Duvid, looking around the room.

Chava looked up from holding the flat person of paper and nodded.

"We must first get through tomorrow without suspicion," he continued. They all sat in almost total darkness. Leah held tightly to Baruch as the adults and Sam pulled the mattresses snug to the imagined warmth of the stove.

The room fell silent and all eyes turned toward Duvid, who stood up and walked to the retrieved wood pile. He grabbed a few of the wooden splinters and tossed them into the stove, stoking the dying embers.

* * * * *

It was slightly after 6:00 a.m. and Froim and Duvid had already left for their work details well before dawn. In the hall, they had shaken off the dried dirt from the prior day and re-wrapped shredded blankets around their arms, then stuffed them into their tattered coats. Their caps were torn and gloves were threadbare with missing finger slots, but they went to dig and lay bricks. Froim silently waved to Chava and Leah, while Duvid gave the sleeping Baruch a gentle kiss on his forehead and a quiet hug to Sam. Then the men were gone, absorbed into the edge of survival.

Clink.....clink.....clink. Sam sat up and heard the slow, repetitive sound of the steel wheels with wooden spokes, supporting the large wooden wagon frame. Early trucks had already cut groves through the sloshy snow, and Sam could hear the clinking sound of the wheels rolling down the cobblestone street until it stopped in front of their building. Through the covered window, Sam heard his name shouted by a couple of voices, getting louder and louder. Even at that early hour, the wagon was never empty and already carried bodies from nearby streets.

"*Gay nish' rous,*" said Leah. "Don't go out there."

"I have to go with them," said Sam, "or the Kapos will come for me."

"*Host es shoyn gezen frirer*," said Leah. "*S'et zan di zelbe zakh.*"

"I know what it looks like and it's always the same, but I can't stay."

Sam's curiosity pulled the window cover back and he saw the boys waiting for him, along with the wagon holding two frozen bodies hauled from the snow.

"Wrap yourself up tight," said Leah. "They can wait."

It crushed Leah to think that all she had for her son were warm thoughts, tighter safety pins, and no breakfast, but she and Duvid had decided it was best to cooperate and keep him occupied. For Sam, he was never given a choice by the adults and the Kapos who entered the apartment. It interrupted the boredom and hunger of the day, and reminded him that it could always be worse for everyone.

"*Tateh* and I still don't like this," said Leah, "but they promised to keep you safe, if you listen and keep your head down." Sam knew that it would give him something to do other than watch his family starve, and he could silently stay within himself without questions. He wondered about the other young collectors and what happened to their family members, but he never asked them. Sam had quietly watched and learned how they survived—staying busy and appearing useful in a self-preservation world.

Opening the door, stuffing a gloved hand into his coat pocket, he felt the soft carrot root end his mother had put in there and told him to save it for later in the day.

It was difficult for Sam to remember the past and impossible to think of a future, but he remembered what his father said at night about believing something better was in the future.

"You see that others have it much worse," Duvid had said, *"and we don't want to end up like that, so we keep moving into the next day, hoping it will be better."*

The wagon work had begun with Sam only working every few days, but became more frequent and eventually every day for longer and longer hours. There were days that the wagon could make a constant circle to the gate with no shortage of corpses to gather and Duvid prayed that he had instilled a survivor's instinct in his son, to live beyond the sure death in his hands.

"Get back before dark," whispered Chava. "Your mother worries."

"Are you wearing both sets of gloves?" asked Leah.

"Got both," answered Sam, as he touched the carrot in his pocket, scurried out the apartment door, and ran out the front door of the building. By the time he had run across the snow-covered street, the other boys were standing beside the icy, muddy wagon.

Mendel and Sol were both in their mid-teens, but had the drawn and serious expressions of battle-worn veterans who had seen more than their parents had feared. Sam had never had friends their age and he viewed them as adults because of their size, while they played and pushed him around like a younger brother.

The older boys were each wearing dark brown coats with a pinned yellow star and partially missing sleeves, but had several shirts and sweaters on underneath for added bulk. Their caps did not cover beyond the tops of their heads and neither of them wore a scarf. They were freezing, too, but didn't care.

"We're backed up from yesterday," said Mendel, "and need to keep you a little longer today. We need to bring them to the gate and meet the truck."

"Ma doesn't know," said Sam.

"She knows you're with us," said Mendel.

Sol put his hand gently on Sam's shoulder and pointed down the street. Sam realized that he hadn't known either of these boys prior to being told by a Kapo to assist them, and he never asked where the wagon went when they were done for the day, but the other boys knew, and that was good enough.

"Sam, whenever you see a snow pile ahead," said Sol, "run and check it, since some of them have been covered up since yesterday and we need time to dig them up."

Sam noticed that the two bodies that were already in the wagon still had snow on their limbs. If they missed anyone, then the body would still be there waiting for them in the morning, only stiffer and under more snow. Neither of the boys spoke much to Sam or to each other, but appreciated that he was much younger and smaller than them, and wanted to be useful.

Since his friend Josh and Josh's family had disappeared, Sam had begun to withdraw into himself to act older. The beggar children pulled in their hands and stared at him from a silent distance as he collected.

Sam had been gathering corpses with the boys every morning for months, but never had to search for the dead. The dead would be taken out of their residences by friends or relatives and brought to the street for pick-up, but could lie there all day and night, and wait for the next day's wagon.

Sam looked down at his boots, buried by the foot of street snow, and kicked at the smooth and flat powder that had fallen. He looked down the street and noticed few bumps along the curb, and began walking in their direction.

"Over here," said Sam, who was only thirty yards ahead and waving his arms. Reaching the corner, Sam saw a pile of clothes against the building and knew that it was a human being. Looking further down the street, Sam could see other bundles under the snow and knew that someone else was dead and waiting.

That was a trade-off between winter and summer corpses. There were more bodies outside in the winter of people who had frozen to death and hadn't been shielded from the elements. The boys noticed that winter had brought an increase of bodies lying in curbs, streets, back gutters, and propped against building corners. The once-a-day wagon couldn't keep up with the demand. The Warsaw ghetto was an open cemetery.

"Wait there," said Mendel. "We're stuck again." Each of the two older boys grabbed a push handle and gave the wagon a shove through the snow.

Winter was only slightly better than in summer, when the warm air was pungent with the rot of people who hadn't been able to wash for a year or more. The street aroma was a mix of littered feces and open walls of urination. There was no neatness about a person who had lost the ability to control his bodily functions, and there was nowhere private to go to relieve oneself or to clean up afterward. People quickly lost any sense of dignity or measure of self-sufficiency. Pride disappeared in the struggle for survival.

The boys noticed that each body smelled different depending on the various stages of decay, and seemed heavier because of the stiffness in the bones, but they never talked about it. The fresh powder did little to dampen the odor of a body, which permeated the snow pile. Even covered by snow, decaying corpses reeked like rotten cabbage and the carcasses spewed a foul ammonia stench that burned in their noses.

Sam covered his mouth with his gloved hand, but there was only death to breathe. Sol pushed the rickety wooden cart through the snow toward Sam, and Mendel walked alongside, scanning the other half dozen snow piles down the street. The cart was a two-wheeled hand wagon, with two legs in front and two in back to steady the load on the flat, five-foot horizontal platform.

The cart quickly became filled with stiff limbs protruding over the edges, reaching out as if they were screaming to exit. Although the bodies were withered or frozen beyond recognition, the boys were gentle and respectful in removing them from the street.

Mendel echoed Leah's comments, reminding Sam to not look at the faces of the dead. Faces were life shadows of starvation, leaving empty sunken expressions. Eyes popped, mouths fell ajar, as if the shrunken skin had pulled them open in a last gasp.

"*Kik nish' on in punim*," said Sol. "Don't look at them."

Sam learned to look away from the faces and focus on lifting the feet when told to do so by the older boys. While a sheet of newspaper or piece of cloth was left to cover the face as the last shroud of dignity, useful shreds of clothing may have been removed by family members or freezing street beggars, exposing limbs and genitals. It was routine for Sam to listen for the simple instructions of, "*Stop here, pick up the body this way, or first turn him over, but don't look at the face.*"

Clink.....clink. As the wagon approached Sam and his first found body, he began to push the snow off the buried feet. There were no shoes, socks, or pants, and only stained undergarments on the man's body. Sam scooped his arms under the feet and the two larger boys lifted the shoulders and arms. Sol supported the head. Sam always had the feet, one under each arm, since the upper body would be heavier to lift. Together, they gently slid the body onto the wagon.

When bodies were to be stacked on top of each other, a fourth boy would be useful to lift the middle part of the body higher, but most emaciated people were too weak to assist.

"Wait," said Sol, as he grunted and struggled to hold the head and shoulders in place, while gathering the outstretched arm. "Let me get a better grip under him."

Any remaining clothes on the body were rags, so they couldn't grab any fabric and expect it to hold.

"Don't drop him," said Mendel, with a loud and piercing crack in his voice. Sam imagined that it had happened once to him. "He'll catch on the edge and slide out if you let go too soon."

Sam bent his knees and got under the legs with a firm grasp of the ankles. After the fifth body, the snow slowed the wheels and it became too difficult and awkward to gently place anyone on the wagon. It was 8:30 a.m. and the boys weren't finished, but the wagon was full and needed to be emptied.

As they moved past the first cross street and pushed toward the gate, the boys spotted one of many other wagons and its collectors moving up a distant parallel street. *How strange*, thought Sam. *In orthodox services, men and women are seated separately; yet now, their half-naked bodies must be stacked together in the cart. It is strange and cruel and doesn't make sense.*

"My uncle is over there," said Mendel. He didn't wave and Sam wondered if he was referring to the collectors or those being collected, but it didn't seem to matter. It was snowing again on top of yesterday's piles.

"They can get that one," said Sol. "We're staying in the direction of the gate, then doubling back down the next street."

Sam slowly marched in front to look for ruts, while Mendel and Sol held tightly to the arms of the wagon, being sure to not pitch any of the bodies off into the snow. Sam realized that they weren't alone in the morning's collection, as he heard the sudden squeal of truck tires turning a nearby corner, sloshing snow against a building that had once been occupied by a butcher.

Empty store windows line the street like vacant bodies, he thought. It was unusual for the private hearse and trucks to be involved in gathering bodies, but the Kapos had been told to clear the pavement and avoid having corpses pile up under the snow or in apartment buildings. The boys were never delayed by anyone wanting to say a prayer for a deceased relative. If a body was taken out of a building, the family might follow crying, but the Kapos would only let them follow for a bit and then force them back. If they were seen by the guards, they would be beaten or shot and left dead on the street, waiting for the next wagon.

"Get over here, Sam," said Sol. "If you get too close, you'll get picked up and taken out to work. This is still better."

Sam quickly walked back to the wagon and the disheveled pile of bodies inside. He grabbed a handle to help Sol push it through the heavy snow. Sam felt a twisted sense of pride that he was able to demonstrate that he was doing something useful.

Down a side street, a Kapo waved another truck to the front door of a three-story brick building. The back hatch popped open and a man and young boy jumped out and entered the structure to retrieve a small wrapped figure and quickly swing it on the truck's pile. The Kapos directed the trucks and wagons to gather the dying ghetto residents, removing them to be stacked like petrified logs in deep, unmarked grave pits. Sam knew about the pits, but had never been required to go there.

Corpses were heaped into different vehicles, but everyone in the ghetto was headed in the same direction. What was meant for adults had quickly become a child's forced undertaking. As the remaining able-bodied men were removed to daily work detachments, trucks and wagon crews were using younger and younger children to collect the departed. Once, a Kapo told Sam's parents, the Germans had ordered him to find boys to fill the wagon. The alternative was that the Germans would take him to do something more cruel or dangerous. Leah and Duvid reluctantly agreed, because they couldn't imagine what would be worse for Sam, but thought he wouldn't return if taken away.

As the boys approached the gate to empty their sixth load of the day, there was an unusual amount of commotion. And the guards were using their extended rifles to keep the wagons and workers in line as they unloaded near the waiting truck. With the help of some distraught relatives, the boys were able to stack eleven bodies on their wagon. A Kapo and guard waved them and their wagon out of line to a corner of the wall, where a number of other guards and a Kapo were standing in the snow.

When they moved aside, Mendel, Sol, and Sam could see the man's body, except it was clothed and he wore a coat and hat. Sam helped the boys roll the man onto his back and with the help of two Kapos. The corpse with bent legs was set onto the pile on the wagon with his shoeless legs dangling off the side. Blood-stained snow remained untouched.

"I hate those Nazis," said Sol. "Sam, don't look at the guards and keep your head down."

After pushing the clinking wagon away from the wall, Sam and the boys arrived at the gate.

"One wrong look and you won't be pushing the wagon," said Mendel, "but tossed into one."

Sam knew that the older boy wasn't kidding. The gate was heavily infiltrated by Kapos on the inside, barbed wire fences in the middle, and armed Nazi guards on both sides.

A truck had pulled up and was waiting inside the gate, and Sam could see that it was already half filled with bundles of bodies wrapped in sheets.

"*Raus, raus!*" shouted one of the guards patrolling the inside wall. "Get out, get out!" He used the back of his rifle to smack down the men to move the corpses onto the truck more quickly. If one of the worker's comrades slowed down the movement and tried to help him to his feet, then he would also be struck. One of the Gestapo officers stood alongside him, resting his hand on his gun belt and pistol. He joined in yelling at the same men who were being struck by the guard. "*Schnell,*" said the Gestapo man. "*Macht schnell!*"

The Nazis didn't speak Polish or Yiddish, but rather used a few choice German words and an occasional gun shot that everyone understood. They wore the brown German army uniform with brown coats and ammunition belts. Their green steel helmets were a dull contrast to the black uniforms, hat, and leather boots of the Gestapo, who walked among the guards with only sidearm pistols.

The guards were visibly nervous whenever workers collected near the gate, and the sound of guns cocking on the rampart could clearly be heard by all. Sam heard shots every night, as the Gestapo moved people off the streets. And when the sound was followed by the painful screaming and crying of family members, everyone was reminded that the Nazis were not there to help people live. When the guards shouted at the Kapos near the gate, it was never a good sign.

"Let's unload," said Sol, "and get out of here."

"Grab him here," said Mendel, pointing at the man's ankles, "and hold the legs over your shoulders as we push them off the wagon."

The top corpse was the man who had recently been shot.

"Don't look at the face," continued Mendel.

Sam noticed that fresh blood had dripped down through the other bodies and onto the wagon tray. Sam only paused for an instant to wipe the blood covering his hands on his coat. *Ma won't like seeing the blood*, Sam thought to himself. He buried his thoughts in pretending that he was holding up the end of some thin branches, covered with a few leaves.

After a few months, Sam felt he had personally cleared a small, dead forest. Other than the Nazi flag, the darkening red blood on his coat was the only true color that Sam could recall seeing in the ghetto.

Unloading near the gate was filled with silent movement. Two scraggy men waited to help empty the wagons and carefully stack the dead near the gate to wait for the removal truck. No words were exchanged between the boys and the men. At the end of a collection route, there could be a dozen or more unclothed bodies in the wagon, with their twisted arms and legs protruding from the sides.

Sam thought back on the delivery truck of chickens with their beaks and feathers poking through the wooden crates on their way to the kosher butcher, and realized that he could never again think of that childhood memory.

With rows of overloaded wagons piling up at the gate, carefully removing each wasted body would be the last shred of decency shown to these unknown souls as they were stacked on the ground. Jews were forced to move dead Jews and briefly checked to see if anyone was still moving. No prayers were offered. Sam was internally perplexed by collecting bodies and that he survived another day. *And was that good enough?* he wondered.

After a long day of methodic passes through assigned snow-covered streets, the boys were starved for any food or warmth and a break from the corpse stench, which had seeped into their souls. The depths of their humanity had become as numb as their hands and feet. Traumatization had been deadened by the volume of stiffened limbs, drawn faces with lice-covered heads, and watching lifeless appendages tossed like kindling onto twisted piles.

The boys could hear a sudden uproar further along the wall and felt the fierce push of armed guards, the clicking of gun bolts, and more shots. This was more than the usual kick someone to the ground or strike him with a rifle butt in the back of the head. A man from the truck detail hesitated and turned sharply to ask one of the guards a question.

The movement spooked the guard, who pulled a pistol out of his side holster, took aim, and shot the man in the head. Without anyone saying a word, the man lay dead in the snowdrift, surrounded by a large, surging crowd.

The boys felt the suction of being pulled into chaos and no-where to run. More shots were fired and the crowd backpedaled into each other.

"Push," yelled Mendel, "and let's get out of here."

Weaving their way through a hoard of elbows, they found the wagon abandoned, waiting for them.

"Say nothing," said Sol, "and don't look back. Unless you want to be next, look down and don't let the Nazis catch you staring at them."

"But . . .," said Sam.

Sol didn't let him get another word out of his mouth.

"Now grab those legs, unload, and keep moving," said Sol.

He pointed at the corpse on top of the wagon, and didn't want to talk. Mendel joined in to help lift the mid-section, which was hung up on the wagon post. Lifting the legs over his shoulders, he accidently knocked off Sam's hat. He didn't think about pausing to pick up the hat or witnessing those who were promptly shot in the head. The bleeding body was very heavy to move.

"Sam," said Mendel, "after we unload at the gate, you can go back to your parents."

Sam was too exhausted to smile, but nodded his head.

"We won't need you anymore today. You should be home."

There were never any "thanks" associated with the wagon work, but Sam knew that at dusk, Mendel and Sol still weren't finished for the night, and were being kind to let him go.

Sam had left the boys and the wagon at the corner and walked until he saw someone lying on the other end of his block. Although the sun was nearly down, Sam recognized the coat and frail body propped up against the wall and the jacket pulled up over the person's head. He didn't want to know for sure, so Sam ran up to his apartment door.

* * * * *

"That sounds like Sam's footsteps in the hall," said Chava. She heard the thumping of boots being kicked against an outer wall and pictured Sam knocking off the snow.

Leah went to the door and shrieked at her first view of Sam. She reached into the hall and hugged him, pulling him into the apartment.

"There's blood on you," said Leah. "Are you hurt?" She held him by the shoulders and pushed him slightly away to better see the blood stains on his sleeves and front of his coat.

Sam shook his head. "Not my blood," answered Sam.

Leah was concerned about his detached response and Sam's numbness to the death in the streets. As he continued to explain the blood, she noticed that Sam was lost in another thought.

"A man was shot and his blood got on me when we moved him." Sam stared down at his blood-covered hands and coat without trying to conceal them, instead dreading the reality. There was no safe place for his thoughts and he was struggling to think of the next day when his father walked into the apartment.

"*Tateh*," continued Sam. "Did you see him? Was that Daniel?"

Duvid quickly walked to embrace Sam, while he looked at Leah.

"*Der mentsh vus di vayst iz toyt, iz geshtorbn*," said Duvid. "Yes, it was Mr. Hofmann."

Sam could not bear to imagine that his reading friend was now one of the collected street dead.

Duvid saw the blood on Sam's coat, but didn't ask about it.

"One of the other wagons stopped for him," continued Duvid. *It's inhuman to be collected like garbage and for a little boy, his son, to be a gatherer,* Duvid fumed to himself.

Sam heard the clink of the other wagon's wheels moving away from his street. His eyes suddenly filled with tears and he began to sob uncontrollably, his thin chest heaving.

Without tears, he had moved countless dead people and seen life murdered out of some of them and yet, that collected body was "Daniel." The ghetto's cold hand ripped open the heart of a nine-year-old boy and left it for a collection wagon.

"I think he has had enough moving bodies," said Leah. "He is strong, but too young to do that."

Duvid heard the wall-thumping turmoil of a body being carried down the apartment hall and out of their building.

"That is enough," said Duvid. He ran his fingers back through his short, slick hair and firmed his jaw, collecting his resolve. "It is time to end it all."

Sam wasn't sure what his father was talking about, but he liked the sound of the finality. The sound of clinks had stopped and Sam privately remembered a prayer for Mr. Hofmann that he heard from numerous families standing in the street: *Yitgaddal v'yitkaddash* .....

When Froim returned and Sam and Baruch had settled down for the evening, Duvid drew Leah and her siblings into the corner.

"It is time to escape this cemetery," said Duvid. "We have four families ready to go with us through the sewer tunnels we've mapped out."

Chava's face lit up in the darkness, while Leah covered her sobs in relief and Froim raised his hands in hope.

"Say nothing about it and trust no one. It will be an interesting meeting tonight."

"We're leaving," said Froim. He wanted to hear the words out of his own mouth.

CHAPTER SIX

DARK DOORS

"**B**ut we haven't seen any of our parents since we brought Baruch home," said Duvid.

"Maybe they got out during the bombing," said Chava.

"They didn't want to leave," said Leah. "With Baruch in my arms, we begged them, but they thought it would pass." She watched the broken candle stub flicker the last moments of light for the evening.

"Let's face it," said Froim. "The only family we have seen is sitting in this room."

"If anyone is still alive," said Duvid, "we would have heard about them. Let's hope that they got out and maybe we'll see them again. But for now, what are we doing here?"

They all exchanged curious glances in the dimness.

"We need to answer for ourselves." His raw question asked for the inescapable, bitter truth.

"We've waited long enough," said Froim, "and I say we go with them."

They knew Duvid's opinion. Although he didn't understand some of the details, Sam had learned to be especially quiet and listen, sensing this was an important decision for their family. The reasons were very familiar to him. During the past month, Sam had been attending late-night meetings with his father, discussing with a group of men about whether to break out of the ghetto. While many of the faces were also clandestinely involved with smuggling and prone to action, there were also older voices present who were strongly against any movement to draw attention.

Sam perked up at the determination in his father's voice.

* * * * *

When Duvid and Sam maneuvered their way down into the subterranean room in a nearby collapsed factory, the door to the space was unlit. Inside, the twenty-five men sat hushed on the bare ground, openly sharing what they had seen happening to Jews in Warsaw and in other German-occupied lands. They individually considered the experiences based on whether these had been personally endured or told by someone trusted who witnessed it. It was never good news.

The room was divided into two very clear sides—each man presented his own view of escaping, huddling near like-minded views. Duvid and Sam never missed a gathering and sat toward the front of the room. It was a life or death discussion.

"*Vart nokh a bisl*," said Sy. "*S'et nit zan shveyrer.*" Many of the elders presumed that if they just waited a bit more, then life would not get worse for their families.

"It will all blow over," continued Sy, "you'll see."

His family had been through the prior war with Germany and he was proud that his family, including his parents and grandparents, never left Warsaw. His full beard was white with untrimmed edges filled with dust from sleeping on the floor.

"And you can't get away from the Germans. Wherever you go, they'll bring you back here, if you're not shot," the old man continued.

Duvid and the younger men didn't think it would get better, but they were unusually quiet that night. Each man in the room had seen the brutality of the Germans and their continued transport of more Jews into the ghetto. With every truckload that stopped at the gates, dozens and then hundreds poured inside to await their fate. There was only the sound of Yiddish unloaded.

"*Yug zekh nisht,*" said Abe, feeling it was too soon and dangerous to do anything. "Why risk putting us all in danger?"

In a deep, sonorous voice, he went on. "I agree with Sy; this will go away. Let's wait and we will see what happens." There was silent head nodding from his side of the room. It was difficult to openly argue with their experiences, while remaining respectful to the side of the room with gray and white beards.

"Let's wait," said Sy again. "It will get better."

Duvid couldn't hold back any longer. "The Nazis have our throats, strangling us. We are building our own brick prison and digging our own graves," he blurted.

He felt a hand on his shoulder to calm him. Duvid recalled hearing the "will blow over" beliefs from his family and Leah's parents. The point of view didn't sit well with the younger side of the room. Sam thought that men with white beards always disagreed.

"Here we go again," whispered Hersz, who sat behind Duvid.

"If you get out," said Chackiel, "where are you going?" Under his cap, Chackiel was bald and had a wide, gray beard with a pencil-thin mustache. He walked with a slow gait, leaning on a cane, but tried to stand tall when speaking.

"There are anti-Semites everywhere and then you must deal with the Germans," continued Sy. "And they don't want to deal with you and you don't want to see them. If you try to leave, you'll be shot dead or beaten into a truck, and they'll toss your busted body back here." His bleak thoughts were firm.

"And remember what happened to Icek's family," said Chil, who sat next to Sy. "He was from a town not far from here where the Germans shot his family dead and tossed the others on a train for a camp. You'll die out there."

"In here," said Leib, "my brother was shot dead in the street for resisting a German trying to throw him in a truck." He lowered his shaking head and scratched at his partially grown-in sideburns. "They left his body in the road as dead garbage and you want me to wait?"

He began to kick away some brick rubble on the basement floor, clearing a space as if intending to step forward, then sat down next to Sam. The dust rose from the disturbed ground and filled the flickering light from the only candle.

Leib looked up and his gaze pierced the conversation, glancing at each face for understanding of the unimaginable.

"Jews are being shot dead," continued Leib, "and are not even being picked up. Everyone's afraid that if they help someone who was shot, they will be shot, too. Why stay where the future is canceled?"

Duvid had been patient, but now had heard enough. He waited his turn and rose from sitting with Sam on a pile of blasted wall rubble on the floor. Chunks of bricks fell from the wall as he pushed away to stand. Duvid hunched his head to avoid hitting pipes and spoke to the divisive question.

"We can't wait any longer," said Duvid. "Whoever wants to try, try to go, say so."

A couple of hands went up and then a few more, and then several more. About half of the men raised their hands, mostly the younger males.

"There is another group who wants to join us," Duvid said in a quiet voice.

The dark and dust-clogged room suddenly felt warm and too small.

Everyone looked at Duvid for more information, but he went silent. "We need to separate those who want to stay from those who will try," he continued. "It's best if they don't know anything."

"We must be patient," said Hyam. His long, white beard seemed to glow in the dark, while his eyes peered out from the shadows of their drawn-in sockets.

"Patience in Warsaw is death," said Benjamin, who had helped carry his father's body to the street earlier in the week.

Those who had raised a hand murmured in agreement.

"Don't tell me that we must starve and watch our boys die," said Duvid. "And don't tell me that Sam must collect your shriveled bodies until someone picks up his bones."

He suddenly turned and began to pace back and forth across the windowless room, repeatedly slapping the back of his hand into the open palm of the other, while ducking the ceiling support beams.

"You talk about God and prayers," Duvid continued. "Doing nothing is saying God abandoned us."

"We shouldn't be talking about this," said Hyam. The elders in the group shook their heads, showing their displeasure. "Wait, just wait a little longer. It must get better."

The light from the single candle tossed shadows into the corners of the room, lighting faces and then hiding them from sight again. There was enough light to see the expressions on the men's faces.

"Sam has risked his life crawling through cemetery tunnels," said Duvid, "dealing with smugglers and being forced to collect bodies for the wagon, and you say it will be better if we stay?"

There was no response.

"Every day, he walks the street with the wagon, picking up the bodies of those who also thought it would get better."

Duvid looked at Sam, who could feel the room getting even warmer.

"My son," continued Duvid, "who is not old enough for his Bar Mitzvah or to carry a Torah, is lifting the stiff bones of our friends and you tell me to be patient."

Duvid wanted to come out of himself with disbelief at the tension and then looked at Sam, who was quietly listening on the floor, taking in the exchanged words.

"Wait for what? I don't want my son to have to pick up your body or mine. Now is the time to leave. More prayers won't make it better."

Duvid sat down next to Sam.

"Maybe, no," answered Reuben, "but I won't give them a reason to shoot me."

"At least we will try and maybe some of us will make it," said Duvid. "It's better than dying here. They will finish us, all the Jews."

Duvid felt the touch on his shoulder again and knew to let the point go. Both sides of the room knew what they were each going to do, some nothing.

"Why must it get better," asked Leib, "when all signs point to starving, being shot, or disappearing? Are you not listening to the reports from others who have been outside? They are collecting the Jews to kill them, not re-locate them. No Jews return to Warsaw after they have been removed. Don't be blind! Are you going to trust the Germans?"

"We will all die," said Duvid, "but I refuse to let the Nazis pick the location and time."

He had faith in the sun rising in the morning, even when no one could see in the darkness.

"If you or anyone else is planning to go," said Hyam, "then say no more."

The glow from the candle reflected against the gazes that darted among the men. No one spoke.

* * * * *

Duvid and Leah did not often have an opportunity to hold hands, but Sam noticed his father holding his mother's small hand—without the wedding ring—and quietly talking to her in a corner of the room, off the mattress. With his other hand, Duvid pointed out the window and in a northerly direction. They had lengthy conversations, but this was private.

"No," said Duvid, "there will be no digging tunnels."

While it had taken several discussions between them, Leah agreed that the timing was right to escape. They finished off the evening quietly talking about what needed to be done to leave and what she needed to know for Baruch.

"Just let me know how I can help with the boys," said Chava. Both Leah and Duvid turned to look at Chava, remembering that there really were no private conversations in the room. Froim just smiled and nodded his head, as if echoing Chava's offer.

* * * * *

December 1941

"Sam, it is very important that you do not repeat anything that is talked about in this room," said Duvid. "You are good at keeping our secrets and this is like the tunnel."

Duvid knew that Sam had heard many of the details regarding the departure, but it was especially crucial that nothing was repeated.

"More meetings?" asked Sam.

"He knows you," said Froim.

"No," answered Duvid, "we just need to be ready and help Ma. She knows what to bring and the clothes to layer, so we can keep our hands free." He knew that Sam understood how this would work.

"I know," said Sam, "we're not carrying anything. Wear it or it goes in pockets and carry nothing, except Baruch." He smiled at his brother.

The adults in the room were in silent awe of his coherent planning and clear eyes.

"Don't be slowed down," Sam continued, "sling it from shoulders." Duvid could hear the memory of Yankle in his son's voice.

He turned to face Froim and Chava, lifting his arms in the air. "Hands free to climb and run fast without dragging anything." He was like a personal escape guide with more knowledge than presumed for an almost-nine-year-old boy.

"How many people are going?" asked Froim.

"Too many," answered Duvid. "I wanted only a couple families involved, but now there are almost forty people. It's too many to be sure that no one talked or was friendly with a Kapo. Each family has someone close they want to help."

Silently, Duvid wondered how many were too many, and how they couldn't say "no."

* * * * *

The middle of the night was as dark as closed eyes and Sam was startled awake by being shaken by his father.

"Get dressed," said Duvid.

Sam jerked upright, knowing what this meant. He saw far fewer people in the street today and figured that his parents made the decision.

"Are we going?" asked Sam, in a hushed breath.

"We're going to try and get out," answered Duvid.

The only promise was the effort. Sam could see the shadows of Leah placing extra clothes on Baruch and laying out two layers of blankets for him. He felt the vague silhouettes of Froim and Chava stuffing their coat pockets with items.

It was a dreary, wet night in early December, and the Warsaw snows and chill went to the bone. It must have seemed like a good time to flee, before winter had trapped the ghetto in the ice.

"Put on as many shirts and pants as you can put on," said Leah, "and still be able to move."

"Once you get up the steps and out the front door," said Duvid to everyone in the room, "don't run, just walk fast. It creates less suspicion if you are spotted."

No one was in sight on the street. They watched and waited for a signal from Duvid. Slowly moving one by one from one corner to the next, they gathered and went into a building where other families were waiting.

"We're only waiting for Mendel and his family," said one of the men to Duvid. Before the sentence was finished, they arrived. Mendel's children were quiet and dragged their feet when pulled by a hand into a dark basement room. The numbers were as many as Duvid had feared.

Sam looked around and noticed there were no gray beards. There was no conversation from the families about how this could be a fatal mistake, since they recognized it was death to stay. Death solved many problems for the ghetto: over-crowding, typhus, starvation, bitter cold, inhuman sanitation, recognizing and stepping over corpses. Attempting a desperate escape was trying to do something about it.

Leah re-wrapped Baruch's layers and Sam untucked his extra shirt.

"Everybody is here," said Mendel, "*Men miz gayn yetst.*" It was time to go; there was no time to waste.

Duvid and his family were the second group in line to go out the basement door, turning left and through another innocuous, unlit door down the hall. Duvid pointed to an open sewer cover into which the first family crawled through into a blacker level of darkness.

"Hang onto the attached ladder and railing," said Duvid.

The circular opening was wide and an easy fit for Leah, even with Baruch bundled inside her coat. The line of families went quickly down the hole, as the men helped the women and children maneuver the clammy slats and collect in an open turn space in the tunnel.

Once everyone was down, Duvid and another man quickly climbed back up the long ladder to slide the weighty lid over the hole. There was no doubt that they were in a sewer. There wasn't a dry spot to stand; frigid storm water clogged with unmentionable and indiscernible debris flowed over their shoes. Dim street light cut straight down and through sewer grates, exposing the long, slimy tunnel.

Duvid's family huddled shivering at the end of the line, waiting for him to climb back down the ladder after closing the lid.

"Walk quietly," said Duvid, "and don't make sloshing noises."

His *shushing* warning was repeated up the line. Damp, rounded bricks lined the sewer and it was tall enough for Sam to stand, but the adults were hunched over in the meter-and-a-half-high tunnel. The procession cast pale shadows along the walls and in the waste water, sometimes blocking the murky light. The string of humanity stretched out as they crept under several city blocks.

The family with children had difficulty holding hands and there was a panicked, whispered echo asking if everyone was still there. Froim, Sam, and Chava led the tight group of Leah, Baruch, and Duvid. The line stretched around a corner and into the murky channel, ending at another ladder.

Sam tried to watch the front of the group, and while he was grateful that he didn't have to burrow through dirt, the earthy, putrid stench was thick to breathe.

Peering through the darkness, Duvid looked down the tunnel to see three of the men in front push the lid off another sewer and climb out of the open hole. The line slowed near a street runoff conduit, when they heard the people in front hollering.

"*Drayt dikh aros, ale mentshn! Gayt tserik! Schnell!*" they yelled. Froim and Chava stopped in their tracks.

"They want us to turn around and go back," said Froim, "Quickly!"

Bam, bam, bam! Shots rang out and the sound reverberated down the wet sewer walls. There was screaming and Duvid's worst fears were coming true. Shots were being fired down into the open hole at the front of the line. *Pop, pop, pop!*

The sounds came from a mixture of rifle and pistol shots, and he saw the sparks of the bullets hitting the metal ladder in front of the line. Something had gone terribly wrong.

While the front men talked about the timing to come up, it was freak bad timing that a passing German truck noticed the popped sewer lid. They picked this sewer exit to be close to woods, thinking that they could quickly run into the brush.

Everyone still in the tunnel could hear what happen next. "*Halt! Halt, halt!!*" hollered the Germans guards, who had jumped off the truck. Shots echoed in the street where the three men had gone up to see if the street was clear.

Bam, bam, bam, bam! The shooting continued from multiple guns and directions. The men didn't come back to their families waiting in the sewer. The only sounds were squealing tires, boots pounding the street, and the German voices shouting into the sewer tunnel, … "*prepare to die!*"

All of a sudden, Duvid's family was in front of the line fleeing the sewer. There was no looking back. Froim grabbed Sam's hand and ran back up the tunnel so fast that Sam was almost dragged along.

"*Schnell!*" cried Duvid. "*Gay schneller, schneller!*" Faster, faster! The rest of the families were pressing upon them as Chava and Froim grabbed Leah's tucked arms and quickly moved her through the channel. Even the women behind them were yelling, but no one could move any faster in the dark and sludge. Froim reached the ladder first, hustled up the rungs and shoved open the lid, pulling up Sam and pushing him through the opening.

After pulling themselves out of the hole, they ran down the streets and back to their building, before soldiers poured into the streets looking for others from the sewer.

It was still the same night and Leah felt that the world seemed darker. Once back in their room, they quietly removed everything that was dirty or wet.

Panic filled the space, shared in silence. The pile of damp clothing was hidden in an outer hallway closet, so no one would be seen with the dirty rags if inspected.

"Pretend you're asleep and don't move," said Duvid. "If we see the morning, do not ever talk to anyone about this. Just go to sleep."

Sam understood absolute need for the secrecy and had trouble finding any sleep, knowing that his father wouldn't stop there. He rolled over on the mattress to find Leah sitting up. The room was beginning to lighten as the sun rose over the ghetto.

"*Zug gurnisht,*" said Leah. "*Tomer eymitser fregt vus di host getin letste nakht, zug gurnisht.*"

Sam understood that it didn't matter who asked about the night, say nothing about what happened.

"*Di'st bloyz geganen shlufn.*" Just sleep.

A couple of evenings later, Sam listened to his parents discuss the shooting.

"They did not return," said Duvid, "and the bodies weren't found."

"No one was going to ask for them," said Froim, "and admit they were there too."

The men had been shot dead and that was the end of it.

"Why did those men climb out of the hole without looking?" asked Sam. He recalled Yankle's instructions for the graveyard.

"That's not the way it was planned," answered Duvid. With a gentle hand, he encouraged Sam to lie back down on the mattress. "Forget it and don't talk about it."

"And why didn't the Gestapo come to question our building?" asked Chava in the darkness.

No one was asleep.

"As far as they know," answered Duvid, "it happened far away from here and near the wall."

Chava recalled their late-night walk to a distant building and now understood why they had walked even further through sewer tunnels.

"Those questioned didn't know what happened, who was involved, or what building we all came from. None of them were from the neighboring buildings. That's why we must continue doing what we were doing before the trouble, and change nothing."

"Are we still leaving?" asked Sam.

Everyone looked toward Duvid.

"Yes, but not that way," he answered. "We've already started the way it should've been done the first time."

Duvid wouldn't say any more and there were no questions.

"Good answer," said Froim.

Each morning, the German labor trucks continued to pick up Duvid, Froim, and others from the building, taking them back into the brick work in the early, harsh winter.

They felt a bit of relief that nothing had changed when the Kapo arrived at the building with the usual threat of filling the daily quota of laborers.

"*Ikh bruch finif mentshn,*" said the Kapo, tightening his brown uniform jacket. "*Kim mit mir, un zey'l zekh opbilding di vant.*"

Duvid was glad to disappear into the work crew of five men and not be fingered for trying to escape.

With Chava's help, Sam bartered between the market and barbed wires to bring back morsels of food. Trading was bleak and the cold, runny German mash from the ration wagon did not offer enough sustenance.

Dead bodies continued to be collected from the street and stacked deep in mass graves, but Leah wouldn't let Sam go with the wagon.

Occasionally, Sam would find himself face to face with the hollowed eyes of an adult who had also been involved with the graveyard smuggling or escape attempt. After an instant of trapped hesitation, no words were exchanged and they both turned away.

Leah struggled to nurse Baruch with the small amount of nutrition that her body could share. She didn't leave the building with him, but tried to keep him active through singing and activities in their room and apartment hallway. Even a ghetto toddler needs to move.

* * * * *

JANUARY 1942

"The mortar doesn't match the dirt," said Duvid, "so please remind me to switch shirts before I get on the truck."

"You only have two," answered Leah, "and I'll watch for the work shirt before you go out."

It was almost dawn and Leah was gazing down at a listless Baruch, lying face down on the decomposing mattress. Chava sat up from huddling with Sam as Froim rose to leave for his truck. She also watched Duvid silently shuttle between the days of bricking openings and walls, and disappearing into night digging.

As he watched his family and friends starve, Duvid knew that not resisting was a sure and agonizing end. Each bucket of tunnel dirt was a promise. He knew that there were a thousand ways to die, but was aware that he needed to find one way to survive and make it through the black days.

The only color that existed in the ghetto was red—the red of the Gestapo swastika armband and blood.

"If it's another tunnel to the sewer," said Leah, "then who gets shot this time?"

Chava was quick to sense her sister's hesitation to try again.

"We were starving before we tried the sewer," said Chava, "and we can't eat books and cloth. Look at us! We won't last another month." They all looked at each other and the decrepit room, and couldn't see a difference. Everyone wanted to go.

"We'll be ready in two more weeks," said Duvid. "It is another tunnel, like the graveyard route Sam used for food, but larger and deeper."

"Deeper?" asked Chava.

"The ground is frozen," answered Duvid, "so we had to go deeper to reach softer dirt. Digging down in the abandoned tunnel allowed us to expand the hole. It's still a stoop, but easier to crawl through with a small group."

Duvid had been digging with another group, much smaller than the first effort, but more disciplined and guarded.

"Will it work this time?" asked Froim.

"This must work for us," answered Duvid. "And when spring arrives and all the snow melts, the Germans will wonder where all the fresh dirt came from."

Froim laughed suddenly and Sam wondered what was so funny.

Duvid held up his forefinger for serious emphasis.

"As I brick up openings in building after building, it's like being forced to strangle my family and then myself," he said.

The ghetto air was putrid, the bodies rancid, and it felt like a matter of weeks until each inhabitant of the imprisoned area would die. It didn't have to be fair or make sense, but it was just that way and everyone knew it.

"Is leaving here any safer for the boys?" asked Leah.

"This was never a home," continued Duvid, "just a holding room until we leave for good."

While there was an unspoken satisfaction of being together, it was a hellish residence and a reminder of what has been lost. Duvid knew that he would probably never see his brothers again, and Leah had to stop thinking about her parents and other family members. There was no point to it and there was no energy to spend on things that could not be changed.

"I know," said Leah, "it just helps me to hear you say it." She reached over and placed her hand on top of Duvid's labor-worn fingers. While he knew that Leah supported his tunneling and sense of timing, Duvid wanted her to push off the precipice of life they were standing upon. There could be no hesitation in escaping.

Sam could see that his parents had huddled together to talk about something private. Their tone was hushed and dire. Duvid opened a piece of paper holding a couple of black and white photographs.

After a few words and glancing at photos, Leah fathomed Duvid's sense of urgency. Sam couldn't hear the discussion or see the photos, but he clearly heard the words *Auschwitz, smuggled,* and *Jews.*

Leah squealed as she open the contents of a dirt-stained, folded paper and dropped them on the mattress. She paused only to gasp and stare directly into Duvid's eyes.

"Where did you get these?" asked Leah in an awed voice.

Duvid explained how the items had been passed from one person to another within their small group, after having been brought into the ghetto to be shared with other Polish Jews. Duvid abruptly ended the conversation, gathered up the photos and gave them to Leah to hide. She understood what needed to be done to have a chance at life for their family.

Looking at her sitting with Baruch lying on the mattress, Duvid couldn't figure out how she had been doing it. Whether running from bombs with a newborn, living in the woods and hiding from Germans, imprisoned and starving in the ghetto, or venturing through escape tunnels, Leah had not taken on the harshness of her life.

Feeling the soft touch of her skin on his rough hand, Duvid wondered how her tenderness endured. He decided to not question what was natural. He had never seen Leah cling to despair. Duvid knew she wouldn't go back prior to the birth of Baruch and say, 'If I would have known.....' For Leah, there were no regrets about creating life, only the determination to preserve it.

"You go on with life," she would often say.

As Chava rubbed Baruch's small back to calm his cough, she could see a lightness in Duvid's eyes and wondered if those were tears building.

"When are we going to try again?" asked Sam.

"Soon," answered Duvid, with a sudden bounce in his voice, "but don't mention it outside this room."

Sam had been listening to the adults from his corner of the floor and understood that the time was approaching. He felt that using his old tunnel would be better than the sewer. Thoughts about his scooter, the horse, and what had happened to other friends and relatives were distant and best left in memories. It hurt too much to think about the way it had been.

He turned his head as he heard the early-morning clinking of the wagon's wheel, reminding everyone that there were few priorities left. "When the wagon leaves," asked Sam, "can I go out and find Gerek?"

"*Gay nish' avek tsi vat,*" answered Leah. "Don't go too far."

"We will stay in front," said Sam.

"*In a pur teyg vet men prubirn aroys tsu geyn fin hir,*" said Leah.

Sam was thrilled to learn they would be attempting another escape within the week, but he also remembered to keep his routine and not be noticed.

"*Zay shtil*," continued Leah. "*Zug gurnisht tsi emetsin.*"

"I know how to keep quiet," said Sam. "Not a word, even to Gerek."

They already knew what to do, and how to help each other put on layers of clothes. There was no conversation about the escape details, except that there would only be one other family.

During the day in late January, Sam couldn't see over the snowbanks, which were well above his head, but he knew it wouldn't matter underground.

* * * * *

Sam was awakened in the middle of the night. He could see Duvid putting his boots on. When his father went to bed fully dressed, it meant a late-night meeting, but tonight was different. Normally, his father would tell him to go back to sleep, but not now.

The day before, Leah had put aside a pile of clothes, stacking blankets, bottles, and chunks of cotton. They all lain down, but no one slept. Sam kept dozing off and waking up.

"*S'nokh nish' yetst,*" said Leah. "Not yet."

"When?" asked Sam.

"*Kh'vel dir ufvekn,*" answered Leah. "We will wake you when it's time."

Sam closed his eyes again, waiting for her tap. He had fallen asleep with his boots on, along with pants and jacket. The long, dark gray coat had big buttons and a large collar, and also served as his night blanket.

When Leah eventually shook Sam's shoulder, he jumped to his feet. Although no one had gloves, Leah wrapped a scarf tightly around Sam's neck. Froim, Chava, and Duvid each picked up their bags, and Leah turned to Sam, handing him strung bags for his shoulders. .

"*Di nemst dus,*" said Leah. "*Farloyg es nisht.*"

"I'll hang on tight to them. Don't worry, I won't lose them," answered Sam.

"All talking stops here," said Duvid.

In the middle of the frozen Warsaw night, their street was eerily silent and absent of any army traffic or guards. Duvid looked out the front door of the building and pointed left, silently leading Sam, Leah with Baruch in her arms, Chava, and Froim.

From their prior nighttime breakout experience, they knew to walk with no noise and stay close to building walls in the deep shadows. Duvid and Sam had become skilled at reading the darkness and nocturnal dodging between shades of blackness.

At each corner, they stopped and huddled in a stairwell or back alley corner, waiting for Duvid to scout a snow path on the next block. After cutting a diagonal route through the streets, they stopped and Duvid held them back in an unlit doorway. No one spoke and they waited.

Out of the shadows, another group of six people appeared and crossed to the nearby corner, as if waiting to be joined. Sam noticed that there were no children in the group. Duvid walked forward and greeted a tall, shivering man. He seemed to be the same age as Duvid and wore a dark, tattered overcoat that had originally been made for fashion rather than warmth. The two men looked at each other's assembled family without comment.

It was an evening of no introductions or names, hoping that the silent, one-way gathering would end safely for all.

"Everyone here?" whispered Duvid. The man looked at his group and nodded his head.

"And you know where to go?"

The man nodded.

The two men hunched together and quietly reviewed the plan. They both paused the conversation and turned in the same direction. They could hear the approaching sound of tires crunching on the frozen snow, but the vehicle turned before entering their street.

"If we make it," said Duvid, "we'll separate, since we are too big of a group to run and not be seen."

"Let's go," whispered the other man to his family. He led them single file, followed by Duvid's family, deliberately separated and fifty meters behind. After weaving cautiously between buildings, they all ducked into an icy, abandoned building that Sam recognized from his smuggling forays.

The mounds of snow leading to the building were higher than he recalled, but Sam figured it wasn't all snow. Little has changed, except there were no silhouettes of lookouts posted at the alleyways or back door. They snuck through the door and down the building's dark passageways.

Once in the basement, Sam could hear the other family, who had gathered in the last side room. Duvid opened the door, revealing the others pushing their way through an immense amount of frozen rubbish in the room. It was full of debris.

Suddenly two other men quickly entered the room and closed the door behind them. They were short, disheveled men with black, unkempt beards. Their hands were encrusted with dried mortar, like Duvid's. They pushed the piles of debris to the side to reach Duvid. The three men embraced, slapping each other's backs. No words were necessary.

"Climb over it," said Duvid to his family, who were waiting at the door. He pointed for them to move toward a cabinet in the far corner of the room. Both families pushed through the piles like digging out of an avalanche. Duvid and the other man slid the cabinet to the side, revealing plywood. Behind the plywood was a rough, hand-dug, earthen entrance.

The hole in the cement wall was filled with more rubbish, concealing a very rough and large tunnel. For months, since the last attempt to break out, Duvid had been slipping out for night digging after his day labor working on the wall. For every day of being forced to lay the bricks that cut off life, Duvid removed a pile of dirt, slowly clearing the hidden passageway.

"Go," said one of the men who had later entered the room. "And we'll go tomorrow."

The two men waited to cover up the hole and then re-bury it under piles of garbage. Each night, different small groups passed on their trust and hope to break away from the Nazi grip.

"*Kim, kim, gey shnel, gey shnel,*" said one of the men remaining behind. He was panicked, urging them to hurry. "*Ikh'l farmakhn.*"

With his offer to close up the entrance behind them, there was no time to waste. Sam pushed his way through the piles to the opening and began to enter the tunnel, excited to explore the expanded tunnel. In the dim glow of a short candle held by the other family leader, Sam could see several wooden slats being used to suspend the ceiling.

Duvid grabbed Sam's shoulder and held him back.

"Wait," said Duvid, "it's different now. Follow and watch."

He turned toward his family with a final instruction. "There is no light in there, so follow very closely."

When Froim entered the tunnel behind Sam, he slowly reached out to feel the height of the dirt tunnel, as if touching heaven. Leah clutched Baruch and slowly shuffled through the tunnel, pinned between Chava and Froim.

"*Bleyb tsizamen,*" said Duvid, "*ale tsizamen. Zay shtil.*"

It was vital to move along as quietly as possible and keep moving, while staying in physical touch with the line. In the blackness, it was too easy to become disoriented and panicked if you separated from the movement. Walking upright, they collided with the sides of mud and dirt and frequently caught themselves on shards of rocks protruding from the ceiling and walls.

Gasps of frustration were highlighted by an occasional groan from someone hitting a stone or wall. Duvid never stopped moving, but would slow down.

"*Iz altding in ordenung?*" whispered Duvid, asking his family if everything was all right.

No one complained.

"*Zol men gayn tsizamen in zay shtil.*"

Other than Sam, they had never experienced being buried alive. They were drawn through the stale air toward the sound of Duvid's raspy voice, focused on quietly moving forward together. With no light, they each gently touched the back of the person directly in front to avoid smacking into them and tripping everyone to the ground.

Escape was the only chance to live and there was no going back. Unlike the sharp-shifting smuggling route, the tunnel ran under the street and came up through a small outlet cut through a snow-covered grass tuft in an obscure and distant cemetery hill.

The walls of the tunnel were tight and after blindly lumbering through the shaft for hundreds of meters, they felt the tunnel begin to slope upward. Duvid could hear a lot of muffled whispering behind him, confirming that everyone was still in line. The clay ground beneath their feet was patted down, but scattered rocks tripped up the path.

"*Ale zenen tsizamen du?*" asked Duvid, looking backward into the blackness. "Is everyone still together?"

"*Altsding iz in ordenung,*" answered Froim from the rear, confirming that both families were at hand in the earthen channel.

The crooked hole at the surface was angled to obscure its opening. Duvid carefully crawled out and turned, pulling each family member out one at a time. The surface hole was surrounded with bushes and a tree screening the opening. Duvid gently pushed the bushes aside to expose a crawl path behind the cemetery bushes.

"Hold these," said Duvid to each of his family members, "but don't snap them."

It was important to not break the ice-covered branches, since others would follow. With his bare hands, Sam upturned the snow to avoid leaving tracks from the hole.

While being forced to brick up doors and windows, Duvid had recognized that the Germans heavily guarded the ghetto's walls and not the cemetery beyond them.

* * * * *

Every day in the ghetto was like the next, an excruciatingly eternity of horror, but not this day. Duvid and his family all seemed to tumble out of the tunnel, focused on the flickering street light beyond the open fence. It had snowed overnight and the fresh powder would leave foot prints. The goal was to get to the outskirts of town, but that would be difficult to accomplish without leaving a trail.

The other family quietly pulled themselves out of the tunnel slit in the cemetery hill. The man crawled to where Duvid had lain down and covered himself with snow.

"*Vi gaysti?*" asked Duvid, pointing both hands in opposite directions. "Which way are you going?"

"*Di zayt,*" answered the man, pointing to the left and confirming what had been agreed. They exchanged a snow-layered arm embrace and firm gaze of confidence.

Duvid and his family went to the right and the other family would go left. The heads of the two families had previously agreed how the move would occur, the number of people included, as well as the day, place, and time to meet, and how to separate.

"*We can only take so many people,*" Duvid had said in a meeting with the father from the other family. Once decided, there had been no further communication until had they met again at the corner.

Secrecy, timing, and numbers were crucial. The other family was also comprised of a mother and father, as well as several older children. They clearly shared the same problems of wearing a lot of clothes and struggling to move.

After the family turned left out of the tunnel exit, Sam never saw them again.

It was still hours until dawn, and they had surfaced in a large, crowded section of the graveyard that Sam had never seen. It was filled with bushes and large headstones to hide behind.

Froim glanced toward the ghetto, but could only see the massive wall that had been erected to stop others from escaping over the fence and through the graves.

"Good-bye," said Duvid, noticing that Froim was looking backward. "We need to get away before the sunrise."

Froim turned and saw a hearse entrance in the fencing at the end of the cemetery.

"There?" asked Froim, pointing at the open gate.

Duvid knew the direction, bit his cracked bottom lip, and rapidly nodded his head. As they dodged between the stones, walking softly to quiet the crunching fresh snow, Duvid suddenly held up his hand and then waved it down for everyone to stop and hide.

Leah had been trying to move quickly, while grasping Baruch with both arms. He was heavier than his infant weight had been when they had fled Warsaw, and Leah was grateful to sit for a moment. The walking movements had kept him quiet and now he started to squirm when they hid.

Leah handed Baruch over to Chava, while she hurriedly searched one of her coat pockets. Leah had a bit of food she had saved for this moment. She licked her finger and put the morsel in Baruch's mouth. Baruch started to groan for more and Chava realized that even making a shushing sound would be too loud. She saw Leah pull out a handkerchief. Leah had anticipated this situation and offered her handkerchief, which was filled with an unknown substance. Baruch tried to stand and get away from Chava's arms.

"Watch," whispered Leah. She wet her finger, dipped it into the cloth, then placed the fingertip in Baruch's mouth. He quickly sat in Leah's lap, quietly waiting for more. The family watched in astonished silence.

The quiet was from a bit of sugar, hidden in the last milk powder shipment Sam had brought back. Sam looked at Baruch and smiled.

Duvid had covertly moved ahead, cautiously shifting through the large monuments and dropping into the snow at the slightest sound. When he reached the open gate, he could see an unlit road leading into the unknown darkness.

It seemed too good to be true, so he watched and listened. The shooting at the sewer exit was on his mind and he wondered if it was a trap.

After fifteen minutes, he crawled back to motion his family to move toward him. No more hesitation or they would lose the darkness. One at a time, Duvid signaled for them to pass through the open gate and cross the empty street.

They each walked tenuously across the slippery gravel road and then huddled together in the snow-filled ditch, waiting for Froim to make it over.

"*Halt zikh un a bisl*," said Duvid. He didn't want them to rush into a crossfire. Duvid gestured to stay down and watch if there was any activity in the area. His eyes flashed like a hunted fox, gazing across the road, darting back into the cemetery, and then forward into the field ahead of them.

"Let's go," said Duvid. He quickly rose and grabbed Sam's hand and began to move across a snow-covered field. The grass was buried under the packed drifts, leaving nothing to hide behind. With no buildings in the farmland or woods to provide shelter, they had to move fast under cover of the last few hours of darkness.

At sunrise, the Kapos would notice that Froim and Duvid didn't report to their work details, and report to the soldiers that their room was empty. A Gestapo patrol would soon discover their trail leading away from the ghetto and wouldn't be far behind with their vehicles and dogs. People who tried to escape and were caught never returned alive.

Feeling the strain of the breakout on his family, Duvid knew that their bolt to freedom might be short lived if their situation didn't dramatically improve. When the snow flattened out, Duvid tried to run a bit, hoping his family could follow in his deep tracks.

After a short jaunt, the heavy panting and the awkward exchanges of Baruch between Leah and Chava drowned out the crunch of the snow. They resumed walking, since they were too tired, undernourished, and frozen to maintain the more rushed pace.

After an hour of crossing the open land, Duvid paused by a lone tree and waited for everyone to catch up to him.

"Try to keep your fingers in your pockets," said Duvid, "or they'll freeze out here."

"Look," said Froim, pointing back at their traveled direction.

"No more city lights," said Chava.

Warsaw and its ghetto had dropped under the horizon. They each rearranged their bags and traded off carrying Baruch.

It had started to snow again, dropping unusually large flakes on Duvid and his family. Sam tried to catch some of the flakes on his tongue and was mimicked by Chava.

"More snow," said Duvid, "but it may cover our tracks out of the cemetery. Let's keep going."

Froim was on watch to spot any farms and pointed out shadows of a distant set of buildings. As they approached the farm, Froim walked a distance ahead to warn if someone was coming from the buildings. It was well before dawn and there were no lights in any of the structures.

"Let me go first," said Froim, "and see who lives there."

"It's too dark," said Duvid, "so wait with us behind the barn."

Froim re-cinched his bags and walked with his family toward the barn.

"You can't knock until sunrise," continued Duvid, "or they'll answer with a gun."

Duvid led Chava and Froim, Sam, Leah, and Baruch around the barn to an open field with mounds of snow-covered hay. At the end of the harvest, the farmer had left a large mountain of hay in the field, with a broken wagon wheel resting against it. They couldn't stand outside, exposed to the elements and patrols, so Duvid and Sam dove into the stack and began to pull out and re-arrange piles of hay.

Within minutes, they had turned the mountain of crisp, snow-capped hay and grass into a temporary shelter.

"We'll climb inside and warm it up," said Leah, prompting Baruch to climb into a crude opening between the stacked stalks. The hidden chamber was icy and the hay poked with its sharp edges, but Baruch curled up against the hay wall. The heat of their bodies in the tight space quickly warmed the hay house and Duvid used some of the loose hay to close the entrance.

For the next few hours, the hay kept out the freezing winds and falling snow muffled the sounds inside the stack. Despite the lack of food, Baruch was quiet and did not kvetch, sitting on Leah's lap and quickly falling asleep.

* * * * *

Duvid had made a hole in the hay wall to watch the farmhouse, and then made a few more to see if anyone was approaching from the distant road.

"Sam," said Duvid, "*gay gib a kik. Zey tsi emets'l kimen.*"

"Yes, I can see anyone walking this way, *Tateh*," said Sam. He sat on his bag, which doubled as a pillow.

The snow had continued to fall during the night, re-covering the haystack. Chava pulled in the fresh snow, so they could wash their hands and chew on it for the water. Sam licked the hay like a cone, relishing its clean taste.

At sunrise, Froim and Duvid went together to the house, but Duvid held back out of sight. Froim knocked on the unlit door, expecting to be run off the land. Duvid saw the door open and Froim go inside. He knew that if Froim didn't come back, they would have to run.

After Duvid had waited patiently for twenty minutes, Froim cautiously walked back outside.

"They're coming back," said Sam to Chava and his mother, dutifully watching out the peepholes.

Duvid and Froim walked back to the hay shelter and Froim openly shared the news. Leah was glad to see the men return and that Froim hadn't been shot dead on the spot.

"It's just an old farmer and his wife," said Froim, "and they would like to help us. Once I told them that we have young children, they said they would take the chance."

Leah's face brightened with the first good news she had heard since the invasion, as she listened through the hay to her brother's every word.

"The man said they heard what the Nazis were doing to the Jews and understood why we were trying to get to the Russian border."

Chava squinted her eyes in the morning haze and looked suspicious at the news.

"They're nice people," continued Froim, "and they want us to come inside the house." He felt peculiar talking at a pile of hay in an open field, but soon Froim heard rustling and saw Duvid push open the bottom part of the hay wall with his ungloved hands.

Duvid bent down and gripped his abdomen with a groan and smile. "I know better than to move like that," he said. "It still hurts."

Froim recalled when Duvid delivered for a seltzer company before the war, his push wagon had been struck by a truck that rammed the wagon handle into his gut. The bar cut into his body and while an operation saved his life, it also removed half of his abdomen and left a large scar cutting across his stomach. When he felt a painful twinge, it reminded him of his second chance. After all of the digging and crawling, pulling his family out of a hiding place for real shelter was the best pain.

"I'm still watching for patrols," said Froim, "so let's walk to the house one at a time."

He gave a "clear" signal and each crawled carefully out of the hay. Duvid was last and Chava carried Baruch, while Leah enjoyed holding Sam's hand walking across the tundra.

The farmer, Lech, a husky, older man with a bristly, dirt-brown beard was waiting outside, wearing a thick work jacket wrapped by a warm horse blanket around his shoulders. He stood near the front door holding a long rake, posed more like a guard than a farmer with a tool. He waved Sam and the others into the house with a wide smile, without taking his eyes off the line of far woods.

After they went inside, Lech stayed outside and waited to be sure that no one had been watching. The people in the countryside had learned to be cautious, too.

Inside the door was his wife, Basha, who quickly moved them into the main room by the kitchen. Her hair was grayish and completely pulled under her faded head wrap. She wore a long dress made of a brown, quilted fabric that lightly touched the floor, along with an ivory-colored apron tied around her thick waist.

When Lech entered, he quickly covered the window to block the view to the interior.

Sam had rarely seen a single home, much less been invited inside. The building wasn't large, but they could afford to heat it in the middle of a harsh winter. Sam had met sharing people in the ghetto, but the farm couple was eagerly friendly without a trade.

Leah was instantly warm, but wouldn't release Baruch from her grasp. Duvid, Chava, and Froim looked at the furniture and carpet spread throughout the room. The kitchen was in an adjacent room, elevated by two steps, and held a large table and two chairs.

Basha was smiling and had put a kettle on the stove when Froim said they had a young child. Fortunately, Duvid and his family understood Polish and could speak to them. The room quickly got so hot from the stove that Sam started to remove the layers of clothes, and Basha hung them to dry.

Lech and Basha wanted to help, despite the obvious risk. Lech walked by and rubbed Sam on the head to comfort him. It was Sam's first moment of relief without having to be quiet and not looking over a shoulder.

The adults began talking and Basha asked Leah many questions about caring for Baruch. They were older than Duvid and Leah, but no one mentioned if they had children. Basha realized that everyone was still standing in the outer room and she quickly cleared the kitchen table to put out food.

"Come in here and I'll get something for you to eat," said Basha. She didn't have to ask twice. Lech had stepped out, but came back inside with a bucket of milk. They all gasped at the sight and stood shocked at the kindness.

Basha led Sam to a stool and poured some milk for him in a metal mug with a handle. Sam looked at Leah for approval of the reality to drink it. He began to gulp down his first taste of fresh milk.

"*Trink nish azoy shnel!*" said Leah. It was fresh and he would have consumed the milk in one immense swig if she hadn't admonished him to slow down.

The grown-ups chuckled at his famished determination. The others quickly consumed the vegetables, bread, and a stew that

Basha had brought to the table. It had been some time since they had seen a whole vegetable or loaf of bread, but Duvid remembered the blessing.

Lech and Basha weren't Jewish, but they understood the need for a moment of prayer. It wasn't Friday, but Leah finally felt relief and gave thanks for having the family together.

"Don't eat too much," said Leah. "If you eat too fast, you'll get sick."

Sam was eating like he had to consume enough to last a week. "Your stomach isn't used to good food," continued Leah, "so slow down and don't fill up."

"There will be more tomorrow," said Basha. She gently rubbed Sam's shoulder as if to reassure him. "We don't have room for everyone to stay inside with us, but Lech will settle you into a good corner of the barn away from the animals. It will be comfortable with fresh hay and blankets, and you'll be safe there."

Lech grabbed two pieces of chopped wood from the stack by the stove and tossed them into the fire.

"You are very kind to us," said Duvid, "and if we can stay just one or two nights, we'll move on."

"That's fine," said Lech, "and best for you, too, since the Gestapo patrols stop by every couple days. It's a warm barn and will keep you from the wind."

They couldn't be seen by anyone outside and Duvid would feel trapped in one building, waiting for the Germans to discover them, but the food and rest for the family were timely and essential. After their ragged clothes were dry, Leah and Basha carried them with a stack of blankets out to the barn.

The barn was a very large, bare wooden structure with a high ceiling and half-walls inside, separating the animals from the hay, milking, and work areas. It smelled like an active farm, and there were no complaints.

"The short walls are so I can see the animals," said Lech, "and so they don't trample anything." There were many dairy cows, chickens, and two work horses that pushed Sam backwards when they rubbed their large noses against him. A large single wall divided the barn and separated the animals from a large pile of grass and hay to feed them throughout the winter.

"It's important that none of the animals are untied or moved," Lech told the family. Tools were hung on nails next to milking buckets, while bins of vegetables and barrels of corn and apples for the animals were neatly shelved along the wall. One chicken chased another and it reminded Sam of when the chickens got loose in the old neighborhood butcher shop.

As the squawking continued and the chickens began to jump up with nervous excitement, Basha and Leah laughed hysterically. The feathers flew and it felt good to chuckle out loud without concern.

Leah had put Baruch down to wander among the noisy animals, but picked him back up to keep him from stepping in things.

Chava and Froim dug deeply into the oily hay until they found a dry layer to smooth out their coats and blankets. They carved out a burrow in the haystack large enough for the whole family to be concealed. Duvid and his family needed to stay out of sight and if anyone approached the farm, Lech would give them a signal to hide themselves and their belongings under the hay.

Both the farmers and the family were at risk of immediate execution by the Nazis if the Jews were found on the farm.

"Give me another bucket," said Lech. "Be careful not to spill this one and put it by the others against the wall."

Basha picked up the bucket by both handles and poured the warm milk into a metal container with a cover. They had a smooth milking routine. The dairy cows were huge, carrying full, round bellies, and they stared at Sam with liquid brown eyes while being milked.

Lech gently moved each cow and tied it to a post in a confirmed area and got a bucket and bench. It was the first time Sam had ever seen a cow being milked; there were so many udders and fresh milk.

* * * * *

Later that day, when it was lunch time, Basha brought a steaming pot of meat stew out to the barn. She had included a ladle and bowls for everyone.

"Will one of you please go into the kitchen and get the bread on the kitchen table?" asked Basha. "I couldn't carry everything at once."

Chava went into the house and came out with a basket of bread. "We like to eat out here during the day," continued Basha, "then we don't lose working time." That night, Basha invited everyone inside to eat at the kitchen table.

"There's lots of bread and fresh butter," Basha pointed out. "Help yourselves."

"The butter is so warm and creamy that it melts on Sam's fingers," said Leah, "before he gets it on the bread."

Froim passed the apples to Duvid to dip in the honey, then poured another cup of milk for Sam, who had been looking at Baruch slowly eating kasha and wheat. Sam realized that it was the first time he had ever seen his mother feed Baruch real food on a plate. It was messy and awkward, but Baruch used a spoon.

Basha ate with them at the dinner table, while Lech stood on the outside steps and kept watch on the darkening horizon. He could see if anyone rode onto the farmland and would have time to come inside and tell Duvid to hide everyone.

Deliveries sounded different from German inspections, and Lech was able to distinguish those arrivals at a fair distance.

"If it's the Germans," said Basha, "I hide the food in here." She showed everyone a fake door in the wall to hide things from the soldiers, but the cubby hole was not large enough for people. "Yesterday, they showed up fast and we tossed most of the food in the wall."

"As soon as their trucks pulled up and the engines were off," said Lech, leaning into the room, "the soldiers jumped out and an officer brought the troops into the house and took our table food and a couple chickens."

"We were lucky," nodded Basha. "They could have shot us and taken everything."

"They'll be back," said Lech, a grim expression on his face.

Leah looked at Duvid, knowing that their warm reception couldn't last.

Before the sun rose, Sam was awakened by the sounds of equipment, boxes, and large, empty, metal milk jugs being unloaded.

"Duvid," said Lech, yelling into the barn. "I want you to meet someone."

Duvid uncovered himself and quickly crawled out of the haystack.

"What was that about?" asked Leah, when her husband returned after the sun had risen. By the time he came back, the morning milking was almost finished.

"Our next move," answered Duvid. "We have to keep going, maybe tomorrow."

"Well," said Leah, "have something to eat. Basha brought over some bread, cheese, and apples."

Suddenly, the side door flew open and Lech ran into the barn. "Bury the food and hide yourselves under cover!" Lech shouted. "I could hear the rumbling on the land."

He took the food and tossed it under a clump of hay. "You have less than five minutes until they get here."

"How do you know it's the Germans?" asked Duvid.

"I can hear their trucks echoing in the open air; it's not wagon wheels and horses. Motorized vehicles are for soldiers and wagons are for farmers."

Lech showed Froim how to conceal the haystack entrance with buckets and equipment, and hide inside beneath the blankets and layers of wheat and hay. Basha forked more hay on the stack so that the pile looked randomly strewn. Then she ran back to the house.

Duvid, Leah and Baruch, Froim, Chava, and Sam knew the drill and remembered the fear.

"Keep your head down and cover your skin," said Sam.

"Breath slow and evenly," said Duvid.

The ground was lightly covered by crusty hay that was brittle from the layers of morning ice, gripping the spikes of straw that protruded from the glaze. Even though they were buried under the haystack in the barn, they could recognize the squeak of trucks braking to a stop near the barn's entrance.

Being buried under the weight of the hay was suffocating, but open air meant death or worse. Each breath was a strain, pulling bits of air through a small, pinched gap between the lips, while trying to not enlarge the lungs so much as to shift the body and twitch the hay. Inhale, exhale and slowly repeat. A muffled sneeze would shatter the barn's silence as sharply as a chandelier crashing to a stone floor.

Leah had tried to dig out space in the dirt in front of Baruch's face so that the hay wouldn't poke his eyes or cover his small mouth. She had draped a piece of cloth over his face and gently held it to soften the pressing hay, but allowed enough air to flow. Huddled under Leah's arms, Baruch twitched unsuccessfully, pressed up against his father.

Sam found that sucking in the frozen barn air through his nostrils was quieter than through his open mouth. He could tell that Leah was working hard to suppress her breath. She could feel Sam's boot pressed hard against the back of her leg and dig into her shin. Lying on her side with both arms wrapped around Baruch, she couldn't even move to push away his boot heel. Every motion vibrated a rustling sound under the crisp hay.

Through a gap at the bottom of the hay, Chava could see a cracked, wooden milking stool resting on its side in the stall next to a waiting cow. Chava, Sam, and Froim were lined up and pressed in tightly behind Duvid. Leah and Baruch were pressed so closely between her family's bodies that it felt as if each breath drew in the hay stacks and barn walls.

Sam could hear his father's last words gently feathered into his ear, "Don't move," said Duvid. "No matter what you hear or see, stay very still."

The large wooden doors were unhitched and flew open into the barn, smashing against the driftwood frame. *Crack!* The oversized hinges held onto the flying wood, but the movement of frozen metal nailed into iced wood rattled the entire barn, raining down dust debris. The winter air rushed in and blew the dried grass on the floor into the wooden stalls.

With his left eye, Sam could look up through the hay to see that both large barn doors had been opened wide. The chickens were disturbed and began to squawk and flutter around the floor of the barn. Lech's mud-caked boots came into the barn, immediately followed by black, knee-high, polished boots.

Sam could not understand the deep voice, but the words were curt and demanding. It was the same sound as the Nazi guards who fired into the sewer tunnel. Duvid's arm was pressed against Sam's side and his hand kept Sam's head from turning. Sam could still see one of the black boots walk to a wooden rail near his feet. The bottom of each boot was scraped against the rail, chipping chunks of manure away from the black heels.

Baruch coughed once and hearts pounded. His mouth was still face down in a pile of rags, swathed in a blanket and in the arms of Leah, but a muffled sound was still a sound. The boots stopped scraping and the heels snapped together.

Froim's hands clenched and held onto Sam and Chava. The squeal of more brakes could be heard. Then they heard the smack of a metal gate flipping open, followed by boots hitting the ground and the clanking of rifles being loaded.

Lech dropped the shovel he was carrying and began coughing with a deep, clogged throat. He pulled down the scarf covering his mouth and continued coughing into the face of the German officer. The relentless coughing was louder and became a stumbling, choking hack. Baruch coughed again, but the baby's cough was enveloped within the louder adult hacking.

Leah held Baruch tighter and pressed his cloth-covered face into the straw on the ground. Any tighter and breathing would stop. Lech gasped for air in between his coughs and wildly waved his arm in the air as if directing that he needed to exit the barn to breathe again.

Smack, smack!! With his thick, leather-clad gloves, the officer began to smack his hand against Lech's back in effort to jar in some air. The sound of the leather glove against the cloth coat made a sharp slap, but Lech didn't wave it off. Still bent over, he slowly led the cough and Nazi out of the barn.

Still coughing occasionally, Lech could see the troops going through his house and another group taking away a cow. Basha was pushed out of the house without her coat and stood with her back to the door, unable to watch the pillaging of their foodstuffs. She was lucky to be outside shivering and she knew it.

Lech swept his foot across the ground in an attempt to sweep a few loose chickens back into the barn, subtly exchanging glances with Basha to be sure that she was unharmed.

"*Sechs Hühner*," said the officer, pointing at the wandering chickens. The commotion was distracting and Lech was glad to grab six more chickens and help the Germans quickly leave. Lech knew that soon there would be nothing to take. Basha watched as the soldiers returned to their assigned trucks with the household plunder and began to load the animals. She heard the sound of the front door slam behind her.

Boot heels stomped down the wooden steps and approached her from behind. She didn't move or turn to acknowledge the sounds.

"Do you have anyone else living here?" asked the German, speaking Polish. "Is anyone staying here with you?"

Basha turned around and looked at him directly in the eyes. "No," she answered with a disgusted look, "just us."

She turned to go back into the house, then closed the door.

* * * * *

Leah wanted to give Basha and Lech something for hiding and feeding them, but Basha refused.

"But you risked everything," said Leah, pulling loose straw out of Baruch's blanket. "Why?"

She suddenly realized that hers might not have been the first Jewish family from Warsaw who had found their farm. From the neighbor contacts to the hidden food and daily Gestapo inspections, this farm was organized to watch out for and hopefully survive the Germans.

"They invaded our country, too," answered Basha, "and this is our way of fighting back."

She returned to the house and began to re-cover the windows so no one could see inside. It had been a long day of seclusion in the cold barn, but Baruch enjoyed strutting with the remaining chickens and Sam was locked in a staring contest with a cow chewing her silage.

"I don't think we can stay here for long," said Duvid. "We leave in the morning."

"Where shall we go?" asked Froim. "Everything is still covered with ice and snow."

"We wouldn't last in the woods again," said Chava.

"There's another farm," answered Duvid, "and another and the next. Lech introduced me to his neighbor, who lives a kilometer from here. It's just a shack, but the Germans will be back here and we need to stay a step ahead of them."

"As long as we're heading toward the Russians," said Froim.

"And if the Germans catch us," said Chava, "they won't take us back to Warsaw."

"That will be our last day," said Duvid, "unless we keep moving."

As the sun set, Leah looked around at the barn structure and realized that living under the hay and between animals had been the safest she had felt since the war started.

"Come inside for some food," said Basha, who had come back to the barn. "Lech, bring the empty barrels for sitting at the table."

Duvid helped him roll the seats to the front stairs, but the barrels were returned to the barn when the food was finished. The Germans could only see the table and two chairs.

"What food?" asked Leah, as she and Baruch walked in the front door. "They took everything this morning."

"We let them think that," answered Basha. She turned around and moved to open the hidden compartment, stacked with vegetables, along with bread and butter from the morning. There was a pot of water boiling on the stove waiting for sliced vegetables and chicken.

After they had shared their meal, Lech suddenly rose to his feet.

"Strange," said Lech, "there's a wagon coming, fast."

He walked to the front door and grabbed his coat and hat. "Let me go out and see."

Basha pulled back the window covering to watch who was approaching in the dark. It was a distant neighbor and she could see from the way he jumped off the wagon and didn't even bother to tie up the horse that he was panicked. It was an urgent ride.

Lech helped the man pull his wagon around and tie up to a post. Then Lech sprinted back to the house, leaving the man waiting by the horse and wagon.

"They're circling back and checking all the farms again," said Lech.

"It's unusual this late at night," said Basha, "but maybe they didn't find enough during the day."

"We can't hide here again," said Duvid. "They will find and kill all of us."

Lech explained in a hurried voice, "My friend heard from his neighbor that the Gestapo was back checking the farms for Jews and then took all of his chickens, food, and supplies. He will take you overland to another place to hide for the night. The Germans are two farms away."

"Let's go," said Duvid, "now!"

Chava and Froim ran into the barn and grabbed all of their meager belongings. They tossed the sacks into the wagon, then jumped onto the wooden plank platform.

Duvid heartily thanked Lech and climbed in with Leah and Baruch, Chava, Sam, and Froim, then made them lie down flat on the wagon floor. Basha ran out to the wagon without her coat and handed Leah some wrapped food for Baruch, along with rags for diapers. The old woman then quickly lifted Sam into the wagon.

"I will pray for your health and safe travel," said Basha. Not waiting for a response, she quickly turned, went back in the house, and closed the door. There was no time for emotion.

Lech grabbed a pitch fork in his bare hands and began to toss hay into the wagon, covering the passengers. His friend held the horse in place until the wagon was filled, then jumped onto the wagon's seat and grabbed the reins. He drove the horse across an unpaved road and the wagon lurched away in blind trust.

CHAPTER SEVEN

CROSSED LINE

"It's dark," said Chava. "There's no one here."

"Who lives here?" asked Sam. Near dusk, they arrived at another farmhouse with an attached barn. No one came to meet the wagon. They saw a small, weathered, gray barn with hay and some equipment inside, but no animals. Shovels, rakes, and farming equipment leaned against the empty stalls.

After a month of hiding from Gestapo death squads and being urgently taken to the next safe house, Sam knew the routine at their fourth farm. They had brought some bread from the last farm and would have to make it last.

"Make a hole in that haystack," said Duvid, pointing at the hay in the barn. "It'll be dark soon and we can't light a fire."

Duvid stayed by the wagon, as Froim helped Chava, Leah, and Baruch down with their satchels. Sam jumped into a snowbank that had drifted against the barn.

"This barn doesn't smell so bad," said Sam.

"No animals," said Froim. "The Nazis probably took the people, too."

As the family fled to the East, the Germans continued to get closer, scavenging farms for chickens, eggs, meat, and vehicles—anything they could use to support their soldiers. Duvid and his family had been traveling since mid-morning in the single horse-drawn wagon. The nameless driver was a very tall and skinny man with light skin and long hair that he whipped around and tucked back in his hat.

When they stopped at the barn, the driver didn't leave his seat or tie up the reins. Duvid stood next to the front of the buckboard and asked directions to the Russian line. The driver talked with his hands, franticly pointing across the field. He snapped the whip and whistled at the horse, which trotted off in the deep snow.

"Was he panicked?" asked Chava.

"Yes," answered Duvid. "It's dangerous to help."

The barn and hay offered shelter from the winds and falling snow, but no heat. Sam slept on the end inside the haystack and was startled awake in the morning by a pushing sensation against his stomach. He looked down into the eyes of a large rat that had nuzzled against him for warmth.

"No animals?" asked Sam, poking Froim to look at the guest.

"As long as you don't bite each other," answered Froim. "Stay warm."

"Wait here and be quiet," said Duvid. He crawled out of the hay and knocked at the door of the small connected house. Two rough-looking, elderly men came out and began arguing with each other, then told Duvid to quickly get back into the barn.

"You can't stay for very long," said the shorter man with untied boots, who must have been startled by Duvid's early knock. "The Germans are close and stop by every day to take something."

"We want to go east," said Duvid.

"Go back inside the barn and don't open the door," said the older man with a stoop. "Hide."

A few minutes later, the barn side door opened and the older man walked in with a tin container of cold milk and a plate of vegetables, bread, and butter. When he approached the haystack, the family emerged from their prickly bower.

"I'm Aurek," said the older man. "And my brother is Iwan."

He looked down at Sam and Baruch, who had begun to explore the barn for any chickens.

"We were told you had children."

"Thank you for the food and bedding," said Chava.

"We don't have much left," said Aurek, "but we'd rather give it to you." He smiled at the boys. "Don't go inside the house. My brother will come out and give you directions."

Leah distributed the food and stored some portions in her bag for later. The milk was quickly finished. Iwan came into the barn and held a rake pole upside down. He began to scratch roads and directions on the ground.

"Here is the border," said Iwan, drawing a line in the dirt. "And we are here." He continued to sketch in the brown dirt.

"Make sense?" asked Duvid.

Froim nodded his head and began to gather his few items.

"It will take a couple of days to go through the woods," said Iwan, "so go east and away from the Germans. Pack fast. You have to go."

Everyone quickly put on their layers of clothes and Leah collected a package of travel food.

"You must go now," Iwan repeated, more urgently.

The barn was close to a dense stand of tall trees, and Duvid and his family disappeared into the frozen forest. The afternoon march through the underbrush was tough and brutally cold. Where the forest canopy sheltered against the snow, the ground was exposed and covered with dense weeds, stones, and thick brush.

While Baruch could already walk, he was still too small for deep snow and compact woods. They staggered through the woods until the trees opened into less dense, snow-covered fields. As dusk came around again, they stopped in a clump of trees, and lay together on a blanket spread on a bare patch of ground.

* * * * *

The night was clear and tranquil. Sam was calmed by the stillness and sat leaning against a tree, gazing at the first star in the black sky. In the ghetto, the stars never sparkled for him.

"Don't talk," said Duvid, "until we know who is near."

It was difficult for Sam to fall asleep, not knowing where they were going and feeling the proximity of the German patrols. They hid in the dense brush, enjoying a taste of freedom.

After a couple of hours, it was still quiet and no one was asleep.

"How long are we going to stay in the woods this time?" asked Froim.

"Until we reach Russia," answered Duvid. "We need to keep moving and stay away from roads traveled by military convoys."

Sam was reminded of their first breakaway from Warsaw, moving in the daylight and from one ditch or cluster of trees to another. Leah began to rock Baruch and gently hum her favorite song, *Timbala*.

After the first week of surviving in the woods, they felt like animals living in the wild.

"Are we gypsies?" Sam asked his parents. "You said that gypsies live in the woods and eat from the trees and ground."

"And some have no real home and are always moving around," answered Leah.

"That feels like us," said Chava, "Jewish gypsies."

"We need food again," said Froim. "In the morning, I will scout ahead for a friendly farm."

Each morning, once the sun had risen enough and it was broad daylight, Froim walked in an agreed direction toward a distant farm.

"Stay low until you approach a door," said Duvid. "Don't be seen until you can see ahead."

Froim would be gone for hours and often return with word that the farmer didn't like Jews and wouldn't stick his neck out for them.

Leah was always relieved to see Froim again, returning to the woods without retracing the same path. Although he had to walk extreme distances, it was important for the farmers to not know their location.

If Froim met sympathetic farmers, he would return with carrots, bread, and small apples.

"Host gemakht git!" said Duvid, *"Dus iz git."* He was always surprised and thrilled by the number of food items that Froim brought back. Froim was always guarded with the farmers, since if they hated Jews, then he could be seized and handed over to the Germans.

Twice, he had come back empty-handed, disheveled, and beaten up. The bruises on his face were not as painful as having his jacket taken away. "They tried to hold me to make points with the Germans," said Froim. "When they said 'we got a Jew,' it was time to fight and run."

On both occasions, Duvid had made them pack up, just in case the farmers had followed Froim. Where he had been threatened by the farmers, Froim returned after dark. Food was often preserved in buckets and boxes outside the actual farmhouse, and Froim watched and waited for the supply room to be unattended. Then he grabbed a container of milk or a tub of butter with bags of bread. He didn't regret feeding his family based on the anti-Semitism of others.

* * * * *

"Can you carry Baruch when we run?" Leah asked Chava. "He was only an infant last time."

"Sure," answered her sister.

Starting at a dark open gap in the woods, they moved one at a time toward Duvid, who signaled at the opening of distant trees. As they settled for the night in another dense area of woods, they shared a bite and drank melted snow.

Chava tried to show Baruch how to melt clean snow in his hands, then poured it in his mouth. Practice was icy on his fingers. Every night, they huddled together in two clumps under blankets. Duvid embraced Leah and Baruch, and Sam snuggled between Froim and Chava. Out in the open, they jumped at every snap of a twig and were startled by rustling bushes. Sound traveled at night and coughs needed to be muffled by their collars and scarves. They all felt sick from the exposure, but tried to keep each other warm like other winter animals. All conversations were a hushed whisper, embraced by thick trees and bushes, while sheltered from the wind and nightly snowfall.

"When we get out of here," whispered Chava, looking at Sam and Baruch, "we'll have a better life and a farm with animals, house, horses, cows, and chickens." That caught the boys' attention, remembering Lech's squawking chickens. "And we will plant and not be afraid because we are Jewish." Chava fell asleep thinking about Palestine.

There were no crops to harvest out of the frozen ground, but looking across the farmland, one evening Sam could see where the winds cleared the snow, revealing scattered green sprouts left over from last season. Those pale green stalks meant one thing. Sam would run low out in the field and quickly dig an onion, carrot, or potato out of the frozen ground. With a proud scavenger smile, Sam collected them in a bag.

When they were deep in a massive wooded area and far away from any roads or buildings, Duvid made a small fire where the smoke wouldn't be seen. Sam was given the honor of tossing the raw vegetable pieces in the burning pile of twigs and branches. With a stick in hand, Sam threw the vegetable chunks into the flames, rolling the pieces in the embers until their skins were black. After brushing away the dirt and ashes with his sleeve, the burnt vegetables had some flavor.

Burnt food was food, best eaten hot. After three weeks in the woods, huddling together for a trace of warmth and dangerously scrounging for any nourishment, Leah sat by a lone tree and reached out in prayer. Sam listened carefully to her whispered words, which were different than his father's daily prayers in Warsaw.

"*Vi bisti, kensti nit zeyen vus zey tiyen tsin indz?*" asked Leah, wondering if God could see what others had been doing to her family. She wrapped her coat tighter and turned back to her family. She saw Froim drawing Sam's attention away from her private moment.

"*Sam, kim aheyr,*" said Froim. "*Ikh'l dikh vazen vi ikh makh dus. Zey dus.*" He offered to show Sam how he whittled sticks with a long knife, lifted from the last farm.

"Protect yourself," said Froim "and always cut into the wood away from you."

Sam watched intensely as Froim searched for a thick and straight stick, slowly peeling the bark to the handle. He held it between his knees and carved the wood into abstract rings and rotating triangles.

In this fashion, Sam learned to make stick utensils for the fire and when they burned up, he happily carved more.

"We need to talk to someone safe," said Duvid, "so that we know we are going in the right direction."

Sam kicked out the small fire and Froim wrapped himself in the blanket from Basha, turning up frozen leaves to cover his legs. Spring weather was not close enough to replace his jacket.

* * * * *

In the morning, Froim went for another long walk in search of a sympathetic farm. He returned just a few hours later without any food in hand.

"There's a man who has offered to help us," said Froim, "if we meet him away from his farmhouse."

He pointed in a northeast direction, curving his hand to show a turn to the edge of unseen property. "No food, but he will give us directions to the border, if we meet him today."

"Let's go," said Duvid. "Wrap up and bring everything."

Within a couple of hours, they sat perched on the edge of the woods near a snow-covered field, waiting for a sign of the farmer's approach. They each faced different direction, looking out for any movement.

"There," said Froim, pointing at the horizon to a very short and round man, bundled up with no skin exposed to the elements. He walked awkwardly and slowly through the snow drifts, frequently looking around in different directions.

Duvid walked to meet him and Sam could hear the Polish conversation echoing across the flat land. There was a lot of pointing and within a few moments, they both approached the waiting spot by the trees.

"This is all we can spare," said the man, and handed a bag of food to Chava. Leah continued to hold Baruch, since he disappeared in the snow depths. "Be well."

The stout man patted the heads of Sam and Baruch and re-traced his steps through the snow back to his farmhouse.

"We're very close to the border," said Duvid. "but wait right here."

Froim frowned at Duvid and was suddenly interrupted by the approaching sound of a loud engine. It was a large flatbed truck driven by the farmer, slicing across the field, churning up the snow drifts under its wide fenders. "And that is how we get there."

"This is better than walking," said Leah with a gleam in her eyes. They all climbed onto the flat bed of the open truck and the farmer took off with his cargo.

After an hour's ride, crisscrossing over other farm properties, the truck stopped near a bridge reaching over a frozen river.

Duvid knew that a sure place to capture Jews trying to escape across the border is at the border. They had come too far to hesitate now.

"If you cross and keep walking," said the farmer, "you will run into the Russians."

He touched everyone and shook both hands with Duvid. The sun had set and with the Germans at their back, Duvid didn't want to stay another night in Poland.

"We must get to the woods over there," said Duvid.

Froim picked up Baruch as they all ran along the open road for fifty meters. Panting, they stopped at the edge of the bridge.

"Listen," said Chava. They heard the distinct sound of engines starting up and faint voices of soldiers.

"It's Russian," said Duvid.

"Look," said Sam, pointing down at a large crack in the snow-capped river. It split the river in two, allowing the moon to illuminate chunks of ice floating on the slick, black water. In the darkness, the squeaking railings of the large bridge guided Duvid, Leah, and their family to a snow-covered road in Russian-controlled territory.

* * * * *

Realizing how exposed they were in the reflection of the moon-lit snow, they immediately got off the road and ran into the black woods.

"The last time we met Russians," said Chava, "they loaded us on trucks and gave us to the Germans."

"I will go alone," said Duvid, "and see if we can get through. Stay together until I get back."

As he reached the outer edge of the woods, Duvid crawled through the underbrush towards the soldiers' voices. He saw that the Russian army was encamped with their tents in rows near cannons on wheels. Each large gun was attached to a 2½-ton truck with a double set of wheels in back and one axle in front. With red stars marking the doors, they appeared ready to move.

Many of the troops were sleeping in the trucks, while pairs of sentries paced an invisible perimeter. Against the reflected snow, Duvid could see them marching in long winter coats with rifles over shoulders.

Froim would like one of those warm coats, regardless of the military insignia, Duvid thought to himself.

"Let's go," said Duvid, whose voice startled his family as he suddenly emerged out of the black woods. "They'll help us."

Even in the darkness, Duvid saw his family jump up and prepare to reach the Russians. He led them through the branches to a rough road, which ended at five posted soldiers.

"They're expecting us?" said Froim.

"*Ponyemayush tsi gavorit po'polski?*" asked Duvid, in a mix of Russian and Yiddish, wondering if the soldiers spoke Polish.

"*Nyet, nyet,*" answered one of the soldiers. The Russian officer, wearing a large furry hat, gestured for everyone to go with him the hundred meters to the encampment, followed by the other well-armed soldiers.

Sam was awestruck by the rows of trucks, cannons, and tanks, as his family stumbled across the military ruts in the churned-up snow and mud. They were waved through an open flap and into a warm tent, where several soldiers lay on mats. A pot-belly stove radiated heat, its rusty chimney stack going out through a cut in the canvas.

Sam and Baruch rushed toward the stove and quickly started warming themselves. The soldiers laughed and waved at Sam and Baruch, while holding tight to their rifles.

Leah unwrapped her frozen boys and placed their ice-encrusted clothes near the stove to dry, while using melted snow to wash them. She didn't understand Russian, but realized by their gestures that a corner of the tent had been cleared for her family.

Some of the soldiers seemed to understand Polish.

"The officer said we can stay for the night," said Duvid, "but we must move on early in the morning."

The soldiers liked two-year-old Baruch and seemed interested in his black hair and big black eyes. One soldier laid down his rifle to hold Baruch's hand and run around the tent with him.

"Those soldiers must miss their families," observed Chava in a low voice.

The men shared their canned army rations, which included juice, potatoes, and vegetables. Froim was especially happy to get another jacket.

The family bedded down in their allotted corner, once again feeling safer and warmer than they had in days.

In the morning, a soldier came in and vigorously woke everyone up. The soldiers in the tent were already gone and orders were being shouted to take the tent down. The Russian army was on the move and Duvid wanted to take his family in the other direction.

"We must go with him," said Duvid, standing by a soldier holding open the tent flap.

After they had quickly re-wrapped all of their rags, blankets, and frayed coats, the soldier guided them through the muddy ruts and onto a tall, empty truck. He was the driver.

"We're not going with the army?" asked Froim, as the truck sped off, leaving the troops behind.

The sun was coming up in front of them on the paved road, and for five hours, they bounced around the back of the truck, changing positions for comfort.

"Grab your things," said Duvid. When the road began to run parallel to some train tracks, he knew they were close to their destination. With screeching brakes, the truck stopped abruptly next to a shabby rural train station. The soldier helped his passengers off the truck and then hastily took off to catch up with his departed regiment.

The unnamed station had one large room with no facilities or information. Duvid's family walked inside and was greeted by the curious, silent stares of dozens of people sitting in small family groups, some elderly and others with children of various ages.

"*Di redst yidish?*" asked Duvid, as he roamed among the families, inquiring if anyone spoke Yiddish.

"*Ye,*" each family said, "*ikh bin a yid okhet.*" They were *all* Yiddish-speaking Jews. Fettered by exposure to the elements and fleeing for their lives, groups of Polish Jews had been brought to the same destination. That night, the wanderers fell asleep exchanging stories on the cold, cement floor, warmed by hearing their familiar language again.

* * * * *

"Everyone up!" yelled a Polish-speaking Russian soldier. "Get outside with your things." He continued to repeat the early-morning instructions as he walked through the rows of sleeping bodies. "Get in line and get on the train."

Baruch tried to nibble the red apple slice that a soldier had placed in his pocket, but he couldn't bite down with his new baby teeth. Leah used her teeth to bite off a chunk and give it to him, placing the remaining fragment back in his pocket for later.

"Where are we going?" asked Chava.

"You are all going somewhere permanent," said the soldier to the men, women, and children slowly struggling to rise to their feet.

"Up, up." Russian soldiers ordered everyone into lines near the tracks, separating single people from families.

Leah scrambled to her feet, picked up Baruch, and walked outside into a family line with Sam and Duvid. Her siblings had disappeared, leaving Leah wondering if she would ever see them again.

Amidst the chaos of hundreds of other refugees suddenly arriving on army trucks, Chava and Froim were put into different lines and corralled onto another train. Soldiers surrounded the station and area leading to the trains, where one soldier was assigned to open a door on each of the thirty boxcars at the same time.

Leah, Duvid, and their boys walked up and down alongside the train, calling out for Froim and Chava, until they were pushed into a boxcar.

"*Froim, Chava, bisti in der car?*" yelled Leah. "*Vo bisti?* Where are you?"

There was no response and she left, not knowing where her brother and sister had been taken. Leah continued to scream out their names into the crowd, while Duvid desperately tried to look out the cargo door and windows.

"There's no one left," said Duvid, "so they must just be on a different car."

Once the refugees had been pressed into the cattle cars by the dozens, no one could move. Round, metal bars covered the two sets of window openings that provided minimal ventilation. While there was a strong barn odor of fresh manure, people sat in their places on fresh hay, after covering the windows with blankets to stop the cold breeze.

Since they were in the front right corner of the cattle car, fortunate enough to be by a window, Duvid picked up Sam to look for Chava and Froim. The large door was slammed and locked. People were forced to squeeze onto the laps of others, painfully moaning to move a leg or shift a body position.

The soldiers did not force the loading with guns or dogs and people seemed relieved to be shipped to the East, away from the war front and Nazis.

"The guard at the door said we were going to a work camp," said Duvid, "to help with the Russian war effort."

Leah and Duvid were uneasy about the explanation and the mode of transportation, until they heard a commotion outside and saw the sudden arrival of another army truck.

Soldiers jumped out with bags of bread and buckets of apples, and began passing the food items through the window bars. It would be a very long train ride.

Several times a day, the train was sidetracked by the army and stood for hours in an open area. Often it went backwards and sat waiting for a military train with Russian flags to go by, carrying soldiers waving with their rifles, covered with blankets and crowded between cannons on four wheels.

Everyone grumbled when the train went backward, meaning there would be another delay. The sound of whistles warning and answering meant the trains carrying the Jews would be moved to the side. At brief station stops, the soldiers would allow a few men to come out and get bread and army rations for their boxcar load. People would gladly eat the condensed sardines by hand, right from the can. No one complained and the cans fit to be tossed out between the window bars.

Modesty was lost after a few days and buckets were used for bathroom needs. It was important that these be emptied and tossed out the last window to avoid splash-back.

When the train occasionally stopped at a rustic village station, the passengers would pound on the doors until the soldiers opened the doors and let people go outside. If there was time, a few people would be allowed out to go to the bathroom and only when they returned, could others go. It was a relay run to the bushes and if people didn't come back in time, often because they had been slowed down by the deep snow, they would be left behind. Soldiers from the next train then scooped up those who had been stranded.

When the passenger train was paused, attempts would be made to reunite with lost relatives.

"It's been several days," said Leah. "How long do we have to be on this train?"

Changing laps and occasionally peeking out a window were the only distractions for Baruch, but he had plenty of people who made funny faces and tried to keep him entertained. Occasionally, the train stopped to let out passengers who had been assigned to diverse work camps, but Leah, Duvid, and their boys remained sealed in the car.

"We're not prisoners," answered Duvid, "and they probably wouldn't shoot if anyone ran off, because there's nowhere to go in the snow."

None of the train's thirty boxcars had heat, but they were moving away from the Nazis and the Russian front, which was now in Poland. The combination of military movement and pushing refugees to the rear of the war felt as though something big was happening, but no one was talking.

"*Tshipitok, tshipitok,*" Duvid yelled out the barred window at a peasant for hot water while waiting at a station stop. If the station had a chimney, then it had a standing fire with hot water. When the train was stalled, Duvid tried to ask nearby Russians to bring something warm for the boys.

Day by day, the snow was getting deeper and the white powder-covered trees got closer to the track. When the train rattled around a curve, Duvid could look back and see deeper snow around the tracks.

On the fifth day of travel, the train stopped at a station covered to the roof with snow and surrounded by trees. A soldier slid open the one cargo door and arctic air rushed into the boxcar. The winters in Warsaw were harsh, but the cold air in Russia was brutally frozen and dry, making it difficult to breathe without coughing.

Sam gasped as his lungs burned and contracted.

"Keep your mouth covered," said Leah, "and breathe through the cloth."

She tightened Baruch's scarf over his nose and mouth.

"Get your things together," said the posted soldier. "You are all getting off."

Other soldiers helped everyone from the boxcar to exit into the snow banks. There were no steps and the snow was two to three meters high with a path cut through the piles that led to a wooden station. A long line of people from a few of the other cars had already formed in the channel leading to the building. There was no alternative direction.

Once in the station, people briefly huddled near the stove and were quickly pushed out the other door and into a line of waiting military trucks. Two escort soldiers rode in each truck.

Duvid and Leah sat on the floor with the boys in their laps, just to keep warm. The driver's door had the white stars of the military, and the dark green canvas cover displayed red flags with a black hammer and sickle.

The truck bumped along the snow-rutted road at breakneck speed, aiming for the dense forest ahead. Duvid and Leah held the boys down in their laps to avoid having them bounce into others or out the open tailgate. As the truck approached a narrow, one-lane wooden bridge, it slowed to a walking pace. The wood creaked loudly as the soldiers looked out the windows to center the ride on the bridge, which spanned a deep ravine between two tree-covered mountain peaks.

Once clear of the bridge, the truck accelerated and in the early afternoon, arrived at an area with snow-covered barracks.

"It's been a stone-cold winter here," said Duvid. "There are no icicles on the buildings."

Sam jumped off the back of the truck and disappeared into the path cut as a walkway through the snow. Duvid chased after him, but only tree tops and roofs were visible. When father and son returned to the truck to get Leah and Baruch, they received their barracks assignment from the posted soldier. The snow-walled path split off for each barracks and led to a side door with a snow-carved indentation for a door opening. The barracks were buried and the snow-filled tree canopy blocked the sky.

They had arrived in Siberia.

* * * * *

The Siberian wilderness itself was the barrier. With only one road, there was no need for guards, fences, or walls. The isolated labor camp had an open space for trucks unloading wood and gathering people. The understanding was clear for the workers and their families. In exchange for being fed and removed from the fighting, they helped the Russians fight the Nazis by working.

In Warsaw, Duvid and his family had seen photos of the alternative.

For privacy, the military barracks were divided into different sections by hanging used sheets. Each building had an open middle area with a cooking stove. All those at the work camp had an individual, wood-framed bed—no hay or dirt as a pillow.

"Aaahh!" said Sam. "It bit me!"

It was his first army bunk and Sam didn't realize that it collapsed if moved. When the bed pinched Sam's finger, Baruch was cautious about his bunk.

The camp had twenty wood-framed, wooden-floored barracks, each holding thirty families. The ceiling had extra beams to bear the weight of the snow. Early on, the children played and swung on the support poles, but they were harshly told not to do so; the adults were cautioned not to lean against the poles, for the guards said that when the roof collapses, it buries everyone inside.

"Sam," said Leah, "walk around and meet some of the other kids."

"Where are Chava and Froim?" asked Sam instead.

Their sudden absence was both painful and difficult to explain.

"We think they got off the train at a different camp," answered Leah. Sadness took energy and there was none to spare. "*Tateh* will find them."

The other children in the barracks were around Sam's age, but Baruch was the youngest. Leah and Duvid soon learned that most of the families in their barracks were Yiddish-speaking Jews from Poland, Hungary, and Romania. When a new family arrived, the men would gather in the evening.

Through the sheets, Sam could hear his father ask about what was happening in the ghetto. "*Vus gayt aros in droysn?*" asked Duvid. "What's happening outside?"

The tone was hushed, but people spoke openly about their experiences with the Gestapo, starvation, removal of children, and the deportation of Jews on trains to camps. There were rumors of an uprising, but it was difficult to get details. Leah and Duvid were grateful their boys were safe.

Adults worked seven days a week without breaks. A few refugees spoke Russian and acted as interpreters between the guards, foremen, and new refugees. Every morning, the workers were reminded to watch for bears, stay in groups, and always wear snowshoes.

The snow was typically four to seven meters deep with no easy way out of a suddenly opened snow pit. The men nodded, remembering what happened the day before when someone disappeared.

The guards' weapons were for dealing with bears and not forcing labor.

Duvid left with the other workers and followed the tractors into the woods, going farther and farther each day. After the workers had cut down a tree, they would spike the end to chains attached to hooks on a truck. The logs were dragged across the snow and back to the camp, where they would be piled, waiting to be trimmed by the women in camp. The foremen operated rip saws to slice through the long trees, turning them into stacks of boards.

Leah quickly learned how to operate one-half of a two-man crosscut saw, while other able women chopped off bark, branches, and end pieces to be used as fuel in the barracks stoves. It was important for the wood-burning stoves to have piles of wood nearby, where it could thaw and easily burn.

The stove was started each morning and provided the heat and cooking needs for the barracks. The fire died during the night and whoever woke up frozen first would re-start it. A pile of wood was always brought in for the night, and when it ran low, Sam got more frozen pieces of logs.

Great piles of split wood were stacked outside the barracks door, but it was plastered frozen from the wind and snow, and had to thaw on the cement stove platform before it would burn. A cement platform under the stove had enough ground clearance between the legs to dry the frozen logs.

In the evening, the workers returned encased in ice from head to toe with snow clinging to their beards, mustaches, eyebrows, and eyelids. Coats and boots were taken off by the door, including hats with ear flaps and visors that came down over the eyes. Their gloves had two layers and extended up over the mid-forearm. The icy apparel was hung across suspended ropes to dry by morning.

After marching all day in the Siberian tundra, Duvid needed help to pull off his frozen boots. The one-piece, military-style gulag boots had no laces and fit tightly to the knee.

"Push straight down," said Duvid. "The boots won't bend."

Sam pulled off his father's frozen boots by straddling the leg and yanking so hard that Duvid used his other leg to steady him.

Duvid's bright red face took time to thaw and return to a normal color. He laid his frozen military-issue gloves and hat near the stove to thaw through to the insignias.

"Where's Abe?" asked Leah. "Didn't he return with you?"

Duvid shook his head. When workers strayed from their work groups, getting lost in the woods or being attacked by bears was common. Sometimes, husbands and fathers did not return after an attack or had fallen through the snow. Little more was said about it.

Grief was shared among the inhabitants of the barracks, but that didn't stop the work. Even elderly grandparents who stayed behind in the barracks tended the stove, read to the children, and made sure they didn't wander off without snowshoes. It was difficult to read, since other than the dim light of a fire in the stove, there was only one candle for light.

The camp had a central kitchen, and when supplies were brought in and distributed to the barracks, the elderly received and stored the items for the families. The basics were abundant, but limited to bread and sturdy vegetables like potatoes, turnips, carrots, and beets.

While Leah was gone, Sam had the very important task of caring for Baruch inside the barracks. Two slightly younger boys in their barracks spoke Yiddish, Eliezer and Nate, but there was no time to play with them and watch out for Baruch. Sam knew he was now like Chava and had to use his imagination.

One day, he remembered he had Froim's knife. "You know how to use it," Duvid had warned him, "but don't let the other kids touch it."

Sam picked up some small branches and began making sticks for swords and cutting small pieces to build houses. The other boys disappeared at night with their sticks to their family area, returning each day for a quick sword fight. It killed time and Leah was glad that no one had cuts.

While Leah was outside cutting logs in the clear area, all of the boys bundled up and made snowmen with sticks for features and sledded with boards. There was no shortage of snow fights, but everything outside was biting cold and brief.

"Be careful, Sam," said Leah, yelling across the open work yard, "it's too high to get down. One of you boys is going to get hurt."

With the fear of falling off the tall snow piles, they moved to the smaller snow hills on top of wood piles. The other barracks weren't directly connected by carved pathways, but Sam could see smoke rising from smoke stacks.

With the typical curiosity of a nine-year-old boy, Sam wanted to know more about his neighbors. He remembered his ghetto talent and began tunneling to some of the other barracks when Leah returned. It took a few days and ended with a surprise pounding knock at a shuttered window.

Since most of the children's time was spent inside, Sam wished that he could cut paper figures for Baruch, but materials were scarce. With a partial deck of cards, Sam wanted to teach him basic numbers.

"Baruch," asked Sam, "*Vuser numers kensti zeyn oys*? Which numbers do you recognize?"

Baruch stared at the dots on the card and followed Sam's pointing finger. "*Ans, tsvay, dra, ...* One, two, three, ... "

Sam held Baruch's finger and patiently had his younger brother repeat the pattern until he could eventually say his numbers properly. There was plenty of time to learn.

The women were outside all day, cutting branches from trees so they could be sent into a planer to make boards. Sam anxiously waited for Leah to return for lunch and to show how he was trying to teach like Chava. Leah was proud that Sam remembered that lesson from the ghetto and not something from the street.

The women came back before the men returned and began to prepare dinner, which most usually consisted of boiled vegetables and soup, rarely meat. While bread was available at every meal, it was harder than a frozen rock.

"Are the Germans still chasing us?" asked Sam one evening when they sat down to eat their meager dinner.

The honest question stunned Leah and caused Duvid to make a 'sshh' gesture with his finger. The sheet walls did not separate conversation in the barracks.

"The Russian army and Siberia are in the way," answered Duvid. "The soldiers are at the Front and we are supplying them with fuel and wood for roads and bridges." He said it loud enough for anyone to hear. "We will only be here until the war with the Germans is done and then we can return home."

There was no timetable, but it sounded hopeful for anyone who might be listening.

* * * * *

SPRING 1942

The arrival of spring meant that the snow level was slowly dropping on the buildings and trees, although it would be mid-summer before the ground was clear of winter, exposing high grass and weeds.

Slush took over the camp grounds. Logs had to be placed on the paths so people didn't sink deep into the mud. The more passable roads brought in more trucks, equipment, and noise, overtaking the expanded open yard.

"As the days get longer, we will start earlier," said Serge, "and finish later."

The face of the logging crew foreman had probably never seen a razor. His light brown beard, sideburns, and mustache combined to form a small shrub on his face, filling in any open gaps between his scarf, coat, and hat flaps. Everything was covered except his eyes.

Serge was slightly taller than Duvid and wore a long, heavy, gray coat, even when inside the barracks. Serge never hollered or wildly waved his arms, but spoke firmly.

"With the snow melting," he continued, "we will cut lower toward the base and have more wood for the women to clear for the saws."

With the sun setting later and orders to get as much wood out before winter returned, the men worked ten to twelve hours each day.

There was grumbling about a later dinner, but no arguments.

"Bears are coming out of the woods for food, so don't wander," they were told repeatedly.

"Good shot yesterday," said Duvid, referring to a threatening bear that wandered into their logging work area.

"And if you find anyone we lost in winter," said Serge, "wrap them up and take them out."

Spring in Siberia was like the end of winter anywhere else. Sam was allowed to be outside most of the day with Baruch and their friends, playing with their sword sticks and kicking cans.

When the men returned at the end of the work day, Serge started a wet snowball fight with the boys and fled for cover into the barracks with Duvid.

"It's Friday," said Serge, "and I have something for you."

Duvid looked at Leah with a curious grin. Serge rummaged into a bag and pulled out cans of candles with two wicks in animal fat, and handed them out to the women.

These would be the first Schabes candles lit by Leah since their apartment in Warsaw.

Duvid walked to the door and yelled outside.

"Sam," said Duvid, *"kim aheyr in m'vet untsindn di likhtelekh."*

Sam and Baruch ran to the door with their muddy and snow- soaked boots. They stared at the can resting on an upturned crate for a table, and his parents standing nearby holding a twig lit from the stove. As others lit their wicks and said the blessing, glowing flames could be seen through the sheets throughout the barracks.

Duvid said another prayer over a scrap of bread and Sam repeated the words.

"Efsher eyn mul," continued Duvid. *"Ven dus, di krig, et zikh endikn, et men kenen gayn tsi Erets Yisroyl."*

There was no wine and its prayer would have to be saved for a better time, maybe in the land of Israel. "We are Jews, even here."

Through the sheet, Sam could hear the anxious voices of two new workers being settled in their barracks and talking about the war, Germany, Jews, and concentration camps. In moments, though, Sam fell asleep, safe and dreaming of tasting anything that had not been boiled, and maybe sweet.

July 22, 1942
The Deportations of Warsaw Jews to Treblinka
Concentration Camp begin.

It seemed that the ground had just begun to thaw when the snow started in early November, threatening another harsh winter.

"Duvid," said Serge, "we need to talk tonight."

He came back after sunset and after twenty minutes of quiet conversation by the stove, Duvid walked back to Leah.

"We have to leave," said Duvid. "Maybe tomorrow, so get ready tonight."

"*Vi gayt men?*" asked Leah, wondering about the destination, but not surprised by the sudden news.

"*Zey hobn nokh nit gezugt vi m'et gayn,*" answered Duvid. "*Ober m'gayt avek.*" While Serge couldn't say where they would be taken, the departure was tomorrow. Two other families with children received the same orders to leave the work camp before winter returned.

"We shouldn't have been here in the first place," said Leah, "but it was safe." Leah grabbed the double-wicked candle and put it in her bag.

"Children and old people must leave," said Duvid, "to make more space for working adults. Let's pack what we can carry, and wash up the boys before we go."

They were not told where they were going in the half-empty truck, carrying the few families and their duffle bags. Baruch was now almost three years old and walked to the truck carrying his bag of clothes and holding Sam's hand. As they passed a group of posted soldiers, Baruch pointed and started grinning and counted the men. The soldier who was driving the truck reached into his side bag, handed a cookie to Baruch, and plopped his large, bushy hat on the toddler's head for fun

Duvid helped Leah and the boys onto the war-torn military truck and sat them down next to a soldier, who was also perching on the hard, wooden bench in the back. Baruch pointed up at the big hat with the red star on the flip-up flap. Duvid shook his head "no."

The truck rumbled off on the snow-covered roads, as small white tornados of flakes were whipped up by a fierce wind. The day-long trip bought the travelers to a large city train station, where the station master gave Duvid papers releasing his family to move about the country, along with some money.

Duvid asked for a pencil and paper to write the details for connecting with people, locations, and follow-up directions. After the routes were explained to Duvid, he was told to get his family on the approaching train.

"Don't stare at people," admonished Leah, for Sam had never seen a train station with glass windows and filled with people dressed in normal clothing. While there were a few workers and refugees in the crowd, the women carried purses and the men were dressed in business suits. They were civilians.

The daily commuter train had wooden bench seats and connected to another train and then another, which took them cross country.

"Where does this train go?" asked Leah, after waiting in stations and traveling for a couple of days and watching the snow diminish.

"A safe place for Jews," answered Duvid.

From incoming workers at the labor camp, he had heard what was happening to Jews in the West. It was a Warsaw trait to be around other Jews, openly pray, and exchange information. He yearned to return to Poland, but he knew that there was only death for Jews within the reach of the Nazis. Duvid's family could only move West if they stayed well behind the Front.

"We still have one more train to meet," said Duvid, looking out the window at the setting sun. Baruch sat on Leah's lap to look out the window at the farms and the animals. The next row of seats was empty and Sam had room to lie down for a nap as the train moved past small homes and crossed over bridges.

In the early evening, the conductor walked the aisle and tapped Duvid, telling him to exit at the next stop. They were the only people to get off at the small, empty station, and told to wait there for someone.

* * * * *

A farmer walked into the cold, empty station room, wearing overalls, a wide hat, and work boots. Fortunately, Duvid had learned enough Russian in the work camp. The farmer approached and spoke to Duvid, and they both started waving for Leah and the boys to load their belongings into his open, private, pick-up truck.

Leah and Baruch sat inside the cab, while Duvid and Sam hunkered down in the open back, huddled between boxes to shield them from the windy chill.

After an hour of bumping along the rutted road, the truck pulled up to a tall mud hut, held together with a wood frame. That was it. Inside was straw for beds. The hut stood at the edge of the farmer's property and had been built for summer migrant workers, who were gone for the winter.

Duvid's family only needed the shack for a few weeks and learned how to keep it warm by tossing dried manure in the center fire pit. During the day, Baruch joined Sam for the job of picking up manure dropped by the cows and horses, and then throw it hard against a barn wall, flattened to dry.

The dried chunks burned easily, and Sam noted that horse manure was best, since the grass they ate did not get as digested as that of the cows. Collecting manure turned into a game for the boys. Leah retrieved water at the farmer's building, so they could wash their hands and Duvid would bring back more buckets of water at night for washing later and in the morning.

To pass the day, Sam also kicked stones with Baruch, who would often swing a leg and fall. Sam was patient, but frustrated by not being able to play with any kids his age. Almost ten, Sam's other responsibility was to keep the fire in the hut going, so the refuge was warm at the end of the day and hot water would be ready to toss in peas or beans for dinner.

Each morning, Duvid and Leah walked to the farm house a half kilometer away. They worked for cash and to pay for the shack and food. Leah helped with the cooking and cleaning for fifteen winter farmhands, while Duvid joined the Russian workers by walking and feeding the cows and horses.

Baruch cried when Leah left for the day, but he stopped when bribed with the bread and honey that she brought back from the previous day.

In those early days of 1943, winter had turned the fields into a flat wasteland. Duvid was paid for their work in Russian rubles, but wanted to go southwest to a city to escape another winter. Sam noticed that his parents were packing again and knew they would be leaving the next morning.

They all jumped back into the farmer's truck and drove a couple of hours southward to a river lined with barges. Duvid was reading his notes for contacts and direction.

"We're going with them," said Duvid, pointing at a long, beat-up barge made of tied logs with a mounted engine in back. The logs were wrapped with rope and roughly covered with oil-stained flat boards.

"Do not talk," he continued. "They're Cossacks and don't like Jews." The barge crew consisted of two men wearing turbans and wrap-around clothes with brown pants tucked into black, polished leather boots. Fur lined their hats and coat collars, while smoke always seemed to be coming out of their mouths.

Duvid had been told to travel the back rivers to be unnoticed, and that these men would do it without questions. The barge's flat boards were totally open, separated into six small cabins by suspended canvas sheets. The stocky, weathered men used poles to steer the barge away from the shallow river banks. The ride was slow and Baruch pointed at the farms with occasional horses and buggies.

There were no roads close to water and Duvid was pleased that they were far enough south in January that the river didn't freeze. They stayed on board for two nights and were let off on the outskirts of Zhambyl in Kazakhstan, where they were able to avoid the local police.

Their travel papers had ended with the train ride.

"Let's split up," said Duvid, "so we don't look like a group or family until we get into town."

Sam went with Duvid and Leah followed at a distance with Baruch, always walking two by two. They reunited when they entered the bustling open market.

"Don't talk and no eye contact." Duvid spoke enough Russian to get information and everyone was carrying something to sell in a market, so they fit in.

"Save the work money for rent," said Leah, "and see what the boys get."

Sam took Baruch's hand and walked to the bread and fruit carts. They had no difficulty looking hungry and vendors were fast to give them food, sometimes having their children give it to Sam. As they walked the fringe of the market and continued to receive food, their pockets quickly filled and were unloaded in Leah's bag.

"I don't like this," said Leah, "but we need food until you find work."

"Hopefully in a couple days," said Duvid.

The boys quickly turned their wanderings into another game and went around to another market entrance and started again. Leah was stunned by the generosity of the Russian market vendors and didn't know if they gave from the heart or to get the boys to move along.

She rationed the collected food for several days, saving a bit for later.

One of the barge crew had directed Duvid to a room for rent. He was shown an empty section of a house that hadn't been shelled. It was on the edge of town, requiring a thirty-minute, hitchhiked ride to the market.

The space was the size of a large garage, but had electricity when the village power was functioning, and an outhouse. Duvid rummaged the rubble and curb debris for a table and chairs, along with straw-filled mattresses.

* * * * *

"Is this meeting safe?" asked Leah. "You won't get arrested?"

"We can't trust anyone, especially if they find out we're Jewish," answered Duvid, "but the boat crew recommended him for documents and work."

Without proper identification papers, Duvid was at risk of being detained, deported, or imprisoned. Using forged documents, Duvid was immediately able to get a job in a Russian military factory, making boots and shoes for the army.

The job alone didn't pay enough for his family to survive, so Leah explored trading in the market, which would require moving closer into town.

"Whether we beg or take from thieves," said Duvid, "we need to survive the day until money comes in from the factory job."

The market was tough and selling was filled with cheating and strong-arm tactics from the other vendors. There were no regrets, since it was stealing from those who had stolen from others. With the government desperately fighting the Nazis, people were on their own to live moment to moment, like fighting for air. It could all end in a blink of the eye and there was no one to trust.

For safety's sake, Duvid, Leah, and the boys moved three times during the year. Duvid's goal was to move West with the Front and get to the Americans. Once under the auspices of the Americans, he would be able to figure out how to get to Palestine. He had heard from his parents that this was the only place safe for Jews.

While Duvid had always done his best to keep the end in sight, he knew enough to tackle one move at a time and keep going behind the war. From town to town, their ragged belongings were quickly worn out or outgrown and replaced with bottom-traded items from the local market.

Through it all, Sam always brought Froim's carving knife, safely tucking it into one of the bundles hanging over his shoulder.

SUMMER 1943

In the light of a late summer night, Sam went outside to meet a neighbor Arab boy and play soccer with a ball made of rags. They didn't speak a mutual language, but they could kick together and only paused when they heard the rumbling of trucks.

The residents of the neighborhood watched as a Russian military convoy went through the main streets, followed by rows of troops walking with rifles on their shoulders. The boys waited and watched them march toward the Front. Kids didn't play war games, instead tossing the ball back in play.

The Gingold family decided to stay in Zhambyl for another winter.

* * * * *

"You must be careful," said Duvid, "and watch the weights and measures."

He handed Leah the second-hand scale, which he had gotten by trading for some army surplus boots.

"It's difficult to cheat the cheaters," said Leah, who had started to trade fabric and vegetables.

"The crowd can be dangerous," said Duvid, "and if there is trouble, Sam, grab Baruch's hand and run away. Don't get caught by the police."

Wherever they started the day in the market, a direction and spot to meet was established.

"Leave everything and run for your life," said Leah, "and we'll meet you."

They all knew what would happen if they left their stall unattended, but the safety of the boys was vital.

"Our things would disappear," said Duvid, "and be for sale on the next table."

He chuckled at the lack of honesty in these markets, recalling it was called "black" because of the shadowy dealings. Here, the police were regularly bribed and most traded illegal goods for money under the table.

Leah scouted out a position for her cart at the edge of the market. Her table was a combination of wooden crates, a board with a scale, graced by her non-threatening smile. She didn't grow the produce, but purchased it from outlying farms. It was extra work to bring it to the village market, where there was much competition, so Leah secured an outer position in the labyrinth of stalls, where people pass by, not wishing to enter the maze. Her table offered some fruits and vegetables resting in egg-shaped woven baskets.

Customers might pay a little more to purchase items right away, compared to the lesser prices inside, but Leah knew how to get the sale first. Leah's extra hustle to make early sales, combined with Duvid's factory pay, still didn't cover expenses for their family.

They had known starvation and didn't want to go back to it with the boys. With the inflated war-time prices in communist Russia, it seemed that everyone needed to do something on the side to add to any regular pay. Another shadow.

When Duvid was asked to front for the black market at the factory and pass cloth and shoes for Leah to sell in the market, he reluctantly agreed. It wasn't a choice. The army shoes with black laces were seconds and would not pass army requirements, while the extra rolls of dark green material were for non-military clothing controlled by the government. If Duvid didn't arrange to move the products, then someone else would or the government would destroy it.

When women customers slowed down to look at Leah's produce, she whispered without making eye contact. "Are you looking for some cloth?" She kept the fabric hidden and most people were too cautious, walking away without responding.

When there was serious interest, Leah would pull out a roll of cloth from under the table, negotiate the price in meters, and quickly measure by holding the material from her nose to the end of her hand. Her diminutive size was an advantage in calculating the distance. The purchased shoes or cloth disappeared into the person's shirt or bag, since they were not supposed to possess any such items.

SPRING 1944

Duvid and the boys were finishing the weekly delivery of army cloth and shoes to stash under Leah's cart when a silent tension rolled through the aisles. Suddenly, vendors disappeared behind their carts and the customers vanished.

Two men came from different directions and fit in with the market crowd, except they had guns under their jackets. There was a simultaneous ruffle of coats, the gleam of pistols, and Duvid was gone. They each grabbed one of his arms and twisted it backward, while Duvid struggled to loosen their grip.

He was tall and strong enough to fight off the strong-arm arrest, but when he felt a gun pressed into his ribs, he relented and was quickly pulled away. It was difficult to know who these plain-clothes police were working for and whether he had been ratted out as a fall guy by competing black marketers.

The vendors knew the routine of the secret police and when the dirt kicked up from the scuffle had settled, they had unflinchingly stood by their wares. Leah couldn't scream and risk being taken away too, leaving the boys parentless.

Leah swallowed her devastated shock and while she was distracted asking nearby traders for help, her merchandise and scale disappeared. The shoes and rolls of cloth were confiscated by the police and her crates were kicked over.

From the corner of her eye, she saw the boys waiting in the distance and then disappearing into the crowd to avoid a connection. From the edge of the market, Sam and Baruch saw their father taken, and remembered to run to the agreed safety spot at the bus stop.

Moments later, when Leah approached them alone, they knew it was real and that they would walk home without their father. She took a sleeve corner of her olive-drab blouse and dabbed at her eyes.

"By myself with two boys?" Leah said, dazed and muttering to herself. When Leah reached out for Sam and Baruch's hands, Sam led them away from the market for the three-mile walk home. She wasn't sure what Baruch had seen and understood, but he was quiet and kept looking at his mother.

Sam thought of his father's plans for a Bar Mitzvah after his thirteenth birthday. Approaching the age of twelve, Sam was now the man of the house without the ceremony.

"*Tateh*?" Sam asked. Leah glanced at him without cutting in on the private thought. He didn't want anything if his father was gone. Sam kicked at the dirt road, struggling to remember one of the last times they enjoyed a moment together.

Before the war, Duvid had taken Sam on the streetcar through the bright Warsaw city lights to see a performance at the Jewish Theatre. "Don't speak out loud until we get to the theater," Duvid had said.

Leah had helped them both dress up to fit into the city bustle without being identified as Jews. Duvid had a white shirt, tie, suit jacket, and a flat, leather hat. Sam had worn a borrowed jacket and Duvid polished his black shoes to match his own pair. Duvid volunteered as stage crew at the large performance hall, and had friends who would allow him to sneak in with Sam. Father and son would be able to sit on the floor near the stage and the live orchestra.

When they arrived at their appointed spot, Duvid told Sam to sit down. It was on a step, but the seat was next to the performers. Duvid knew that the view would be a lifetime experience for his son, and he sat on the floor next to him.

That night, the hall had been packed as Molly Picon took the stage. She had been working in the area making a movie and came by the theatre with her troop to sing Yiddish songs. "Yankle mit a Fiddle" was her first number and Sam was in awe of the performance. During a break from singing, another performer walked onto the stage holding a long cane, wearing a straw hat and wide smile.

Sam wasn't familiar with Maurice Chevalier, but was enthralled by his rendition of "Yiddishe Mama." Molly returned to the stage to thunderous applause, and sang "Ikh hob dikh tsufil lib, nisht a klayne zakh." (I Love You Much Too Much; It's Not a Little Thing). *At the end of the performance, Duvid and Sam smiled at Molly. She exited the stage and turned to smile back at both of them.*

Sam now feared that his father was just a memory, too, like that 1938 moment.

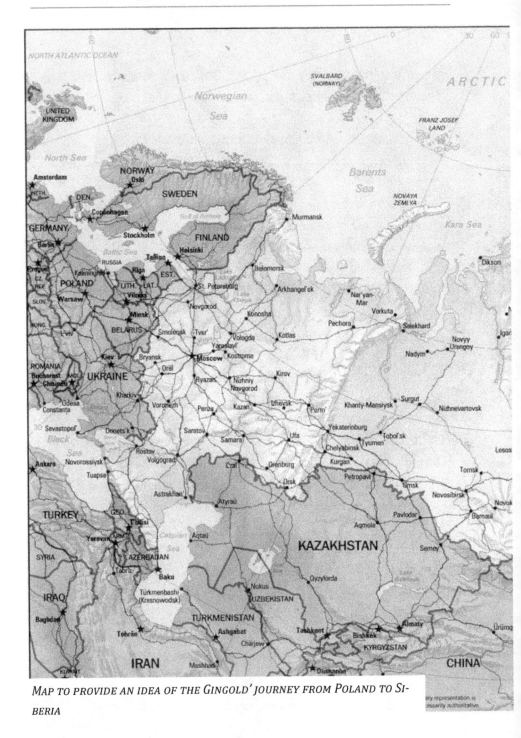

MAP TO PROVIDE AN IDEA OF THE GINGOLD' JOURNEY FROM POLAND TO SIBERIA

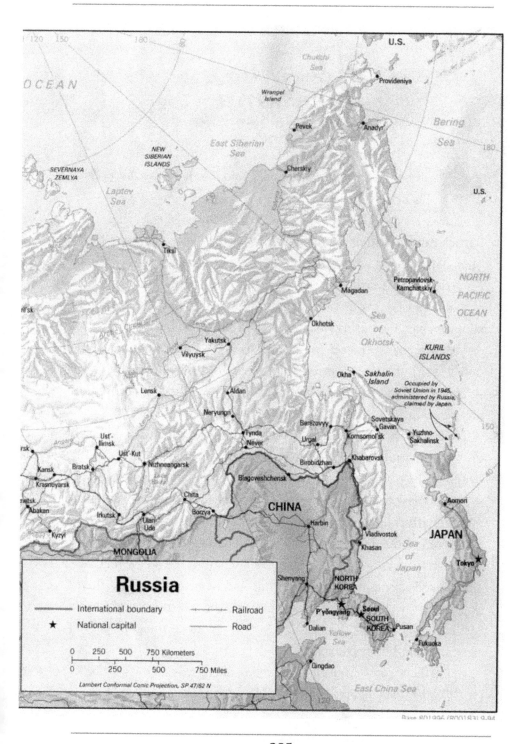

CHAPTER EIGHT

THE SWITCH

"I'll be back before dinner," said Leah. "Stay here with Baruch."

"Where are you going?" asked Sam. "We'll come, too." Baruch ran to Leah and started to cry, clutching his mother's thigh. Their father hadn't returned by morning and no one talked about his arrest in the market.

Leah paced around the room talking to herself, trying to suppress gasping outbreaks of tears in front of the boys.

"We've got to find out where he is," said Leah. "I'm going to the police station." She was afraid to ask the authorities for any information and risk being picked up, too, but feared Duvid's absence more.

Leaving Sam in charge of Baruch, she walked outside and crossed the muddy road to the pump, returning with water for the evening. She placed the bucket on the table and left for the station.

Sam knew there was no time for soccer in the remaining warm summer afternoon. He never thought too much about their current two-room home, but everything reminded Sam of his father. From the beaten-up table and chairs in the kitchen to the straw mattress that poked all night, everything that had been obtained by Duvid was suddenly special. It was easy to make the mattress comfortable by flattening the straw stuffing, but he couldn't imagine getting used to his father's absence.

Like the weather, nothing seemed to change.

"*Tateh?*" asked Sam, as he heard the door open.

Leah was alone. "No one could find him in any records," said Leah. "It was like they didn't take him."

Sam was bewildered. *How could his tateh be lost?*

"I will go back in the morning," continued Leah, "and find someone in charge."

For several days thereafter, Leah went to the station every morning, demanding information about her husband. When officials finally admitted to Duvid's detention, they told her that he had already been sent to an unspecified communist prison to await a trial date. The court's backlog was bottomless and stagnant.

"You didn't pay them off?" asked Natan, a Jewish refugee from Romania who had traveled on the train to Zhambyl with Duvid and his family. Natan lived in a neighboring building with his wife and three teenage children, two boys and a girl. "They're all crooks and you just have to pay the ones in charge."

Natan spoke in Yiddish and was as tall as Duvid, but much thinner. Before the war, Natan had been a government employee. Through the grapevine, he had heard about Duvid's arrest and stopped by one afternoon to share his knowledge with Leah and Sam about how courts operated in Russia.

"They may have taken the shoes and cloth rolls as evidence against him," continued Natan, "but when they sell it for themselves and the evidence disappears before trial, they should turn him out."

"They don't have a trial date," said Leah, "and they won't say where the prison is located."

"*Tateh* is in prison?" asked Sam.

Hearing his father's name, Baruch perked up while sitting at the kitchen table, but didn't understand the details. "*Tateh?*" said Baruch. He looked at the door and repeated the call for his father.

"When they can't get any more out of him and the evidence disappears," said Natan, "they might let him go."

Leah looked at Sam and Baruch, who were waiting patiently for any dinner. "We need a different spot to sell our things," said Leah, "but I need to sell in the market again or we starve."

Early the next morning, Leah trudged to a nearby farm with the boys to get produce for the market. Leah found a different spot on the edge of the market and a hundred meters away from other food vendors. With used crates and a borrowed scale that had to be returned every day, Leah set up her fruit and vegetable table.

It took several months for her vendor neighbors to sympathize with Leah and understand that she wasn't a threat to their sales. To break up the daily boredom, they enjoyed watching Baruch run through the aisles.

SEPTEMBER, 1944

"In a week, we're moving to Tashkent," Rayna, Natan's wife, told Leah one afternoon. "You all can join us."

Leah was wondering why they both wanted to talk to her that night, and she thought that Duvid would approve of their being near another Jewish family.

"We've talked it over," continued Natan. "You can't be alone with two kids, so come with us."

"Let me think about it," said Leah, "and I'll tell you when I get back from the market tomorrow." She knew that Duvid could find them if she left word with neighbors. What was the point of staying if they might not survive?

Leah bounced her thinking off of Sam to see if he had a gut reaction to the offer, and any sense of his father's timing. "Sam," asked Leah, "*vus kleyrsti?*"

She wanted her older son to have an opinion about leaving with Natan's family. Since she didn't know where his father was imprisoned, there was good reason to keep going West.

After much deliberation, Leah told Rayna that the Gingolds would go with their family if they could wait a few weeks. She wanted to try and get word of the move to Duvid and earn a little more money from the market. The home possessions would be abandoned as they had found them, pieces of life for the next family.

Both families agreed on the morning to meet at the train station to catch the noon train. Rayna and Nathan were already there with their two older boys and young teenage girl, surrounded by their bags. Leah proudly counted out money for her share of the tickets and Natan took it to the counter to purchase seats for everyone.

"Everything is taken care of," said Natan, "except they just canceled today's train." Leah's stomach dropped as she looked at Sam and Baruch, who were both eager to begin the journey to Tashkent.

The two families sat on the cement floor in the corner of the station, near other families who appeared to have been sleeping there from the prior night. It would take a couple of days to work the unreliable connections, but there was no other safe option for either family.

The war continued to rage on.

* * * * *

"Is this all ours?" asked Sam, looking around their new quarters.

"No," answered Leah, "we get the unit on one side, and that's enough for us." Although their place seemed larger than the prior residence, it felt emptier.

Leah had agreed to split the cost of renting a two-residence cement-block house, which had been painted a dark gray, with Natan's family. The units had a kitchen with two rooms, each with beds and a dresser. There was hot water in the kitchen, a stark improvement. The space was inexpensive, since it was outside of town and required hitching a ride into the village and the market.

To help cover the cost, Natan rented out the two unused spaces in the garage.

Another improvement to their living situation was new neighborhood friends for Sam. Twelve-year-old Sam first noticed Sarah, an older girl who was tall and thin. She always had a smile and a wink for him, laughing at things that only she thought was funny. She liked to wear a white shirt with a collar sticking up and a long scarf, while watching the boys play soccer in the street.

Leah took Baruch with her to the market and cautioned Sam to only play with the other kids from the area, avoiding transient strangers looking for shelter or money. The war had produced desperate refugees.

One of the neighborhood boys was a Russian teenager, Arkin, who had come from a distant farm. As the work on his family's farm slowed for winter, his parents were glad to let him go to the edge of the city and play soccer with other boys. Arkin was instantly accepted, since he had a soccer ball with air inside. An early winter snow didn't bother Sam or stop anyone from playing soccer.

Arkin also brought his German Shepherd, named Igor, who pulled a sled across the flat, open, snow-covered fields. Two boys could fit on the sled and when Igor saw a chicken or rabbit to chase, the sled would fly across the frozen surface, often getting wrapped around a tree.

When Baruch came home from the market, there was room for him to squeeze in between the boys on the sled and hold on for impact. Igor thought he was one of the boys and joined in the soccer game. Arkin brought stuff on the sled that his parents thought Leah could use or trade in the market. Whether it was cream cheese in a kettle, outgrown jackets, or random clothes, Leah could sell anything.

As winter deepened and the snow increased, Arkin brought steel-rod hooks for all of the boys. With the meat hooks in hand, they learned how to chase and clasp a truck bumper, sliding into town on the snow. Since the roads were never plowed and packed down quickly, it was a fast ride.

One day, neither Igor nor Arkin appeared. A week went by without seeing Arkin and realizing that no one knew the exact location of his family farm, they couldn't check on him. Sarah came every day, asking if anyone had seen him, but he wasn't there. Then one frigid morning, Sam and the boys were having a snowball fight and in the distance, they could see Arkin slowly walking with Igor.

Sam and his friends ran to catch up to Arkin, calling his name. "Where have you been?" asked Sam.

"We haven't seen you for a while," said Sarah.

"I had to take care of Igor," answered Arkin. "Igor's a she and had five puppies."

Jaws dropped and everyone stared at Igor. Arkin explained, "I couldn't leave her until she could walk."

Baruch's plea for a puppy went into the night, but Leah continued to say no.

"I'm glad Arkin is back," said Leah, "but we won't be here too much longer, so the puppies have to stay with their mother."

Even with all of his adult experiences, Sam realized there was still a lot to learn about life, but neither he nor his brother was prepared for the next twist.

* * * * *

NOVEMBER 1944

There was an early-morning knock on the front door. The cold night had frosted the metal handle and it was too cold to wing the door open before knowing who was pounding.

"*Dus iz a mentsh ba deyr tir,*" said Sam. He could see out the angled corner of the front window that there was a big man at the door, who continued to knock.

"Ma!" Sam called, not wanting to let in a stranger.

Wrapped in a blanket, Leah came running toward the door as the morning sun lit the man's face.

"*Deyr tate'z gekimen!*" said Sam. "It's *Tateh!*"

"*Tateh?*" asked Baruch, looking at his brother.

Leah whipped the door open and then crashed into Duvid with a crying hug, embracing lost time. Sam and Baruch couldn't believe their morning eyes and joined in a clenched hold on their father's legs.

"I found you," said Duvid. Standing outside the door, they didn't recognize him with longer hair and a full beard, but it was him. His face was drawn and his drooping, ragged clothes smelled of rot. They were the same clothes he had on when he was taken six months earlier. Duvid hadn't seen the light of day since then, and struggled to stand and hold his family. His appearance reminded Leah of when they left Warsaw, and it was a great relief to see him.

"Thank God you're here," said Leah, tears still streaming down her face, while she took out some food left over from yesterday's market. They never talked more than that morning and when word got out that Duvid had returned, Natan gladly offered him some of his clothes so that Duvid could burn his jailhouse rags.

Sam and Baruch wouldn't leave their father's side, as he explained his return. "After holding me all of these months," said Duvid, "they couldn't find documents of why I was there." Duvid knew it was about the black market's sale of illegal military items, but with no evidence, it made no sense. There were a lot of jailed people in one room for the hearing day.

"I took up jail space," continued Duvid, "and without any documents or evidence, the judge told me to go back to my family."

"How did you find us?" asked Sam.

"They moved me to two different prisons," answered Duvid, "so I had to retrace your move and ask our old neighbors back in Zhambyl."

Duvid didn't want to go back to selling at the market, so the next day, he began to look for winter work with farm animals, since the cold didn't bother him.

SPRING 1945

"There's news," said Duvid. After a shortened day of work on May 8th, Duvid burst into the house with a large smile and a Russian newspaper under his arm. Celebrations had broken out in the streets at the announcement of Hitler's death and Germany's surrender. "This changes everything for us."

All night long, the Russians fired guns and blasted cannons in celebration. The streets were filled with soldiers hanging out of parading infantry trucks, yelling and waving Russian flags. The drinking lasted all night.

"When things settle down," said Duvid, "maybe we can go home to Poland or travel to Palestine." He was certain that they should leave Russia as soon as the armies stopped moving and returned home.

Stalin had made a public decree that with documentation, all displaced people could go back to the place of their origin. When he heard that the British were letting in some Jews, Duvid figured that they must get out of Russian control.

Rumors were flying and unfortunately, returning to Poland was not an option, since refugees and returning troops said all Polish Jews were dead and the cities leveled. It was unimaginable, but repeated over and over again with no evidence to the contrary. All reports were that Jews were dead everywhere.

Leah and Duvid continued to talk late into the evenings about what they should do. They couldn't move backward, but couldn't ignore the information and news stories pouring out about extermi-nated Jews.

Leah gasped at recalling the photos she had received in the ghetto.

"We couldn't force them to come with us," said Duvid. "Remember, we tried to convince them."

Leah wanted to go back to Warsaw and see if her parents survived.

"I should have stayed with them," said Leah.

"No," said Duvid, "you had just had a baby. We also got Sam, Froim, and Chava out. It was the right decision."

Leah cried, "We can pray that we'll see them again."

On a scrap of paper salvaged from the market, Duvid drew a rough map of Germany and Poland, pointing to a destination city that would get them closer to the Americans in Berlin.

"Tell Arkin to bring his wagon," said Leah to Sam. "We want to give his parents some things we can't take with us."

"Where are we going?" asked Sam, who had stopped cutting wooden shapes for Baruch.

"Your father has a town picked out for us," answered Leah. She couldn't share any information regarding the plan to leave Russia.

"We're leaving in a couple of days, so ask Arkin to bring his wagon and you and Baruch can help him load things."

Everything from a child's chair to carved sticks made with Froim's knife, along with furniture his parents accepted, filled Arkin's wagon over several days of moving loads. It felt fair to Leah, especially considering all of the items and food given by his family.

For the first time in a long time, Sam had friends like Arkin and Sarah, and he found a way to say goodbye.

"I'm going to miss watching you play soccer," said Sarah.

"Who am I going to pass to?" asked Arkin.

"Just don't hold onto the ball too long," answered Sam, "and take more shots."

* * * * *

The Gingold family quietly moved with little more than the clothes on their backs and some food tucked away for the trip. To Baruch's disappointment, their move did not include a full-grown German Shepherd puppy.

Duvid was very confident about the direction he was told to follow—a northern route toward Szcaecin, Poland, which was controlled by the Russians. Its proximity to Warsaw helped keep the dream alive that relatives might have survived the war. The reality was that Szcaecin was on the border with Germany and not far from Berlin, which had been split up into four zones by the Allies.

When he received departure papers, established by Stalin's order, Duvid put down Szcaecin as the Gingold's original home. When the document was stamped by the local Russian officials, they were free to leave Tashkent.

"As Jews, we may never be welcome to work or stay anywhere," said Duvid. "We just need to keep moving to the Americans in Berlin."

"I've packed all the food left from the market yesterday," said Leah.

Without money for train tickets and having to cross thousands of kilometers of war-torn countries, it would take months to reach their destination. It was critical that they get out of Russia before the borders were closed again.

After several days of hitching rides from passing trucks, one of the first stops was in a high mountain town in Uzbekistan. That very evening, the town began to flood from the annual mountain snow melt, and Duvid and Leah had to guide the boys to climb a ladder onto the roof of an A-frame building. They stayed overnight on the flattest part of the roof, because the raging flood waters were clearing out the town, pulling along furniture, tables, mattresses, and people. With a constant "*ssshhhhh*" roar, everything was picked up and taken away, leaving a stripped streetscape.

"Everyone has different problems," said Duvid, "and when the streets open tomorrow, we keep moving." The roads were backed-up with military convoys, civilian trucks, and refugees on the move.

While traveling through Uzbekistan, Leah would sit Baruch and Sam by the roadside, seeking sympathetic drivers with room for a family.

"Sam," said Leah, "*nem du okh in gay bay der strassah, et men zeyn oyb itlekh't nemen dikh.*" Sam and Baruch would stand at the road and wave at drivers, with Duvid and Leah behind them holding the bags. One out of five trucks or buses would stop and take them to the next town, where they might work for a couple of weeks to make enough money to move on. It was slow going, but at least they were traveling in the right direction.

When a truck stopped, Leah didn't hesitate about jumping into the cab, while Duvid and the boys climbed in back with the bags. Leah used her market experience and was comfortable negotiating any cost. Most drivers were kind enough to drop them at the next town, where they would wait for another ride. Some rides were more informative than others.

At one point, a half-empty troop convoy truck picked them up with another refugee family. The soldiers, casually holding their rifles, spoke freely, unaware if their passengers spoke Russian.

"There were piles of Jew bodies," said the soldier, who had camouflage dirt all over his face and hands.

Duvid frowned at Leah and the boys to not respond.

"It was a massacre," continued the soldier, "and I saw a lot of dead kikes."

Duvid didn't know if Baruch understood, but he kept his head down, anxious to get off the truck.

* * * * *

SUMMER, 1945

Duvid, Leah, and their boys finally reached Szcaecin, in Russian-controlled Poland. They immediately saw that the whole town appeared bombed out and many residents were missing. Rent would temporarily be free, since many buildings were in shambles and abandoned.

Duvid led his family to the first floor of a bombed apartment building where there was a standing roof and walls for one unit.

"The faster we clean out the bricks, glass, and splintered wood," said Duvid, "the sooner I can look for furniture."

There was no electricity or water running in the village, but the unit was dry.

"This isn't better than Tashkent," said Leah, "but I'm so glad you are back with us." She gave Duvid a quick hug.

Other scavengers were looking for shelter and Duvid knew that without any authority in the city, it was first-come, first-claim, so he secured the door. Duvid began to look for a mattress and useful pieces of clothes.

"I'll take Sam and Baruch," said Leah, "and find a market."

The boys appealed to vendors for some food and being hungry too, Sam and Baruch understood the routine and necessity. There was a water pump in a courtyard and a stove in the unit, but Duvid would need to break up some of the splintered wood to boil water for cooking.

The city was struggling to recover with the help of Polish government officials who had run the city before the invasion. Slowly, streets were being cleared and shops opened, offering some temporary work for Duvid.

"Can I work for money?" asked Sam. He didn't like begging for vegetable pieces in the market. Sam wanted a job like his father. "I want to help."

Sam learned that they wouldn't move again until his family had earned enough money to pay drivers who stopped for them. More money meant the faster they could leave.

"Businesses are paying to sort out bricks and glass," said Duvid. "There is a collecting station down the street paying cash, depending on the weight."

With his mother selling in the market and his father clearing the streets, Sam decided that he and Baruch could help, too. He found a wagon and with Baruch, collected broken glass from windows and bottles to sell to the recycling station. More money was paid for whole jars or bottles. Baruch gathered and placed shards of colored glass into separate piles. Even with their hands wrapped with cloth, Baruch and Sam cut their hands many times picking through the sharp edges.

At the end of the day, all money went to Leah to divide for buying produce for the family and to be saved for transportation and border crossing bribes to get out of the country. In two months, they would leave Poland for good.

SEPTEMBER, 1945

"Are they still talking about it?" asked Leah, when Duvid returned from his day of sorting fractured bricks from whole ones. He stretched to arch his back, opposite of his bending stoop at work.

"Every day," answered Duvid, "someone on the brick crew wants to get near Berlin, but they don't know how."

In Berlin, there were organizations formed after the war to move surviving Jews out of Europe, but you had to get there and no one was openly talking about how to do it. Duvid had been meeting someone late at night, but didn't want to share the details of the planning. Just like the ghetto, it was best if few people held information, and Leah never asked. Trust had few questions.

"What's America?" asked Baruch, walking in the front door with Sam from a long day of collecting glass bits.

"It's a safe place," answered Leah.

The name didn't mean anything to the boys, other than hearing other people talk about it.

"Get to sleep right after dinner," said Duvid to the boys, "because we have enough money to smuggle ourselves out."

Sam and Baruch looked at Leah for confirmation. "We'll wake you when it's time to go."

At 3:00 a.m., the boys were gently roused. Each of them had one bag, stuffed with as much clothing as possible, leaving everything else.

"Are we going into tunnels?" asked Sam.

"No," answered Duvid, "there's no underground."

The cover of darkness would have to be enough concealment for the parents and young boys to slip out of town.

"Will there be shooting?" asked Sam.

"Hope not," answered Leah. "You remember everything, Sammy, don't you?"

"He'll never forget," answered Duvid. "Just stay close and don't say a word. Not a sound."

Duvid crouched down to Baruch's height so he could be eye to eye with his younger son in the darkness.

"*Shah*," continued Duvid, holding his fingers to Baruch's lips in a shushing gesture. "Just hold onto to Ma and be very quiet."

Now that Baruch was six years old, Duvid couldn't believe that they were running again. He looked at Leah and held his jaw firm with the confidence of this being the right time to go. Neither spoke a word, but Leah nodded that she was ready.

Leah picked up Baruch with her right arm and stopped. She shook her head and lowered him back to the ground. She unslung the satchel that was hanging over her shoulder, and unhooked the opening.

"With every move," said Leah, "Baruch gets heavier and now this bag is too much."

She pulled out her favorite cooking pot and tossed it with a couple of ragged pants and shirts onto the ground.

"It's still warm weather and I shouldn't need so many clothes. And there's no time to cook while running."

Duvid smiled at her practical assessment and with his foot, pushed the pile against the wall.

"Shhhhh," said Baruch.

"He learns fast," whispered Duvid.

With the bribes paid and under the cover of night, it was time.

* * * * *

After the second clandestine stop, the Russian army truck with two uniformed soldiers brought the twenty-five passengers to an unmarked dock and quickly unloaded them. Without a word, the soldiers and truck were gone.

"Hurry," said the two men working the boat and jostling the people on board. With his hard-earned cash, Duvid had paid the agreed amount of Polish slotys for each person, days before the event. He was relieved to see the boat and crew.

"Be quiet," said the taller crew member, "and sit on the floor." The passengers sat on the deck of the cargo barge and hunched low behind the gunwales.

"Run!" said the husky skipper suddenly. "Get off the boat, now, and run."

Confused, everyone was told to get off the boat and hide in the woods, even before the engine was started. A lookout for the skipper signaled that he saw the reflection of spot lights on the water.

A boat with border guards was approaching.

"Where is the truck?" asked Leah. She stepped off the gunwale onto the dirt shoreline, still holding an overstuffed sack of clothing and Baruch's hand.

"It's gone. They ran, too," cried Duvid. "Drop the bags and run for the tree line. I've got Sam."

They dropped everything and took off with the rest of the group and dove into the thick woods. Some of the adults kept pushing their way through the trees, while Leah and Duvid hid behind some dense bushes and pushed the boys flat to the ground.

"Keep your face to the ground and don't show your eyes or skin," said Duvid.

This is too familiar, thought Sam.

Leah tried to quiet her heavy breathing and put her arm over Baruch's head. They all disappeared under the spotlight beams piercing the woods. When the lights were cut, Sam could see eight border guards with rifles in hand, forming a semi-circle around the two boatmen.

"What are you doing here at four in the morning?" asked the pencil-nosed commander.

"We're not going anywhere," answered the skipper. "Just trying to fix the boat. Search it if you want."

The guards found nothing, since the crew had quickly tossed all of the bags into the dark river. The spotlight was fixed on the woods and missed the personal debris drifting upstream. Duvid heard the bags splashing into the black water and was later relieved to register the sounds of the rifles uncocking.

After the guards left, the skipper walked into the woods to find his hiding passengers.

"We're not going," said the skipper. "They will be waiting for us at the first turn in the river and they may still be watching the boat now, waiting for some movement."

Duvid stood up and began to brush leaves and dirt off his pants. "It's not safe and we'll be shot on the spot."

Leah picked up Baruch and held Sam's hand. "The river is a nice place for them to toss bodies after they confiscate the boat," continued the skipper. "It's not worth my life or your family's." Everything useless floated or sank in the river.

"The deal is dead," said the skipper.

After months of work, saving, and waiting, Duvid couldn't believe it.

"You had better get away from here before the sun comes up," said the skipper

"Fine," said Duvid. "Just give me my money back." He grabbed the skipper by the collar and pressed his face close enough that the men could feel each other's misty breath. "It took months for all of us to come up with the cash to pay you to leave us in the woods. You said that you have done this before without being caught. This was not the deal."

"I've not been caught," said the skipper, "because I know when to drop everything and run. I do not have your money."

He tried to push away from Duvid, but couldn't break his grip. "I don't carry anything on me, since the soldiers will just take it. Search me. I'm only paid when I return. Your money is with Viktor," said the skipper, "if you can find him."

Duvid let go of the skipper and pounded his fist into the palm of his other hand in frustration.

It was pointless to argue and Duvid knew they would have to find a different way to reach the next square in the survival game. With each step to leave Poland, Duvid watched a mounting wave of refugees pour into the town, each scratching to move away from war wreckage.

After Leah, Duvid, and the boys walked several kilometers back to town and into their old broken-down building, Leah started to laugh, joined by Duvid. "Good thing no one moved in while we were gone," said Leah. She began to pick up their clothing, cooking pot and dishes.

"And no one took the stuff we found," said Sam.

"I'm hungry," said Baruch.

"He's six," said Leah, "and eats like ten."

She opened the cupboard and took out some vegetables that they left behind.

"We need water," said Leah, handing the bucket to Baruch, "and then we all need to get back to work."

While Sam and Baruch were happy to see their friends again, Sam wanted a bigger wagon to collect more items for more money. They searched surrounding farms and found a larger wagon resting on some roadside rubble. Unlike he had done with the clinking Warsaw wagon, Sam filled and pushed this wagon with hope. He discovered that bombed-out stores had the best glass and bottles, if he ignored any danger and crawled through the rubble to get inside.

Baruch and Sam never encountered anyone protesting or competing to enter those buildings. Their wagon quickly filled and with its large metal wheels, could be pulled by the one handle and moved with a push from behind. Baruch helped move it to the scale, where long lines of people waited with carts filled with wood, metal, and steel sheets, stoves and pipes. Some people used baby buggies or whatever had wheels, rolling their scavenged items onto a truck scale to receive cash.

Relying on her pre-war Warsaw experience, Leah found work in a re-opened bakery and brought home her pay, along with bread ends, half muffins, and thick baguette pieces. Duvid returned to the factory, working a double shift sorting brick scraps to be recycled. Even with their combined effort, it would still take months to accumulate enough money to get across the border, probably after winter. All family money was kept by Leah, because Duvid didn't trust any place other than the money belt she had sewed into her pants.

MAY, 1946

"We need an unstoppable way to go across the border and get to Berlin," said Duvid.

"Can you trust these people?" asked Leah.

While avoiding being shot by border guards was vital, not losing months of cash to unscrupulous smugglers was important.

"They won't share details," answered Duvid, "other than not returning with the people they took. Tomasz arranged the contact and people trust him."

"Are we leaving again?" asked Baruch, listening to the quiet evening conversation. Leah thought he was old enough to understand the importance of secrecy, when she realized that Baruch wasn't much younger than Sam when he started smuggling in the tunnels. "I won't tell anyone."

Since he spent his days with Sam and evenings at home, Leah and Duvid were confident in Baruch's learned restraint.

"Sam, would you like to come with me tonight?" asked Duvid. "I need to pay them in full tonight and get instructions, before we leave tomorrow night."

Sam nodded.

When Leah, Duvid, and the boys quietly slipped out in the middle of the following night, they didn't bother to say good-bye to anyone, unsure of a successful departure. They met ten other families at the designated side road. They waited with their bags and were being pushed into a large, canvas-covered Russian army truck by two uniformed soldiers.

"Gingold, four!" said one of the soldiers. He checked off each family before they were hustled onto the truck.

Climbing on top of their belongings, people were cramped and had their heads tightly pressed against the canvas. The truck was so full of people that Leah endured someone's heel jabbed under her rib cage. The canvas was tied down tight and the hatch was slammed closed. There was no talking.

"Do not speak, move, or open the canvas to show yourselves," said a soldier. He got in the truck cab with the other soldier, started the engine, and took off into the darkness.

It was difficult to settle in sitting on top of each other, and Sam was tightly entangled in his father's legs. Some passengers layered like logs and others sat in balls. Sam realized he was surrounded by Jews, because they were complaining in Yiddish about every bump in the road and heel in their side.

"*Gay tsi rekhter zat!*" said a woman.

"*Shtip a bisl tsi deyr linker zat!*" said her husband. "*Nem di hent tsi deyr anderer zat!*" Moving a limb to the left, right, or to the other side didn't help. It was an overcrowded ride of moaning.

The monotony of the three-hour drive on dirt roads through the woods was only broken up by large bumps over roots and branches scraping the canvas.

Shortly after dawn, the truck stopped and the two Russian soldiers exited the truck cab. The officer wore rows of medals with ribbons on the left side of his jacket and epaulettes on his shoulders and hat, while the soldier was plainly uniformed. The officer started walking up the road and the soldier stuck his head into the back hatch opening.

"I will open this up so you can breathe," said the soldier, "if you don't move. This is an important checkpoint." There was immediate silence in the truck. Everyone could hear the checkpoint conversation, followed by the officer walking back to the truck through the woods.

"We're leaving," said the soldier, "and I have to close this up."

The truck moved and the conversations continued.

"They're on a schedule to get to the paid-off guards who will let us through the checkpoint," said Duvid softly, his legs cramped from the close quarters.

When the truck moved forward, Sam looked out the back opening to see the dropped arm of the checkpoint. As the truck moved quickly down the paved road, the canvas began to flap and rattle. Within two hours, the vehicle slowed down, went off the road, and drove deep into the woods. The passengers could feel tree roots and branches again.

When the truck stopped, both uniformed men walked to the back hatch and began to roll up the canvas.

"I can't open it the whole way," said the soldier, "but enough for fresh air. These are neutral woods," he continued. "The bathroom is any tree or bush."

He unclamped a big water barrel with a spigot from the side of the truck, and placed a stack of cups on top. The passengers stared at each other in amazement. The Russian soldier stood in front of the thirsty group.

"We will be here a while," said the soldier, "so rest, stretch, and relax, but don't wander. We won't look for you when we leave, and stay out of sight of local people or other military." It was easier for soldiers to shoot at people, rather than ask their business.

Pairs of refugees ran into the woods, searching for a bathroom spot. The group waited for hours and took naps on the grass. Sam and Baruch ran around with the few other kids, throwing sticks at each other and playing hide-and-go-seek in the area.

"Chase me!" said Baruch, hiding behind a tree.

"Sam, try to wear him out," said Leah, "so he will lie down and rest."

Baruch had weeks of stored energy ready to burn in the woods. Everyone watched the children play while they rested at the edge of the woods, waiting for instructions. Eventually the children returned exhausted and collapsed next to their families.

The Russian officer was short and husky with a square jaw. His uniform jacket sleeves were tight with solid muscle. It took little effort for him to lift women and children on and off the truck in one swift move.

The soldier was taller and skinny, wearing a baggy uniform that looked like it belonged to someone else. He spoke quietly and took orders from the officer. They seemed to move together as a team, although the officer started and finished each move. It was not their first trip as an organized network within the Russian army. For them, it was a side job and since they knew the guards to payoff, the game was worth it.

The soldier had dark, inset eyes, probably from lack of sleep. The officer looked fresh with rosy cheeks with pressed clothes and ribbons. Even his shiny black leather boots looked fresh and unused, while the soldier didn't have boots and wore brown laced shoes. His brown waist gun belt didn't fit well and was awkwardly attached.

In the late afternoon, both Russians leaned into the truck cab and began to visibly change out the paperwork in their wallets. Only a few of the adults knew what was about to happen. The officer and soldier each carried a bag and went behind the truck and out of sight. The group could clearly hear them talking, but had difficulty understanding their conversation.

"What are they saying?" asked Sam.

"I can't understand them," answered Leah, looking directly at Duvid.

Although Leah had never been fluent in Russian, she felt there was something different about their speech. She walked to the truck to eavesdrop, but was unable to decipher a word.

An older woman approached Leah. "It's English," said the woman. "They're Americans."

Leah was confused and shocked. Duvid smiled.

At that moment, the men appeared from behind the truck, both wearing American uniforms. They were both American officers, wearing olive-drab clothes with peaked hats, along with side-arm pistols and shined shoes. The short officer was a captain and had more medals on his chest, as well as bars on his collar and hat.

Along with most of the group, Leah was surprised and delighted at the sight of Americans. Having no one to fear was an unfamiliar sensation for Leah. The captain continued to speak English, asking his tall lieutenant to explain what was next for the passengers. The switch was complete.

"Does everyone have their people?" asked the lieutenant, continuing to speak in Russian. "Let's get going. You are cargo to the guards, so no peeking out of the canvas."

He motioned for everyone to gather, while continuing to look at his watch. The right people would only be in the right place for so long and then the deal would be dead.

By late afternoon, the overstuffed truck reached a paved road and picked up speed. As they approached another checkpoint, the truck stopped and the lieutenant walked back to the opening above the hatch.

"Stay down," he said, "no talking. We're almost there."

The crammed truck was filled with the anxious smiles of shared anticipation. Although the truckload of people didn't understand the English conversation, they knew it was friendly. The captain stayed in the cab, flipping through papers, and awaiting checkpoint clearance. The lieutenant returned with three American soldiers, each carrying a rifle on his shoulder.

After saluting and speaking with the captain, they examined his papers and saluted again. They proceeded to lift the canvas to look at the refugees, who remained silent during the inspection. As the soldiers returned to their post, the lieutenant quickly jumped up onto the driver's seat and re-started the engine.

The silent adults and children on board could feel the same hunger for freedom. As their truck passed the gate and accelerated into the dark, they looked out the back hatch and saw farm buildings and the passed checkpoint.

The back draft from the accelerating truck pulled and lifted the canvas, revealing flashes of lights from a distant city. Standing on the bouncing truck bed, one man pulled out a knife, sliced open the loose canvas, and stuck out his head.

"I can see Berlin!" said the man, who was pressed between his wife and teenage daughter. Every person in the truck cheered and started to pull down the ripped canvas for a view of the American side of Berlin. A chant of "Berlin" rose from the back of the truck, as people burst out crying.

"*Got tsi dank*," said Leah. Thank God! She couldn't believe her eyes and looked at her family for confirmation of the moment. "*M'iz gekimen tsi deyr amerikan zayt. Got tsi dank!*"

It was the American side and she knew that God deserved the thanks. With the canvas gone, Duvid picked up Sam and sat him on the cab of the truck, while holding onto Baruch. who was trying to climb up as well. Baruch looked out with his mouth open, turning his head back and forth. Everyone else stood on their bags and kids were picked up by their parents. Smiles that had not been seen since before the war filled the back of the truck.

It had been almost a year since Germany surrendered and most of the roads had been cleared. The city was a mixture of large demolished buildings on one side of the road, and gardens and homes on the other. Street lights were on and streetcars hummed along, packed with people hanging out and holding on for a ride. Some restaurants already had tables outside with people seated, wearing clean and tailored clothes.

U.S. army jeeps with MP patrols passed in front of a big building with dozens of men and women in U.S. military uniforms walking up and down the long flight of front stairs. The truck pulled up to a gate. American soldiers with shiny helmets approached the cab and greeted the officer with the medals. They all shook hands and laughed with expressions of "he's back."

The soldiers opened the back hatch to unload the passengers, grabbing the children to lower them to the pavement. A large soldier with a big smile waved at Sam to come closer, and then reached out to him and Baruch. The boys didn't understand a single word he said, but knew his tone was welcoming. Other soldiers took the bags and lined them up on the walkway and saluted the officer with the square jaw. He returned the salute, smiled at Sam and gave Duvid a thumbs-up. The officer and junior officer jumped back into their truck and without any comment, took off.

"The Americans seem happy for anyone who can escape the Russians," said Duvid.

"It's the first time people are happy to see us," said Leah. Other soldiers talked and smiled at the boys, until they were ordered to get all of the bags. Holding the hands of the children, the soldiers brought the families into the building. The large soldier who had taken the boys off the truck held Sam's hand, while Sam grabbed Baruch's hand. Duvid and Leah held onto each other's hands.

The marble floor in the lobby was shiny and everyone was directed to a table with people waiting to ask questions with the assistance of a Yiddish interpreter. A middle-aged man wearing a suit and tie directed the soldiers to assemble the bags and in Yiddish, told the families to get in a line. A woman seated behind the table patiently waited to get a family history from Duvid.

He shuddered remembering the start of the war with its bombs, strafing, and ghetto survival. Duvid explained their hiding from the Gestapo in the farmland and woods, distant travels and efforts to reach the Americans. Sam, Leah and Baruch listened as he spoke.

"Don't be afraid," said the interpreter. "Tell them the truth and no one is going to hurt you anymore. You will have food and rest, and your family will be safe."

The soldier was still holding onto Sam's hand and brought him and Baruch to a table. As the soldier went down on his knee, Baruch could see his own reflection in the shiny helmet. The soldier smiled at the boys, reached into his inside pocket, and pulled out a Hershey bar. This he gave to Sam. He patted Sam's head and said something.

Sam didn't know what he had been given, so he put it in his pocket, saving the sweetness to share later. It didn't matter that they hadn't eaten anything all day or that the travel had been hard, because Sam and his family were not facing fear. It was over.

They had come out of the Holocaust of World War II with nothing—except everything that mattered.

Leah and Duvid's third son, Jacob, was born on November 14, 1946, while they lived in Greenwald, an American DP (Displaced Persons) Camp in Berlin.

Duvid checked the refugee lists and discovered that Chava and Froim had lived in another Siberian camp and migrated to Palestine. Chava's dream in the woods came true.

When Sam turned thirteen, officiated by the Greenwald Rabbi, and in the presence his father, mother, and brothers, Sam had a Bar Mitzvah.

Before you read the Epilogue, I respectfully request that you first re-read the short prologue of this book. It may appear clearer to you now and bring full meaning to the Epilogue.

EPILOGUE

The windows in her room at the Milwaukee Jewish Home and Care Center overlooked the gentle waves of Lake Michigan, but Leah remained gripped by a time when being calm was an unknown luxury and life was a promise. The new LG flat screen television on her dresser was a closed window and the screen remained dark to the world, as she waited for a reason.

"Last night," said Leah, "I had a dream that I was back in Warsaw, shopping in the market with my mother."

Her gaze shifted, as if stunned by the sharpness of the vision.

"Friday mornings, we bought ingredients for *cholent.*"

Her grandson, Jeffrey, listened intently to Leah's vibrant memory and pulled his chair a little closer. His mid-week afternoon visits were a great time to learn about her experiences and how they influenced the life he knew as the child of a Holocaust survivor, Sam's son. There were many unanswered questions.

"We would leave a full pot of chopped vegetables," she continued, "to warm overnight in the baker's oven until early *Schabes* afternoon."

Her eyes sparkled at the thought of the aroma and her mother's presence.

"First, we brought the vegetables home to cut," she continued, "and I remembered dreaming about mixing the ingredients with her."

When her eyes welled with tears, she stopped talking. The memory was from a time before the ghetto, but the vegetables were still fresh. She lightly chuckled at herself, wondering why in her nineties she now had a dream about a Warsaw childhood morning.

Leah's early and tender memories were buried, embedded with reminders of her harsh life. Although she smiled when friends commented on her soft skin, she would look at her hands, reminded that her fingerprints had been permanently rubbed off while cross-cutting logs in the Siberian winter.

As she glowed in the market memory, Leah was overcome by the horror of the ghetto, indelibly linked to her lost family.

"Hitler took everything from us," said Leah. A grim and pained expression suddenly transformed her soft face and she looked directly into Jeffrey's eyes. The cholent memory was ripped from her in a cold, unchangeable instant.

"The Jews had nothing. We had nothing left. Hitler took everything."

It was true, but she had outlived the Fuehrer and her way ahead was littered with traumatic remembrances as crystal-clear as the clink of the death wagon. Ever since Warsaw was bombed on the day Baruch was born, Leah lived in reverberating shock. When their third son, Jacob, was born in the U.S. army re-settlement camp in Berlin in November 1946, Leah and Duvid awoke to a survivor's life, moving with her expanded family to America.

When Jacob unexpectedly died in 1973, Leah went numb, as if the Holocaust had never ended.

"Froim and Chava were lucky to make it to Palestine," said Leah. "We were all lucky to get out alive."

Her grandson wanted to shift to good news that might bring back her smile.

"We didn't tell you about this summer," said Jeffrey. "Terri and I are taking the girls to Israel." Leah perked up and turned toward her grandson. "It will be our first family trip there and we are meeting Froim's family; his son, Yitzchak, and his family, as well as their children and grandchildren."

He looked at the family photo collage above her bed, framed around a color image of Duvid and Leah embracing each other at an anniversary celebration.

"This summer?" asked Leah. Froim and Chava had already passed, leaving Leah as the last surviving sibling from Warsaw, but Jeffrey couldn't let it end there. He knew nothing would lessen her burden of carrying Holocaust memories, but a family connection was proof of survival.

"Yes," answered Jeffrey. "It's all set. We're meeting everyone for dinner in Haifa."

"How did you arrange it?" she asked. "Only Froim's daughter-in-law speaks English."

"It wasn't simple," answered Jeffrey. "We had friends translating the Yiddish and Hebrew. They made dinner reservations and hopefully, we all end up at the same restaurant on the same night."

Leah's smile returned.

"I haven't met Froim's grandchildren and great-grandchildren," continued Jeffrey, "It'll be like re-connecting a puzzle."

Continuing the family bond was vital to Leah's spirit and one that she embraced. However, there was still a large open gash in her life that seemed irreparable. The holocaust was over and Leah had not seen him for decades, but Jacob would appear in her room.

* * * * *

May, 2005

"*Bobe*," said Lainie to Leah, her grandmother. "Rob and I want you to meet someone."

Sam's daughter and her husband, Rob, stopped in for a visit. It had been less than a month since Lainie had left the maternity ward, but her youthful exuberance for the introduction vaulted the generations to her grandmother. Rob was shining as proudly and as brightly as his red hair, and walked into the room holding the carrier. He gently placed the car seat on the edge of the bed and Lainie reached over to unclip the seatbelt.

"We talked to Dad about it," said Lainie, "and decided to name him after your youngest son, Dad's brother, Jacob."

Leah hadn't heard the name Jacob associated with life since that shredded day in 1973. She was stunned by a moment too painful to remember, but when she looked into the infant's half-open eyes, Leah beamed and her cheeks reddened with emotion, as her eyes filled with tears. Leah realized that severed connections can be re-born and sharing painful memories was an answer to her life.

Her great-grandson, Jacob, was life. Leah decided that there should be no final witness to the Holocaust, so without hesitation, she revealed the path to her grandson, Jeffrey, as a gift to future generations.

When Jacob was two years old, Grandpa Sam brought him for a visit to Leah's floor in the nursing home.

"I think Jacob looks a little bit like the first Jacob," said Leah. "He smiles all of the time, too."

"I see it," said Sam.

"He has a happy face," said Leah. Peering at the infant brought her back to one of happiest times in her life, when she imagined that her third son would have a good life and maybe not have to fight for it every day.

A typical toddler, two-year-old Jacob dashed around in the nursing home hallways, but he instinctively looked back to see if Leah's wheelchair was following. She laughed so hard at the sight of his tush wiggling down the hall that Jacob laughed out loud too, although he didn't know why.

* * * * *

MILWAUKEE, 2008

"I finished clearing out her room and taking down the photos yesterday," said Sam, "and found this."

He held a torn, faded envelope and handed it to his son, Jeffrey. "It was buried in a drawer, under some oranges, sugar packets, and plastic-wrapped crackers."

Jeffrey carefully opened the worn paper and pulled out the few black and white photos, expecting to see old family images.

"Auschwitz ovens," said Sam.

Jeffrey was frozen and shocked by the find in her drawer.

"She's had them forever," said Sam, "and brought them back after the war."

When Duvid died of leukemia in 1983 and Leah decided to move into the Milwaukee Jewish Home, Sam remembered placing the envelope in a moving box.

"Why keep them?" asked Jeffrey.

"She couldn't forget what brought us here," said Sam, "and wanted us to remember and be thankful."

When Sam had crawled through the escape tunnel in the ghetto, he never saw a light at the end of the tunnel. His parents knew that as long as Sam kept pressing forward, their son was the light. For Leah and Sam, *survivor* continued to be a living word pointing forward, to be shared with a few bits tucked away for later.

AFTERWORD

1951: Duvid, Leah and their three boys—Sam, Baruch, and Jacob—moved to Milwaukee, Wisconsin.

Chava moved to Palestine and married Slomo Sher. They had two girls, Rivka and Sara, and one boy, Joel.

Froim moved to Palestine and married Rivka. They had one son, Yitzchak, who lives with his family in Haifa, Israel.

Sam Gingold, Jewish War Veterans (Commander, retired), LUTCF, married Sue. They had three children—Bruce, Jeffrey, and Lainie DeJong (Rob). He was remarried [Jill] and they lived in Shorewood, Wisconsin. Sam died on July 14, 2018. He was surrounded by generations of his loving family, exactly the way he lived.

1972: Jacob Gingold, graduated from Northwestern University with a B.S. in Mechanical Engineering.

Baruch (Bill) Gingold, PhD, MHA, CSA, CHE, QMHP, QDDPT, married Phyllis and currently lives in Urbana, Illinois. They have four children—Steve, Shara Meisinger (Phil), Tamra, and Jason.

Photos

Leah (nee Weintal) and Duvid, wedding photo,
Warsaw, Poland (1932).

SAM GINGOLD, AGE 2,
WARSAW, POLAND (1934).

BARUCH AND SAM
GINGOLD,

BARUCH AND SAM GINGOLD
POSTCARD FROM GERMANY (1950).

BARUCH AND SAM GINGOLD,
BERLIN, GERMANY (CIRCA 1946).

CHAVA WEINTAL   *FROIM WEINTAL*   *DUVID GINGOLD*

DUVID GINGOLD, IDENTIFICATION PAPERS, BERLIN, GERMANY (1948).

LEAH AND JACOB, MILWAUKEE (LATE 1950S).

(L TO R): SAM, LEAH, DUVID (REAR), JACOB (FRONT), BARUCH, MILWAUKEE (1952).

JACOB GINGOLD (MID-1960S).

DUVID AND LEAH, MILWAUKEE (1970S).

BARUCH GINGOLD (2014).

CHAVA, SAM, AND FROIM, ISRAEL (1988).

*JEFFREY GINGOLD AND FAMILY WITH FROIM'S SON, YITZCHAK (CENTER BACK)
AND FAMILY WITH FRIENDS IN ISRAEL (2010).*

SAM AND JEFFREY GINGOLD (MILWAUKEE, 2014)

SAM AND GRANDSON JACOB DEJONG
YOM HASHOAH CEREMONY (2015).

RESOURCES

Generations of The Shoah International

Jewish Museum Milwaukee

Nathan and Ester Pelz Holocaust Education Resource Center

Polish Center for Holocaust Research/*Centrum Badan nad Zaglada Zydow* (www.ghetto.pl)

Steven Spielberg Film and Video Archive

United States Holocaust Memorial Museum

Yad Vashem: The Holocaust Martyrs' and Heroes' Remembrance Authority

REFERENCES

In Those Times There was Darkness Everywhere, by Elie Wiesel, in Rittner, Carol R. S. M., and Sondra Myers, Eds. *The Courage to Care: Rescuers of Jews During the Holocaust.* New York: University Press, 1989.

Obersalzberg Speech, by Adolf Hitler, August 22, 1939.

About the Author

J effrey N. Gingold is an interna-
tionally acclaimed and award-
winning author, and published
freelance writer. Jeffrey has been
interviewed on national television,
public radio shows, in magazines,
and numerous global publications.
He is an outspoken advocate for Holocaust education who shares
his father's epic survival and unforeseen life twists in the Warsaw
ghetto.

Jeffrey donates 100 percent of his author royalties from this
publication to Holocaust education and research.

He lives with his wife, Terri, and two adorable daughters,
Lauren and Meredith, in Milwaukee, Wisconsin.

Please contact the publisher at info@henschelhausbooks.com
should you wish to communicate with the author. Thank you.